The Middle West in

American History

1556-B3-95

BY   *00*

DAN ELBERT CLARK

Professor of History
University of Oregon

THOMAS Y. CROWELL COMPANY
ESTABLISHED 1834   NEW YORK

FOREWORD

THE American frontier was more than a century old when pioneers first pushed through the gaps in the Appalachian Mountain ranges to begin the conquest of the Mississippi Valley, but their coming endowed the westward movement with a new character and touched the invaders with a new magic. Always before, as they marched westward, a forbidding barrier loomed before them, narrowing their horizons, restraining their vision. Now the vast interior of the continent was theirs to conquer. Now the opportunity for self-betterment that always attracts men to frontiers was temptingly real. Lured by these unparalleled prospects, the pioneers moved forward in one of the major migrations of world history, shouldering aside the Indian occupants, defying the Spaniards and the British who disputed their ownership, and ignoring the Easterners who tried to hold them back in the interest of an orderly settlement pattern.

Within a half century the interior was occupied, but the pioneers' coming was of more lasting significance than this brief time span would indicate. Separated now both geographically and psychologically from the traditionalism of Europe and the East, the frontiersmen were able to rear in the continent's heartland the first truly American civilization, differing markedly from that of the Atlantic seaboard. There, amidst the forests and prairies of mid-America, were nurtured those traits and institutions that most clearly distinguished the people of the United States from their Old World ancestors. There an "Americanization" of men and customs took place.

The pages of this book tell the story of that transformation in a very personal and a pleasantly unique way. Appearing originally as the central section of Dan Elbert Clark's well-known volume, *The West in American History*, they enlightened a generation of students after their first publication in 1937. Revised now to embrace the findings of later scholarship, they provide a sound and comprehensive view of the settlement of the Mississippi Valley that will prove equally enlightening to a new generation of readers. But their significance transcends the mere transmission of historical knowledge, important though that may be. Few books about any region of the nation mirror such warm affection, or convey such a sense of intimacy with a segment of the past.

The manner in which Professor Clark tells his story is as pleasing as the warmth that lends enchantment to his words. He scorns traditional chronological patterns, and he is clearly little concerned with the political and military events that have received such emphasis from other authors. Instead his concern is with the people, with the backwoodsmen and small farmers and pioneer merchants who made up the bulk of the westward-moving population. How did these men and women reach the West? What roads did they follow and what vehicles did they use? How did they clear their land? Did they succeed in their grapple with nature, or fail? What were their social activities and cultural interests? These are the questions that intrigued Professor Clark, and this book shows the extent to which he was successful in finding answers to them.

In his quest he employed two unique devices. One was to stress the evolution of various social, political, and economic practices; he deals successively with the migration of peoples, the fate of the displaced Indians, the emergence of a workable land policy, the creation of economic and governmental institutions, and the growth of social and cultural interests. His emphasis is constantly on the real frontier, not on the frontier that emerged in the minds of later romanticists who saw the West as a clover-scented Eden or the superrealists who viewed it as a sink of barbarism. His readers meet and come to know the actual pioneers who served as heralds of civilization in their conquest of the wilderness.

This stress on realism was possible only because Professor Clark, unlike many authors, immersed himself in the contemporary writings of the period that he described. His pages mirror a lifetime of reading in travel accounts, diaries, reminiscences, letters, and newspapers. From these he distills a record of the people and their history that is as intimate as it is unique. The reader journeys westward with the pioneers, curs-

ing with them the miserable roads, listening with them to a
piano as they walk through the streets of Pittsburgh, seeing
with them the countryside that unfolds before their eyes,
counting with them the wagons waiting to be ferried across the
Mississippi. Few books on any region boast such a wealth of
local detail, or such a rich collection of quotations from the
pioneers and their observers, as this one.

The result is a volume that is as readable as it is inform-
ative, and one that transmutes the westward-moving migrants
from digits in columns of figures to warm-blooded human
beings. By sharing their hopes and their dreams, their tribu-
lations and their disappointments, their successes and their
failures, today's reader can understand his pioneer ancestors
and can better appreciate the sacrifices they made in subduing
the nation's heartland. He can better understand the America
of today as a result.

RAY ALLEN BILLINGTON

The Huntington Library
January, 1966

CONTENTS

CHAPTER I

AMERICANS TAKE POSSESSION

THE history of the American West is the history of the westward movement, of the effect of life in a frontier environment, and of the problems, local and national, arising out of the needs and demands of western settlers. In character, volume, and rate of progress the westward movement in America is not fully paralleled elsewhere in the history of the world. Conquering hordes have swept over many lands. Colonial projects, fostered by rulers and statesmen and governments have been numerous. Nowhere else has so large an area been settled in such a short period of time almost entirely through the work of individuals moving singly or in small groups and of their own volition.

East of the Appalachians, settlements had been gradually pushed back from the tidewater regions up the river valleys, into the piedmont sections and the upland valleys, and finally across the mountain barrier that had so long seemed to close the way. That process occupied a century and a half. We shall now see how the small stream of settlers through the mountain passes swelled into the proportions of a torrent that spread with amazing rapidity over the vast interior valley and, within seventy-five years from American independence, deposited outposts of settlement on the Pacific coast. Land-hungry Americans had no intention that the fertile territory beyond the Appalachians, made a part of the new nation by the Treaty of 1783, should remain the haunt of Indian tribes and the hunting-ground of fur companies.

THE FIRST THREE DECADES

Anyone who will consult the census reports for the three decades following Yorktown will discover ample evidence of the

1

rapidity with which Americans entered into possession of this rich domain. In the first federal census in 1790 the regions soon to be known as Kentucky and Tennessee showed populations of 73,677 and 35,691, respectively; and there were small settlements across the Ohio in the Northwest Territory. Ten years later, in 1800, the population of Kentucky and Tennessee had increased three-fold, or to 220,955 and 105,602, respectively. By this time the Northwest Territory had been divided. The portion soon to become Ohio had 45,365 inhabitants and there were 5,641 in Indiana Territory. In addition there were 8,850 people living in Mississippi Territory, which then included Alabama. By 1810 Kentucky (406,511) and Tennessee (261,727) had again more than doubled in population. Ohio now had 230,760; Indiana Territory, 24,520; and Mississippi Territory, 40,352. Further spread of settlements was indicated by Illinois Territory, with 12,282 inhabitants, and Michigan Territory with 4,762; while in the Louisiana Purchase region 76,556 inhabitants were enumerated in what became the State of Louisiana and more than 20,000 in the present Missouri and Arkansas.

Figures may satisfy the statistician. By their use it would be possible to plot graphs or draw shaded maps showing the rapid growth and spread of population in the West. But at best figures and graphs and maps are cold and lifeless and purely objective. To gain a subjective view, a vivid picture of the great movement of humanity reflected in these census reports one must go to the writings of those who saw this movement when it was actually in progress. Letters, diaries, journals of travels, early histories, items in newspapers—these are the sources from which we may gain first-hand glimpses of the process and volume and rapidity of western settlement during the early years of the Republic. The selections which follow are merely illustrative of the pictures these sources reveal.

Chief Justice Robertson of Kentucky in an address quoted by Thomas Speed, the historian of the Wilderness Road, told of the "tide of emigrants, who, exchanging all the comforts of their native society and homes for settlements for themselves and their children here, came like pilgrims to a wilderness to be made secure by their arms and habitable by the toil of their lives. . . . Cast your eyes back on that long procession of missionaries in the cause of civilization; behold the men on foot with their trusty guns on their shoulders, driving stock and leading pack-horses; and the women, some walking. . . . others riding with children in their laps, and other children swung in baskets on horses. . . . see them encamped at night expecting to be massacred by Indians. . . . This is no vision of the imagination, it is but an imperfect description of the pilgrimage of my own father and mother, and of many others who settled in Kentucky in December, 1779." The same authority states that Rev. Lewis Craig's church from Virginia moved in a body to Kentucky in 1781. He quotes also a statement by Peter Cartwright who moved to Kentucky with his parents about 1783: "It was an unbroken wilderness from Virginia to Kentucky at that early day. . . . There were no roads for carriages, and though the immigrants moved by thousands, they had to move on pack-horses."

The close of the Revolution was followed by a great outpouring of people into Kentucky, especially from Virginia and North Carolina, with smaller numbers from other eastern States. Contemporary estimates indicated that as many as 12,000 men, women, and children toiled over the Wilderness Road or came by the Ohio River, in 1784, and 30,000 in 1787.

In 1796 Francis Baily, an English traveler, was on his way westward through Pennsylvania. "I have seen ten and twenty waggons at a time in one of these towns," he wrote, "on their way to Pittsburg and other parts of the Ohio, from thence to descend down that river to Kentucky. These waggons are loaded with the clothes and necessaries of a number of poor emigrants, who follow on foot with their wives and families, who are sometimes indulged with a ride when they are tired, or in bad weather."

When he reached Kentucky the following year Baily was impressed by the progress which had been made, not merely in the number but also in the character of the settlements. "Those ranks of men who form the first and second classes of society have moved off," he wrote, "and left the country for the most part to be possessed by those who have been brought up in all the refinement and civilised manners of their brethren

on the eastern side of the Allegany mountains. From a few
straggling settlements scattered over this vast territory, whose
inhabitants were obliged to shut themselves up in block-houses,
and establish their right by the point of the sword, who ranged
lawless through this wilderness, every one doing that which
seemed right in his own eyes—there have arisen . . . fertile
fields, blushing orchards, neat and commodious houses, and
trading towns, whose inhabitants have imposed upon themselves the just restraint of mild laws, and who, increasing in
numbers, can lie down secure and free from all apprehensions
of the tomahawk or scalping-knife. Such has been the wonderful progress of this country, to have implicit faith in which, it is
first necessary to be a spectator of such events."

Across the Ohio River at the mouth of the Muskingum the
Ohio Associates from New England founded the town of Marietta on April 7, 1788, thus forming the advance guard of the
stream of emigrants who soon transformed that region into a
land of homes and farms. "During the winter of 1787-8,"
wrote James H. Perkins, "their men were pressing on over the
Alleghanies by the old Indian path which had been broadened
into Braddock's road. . . . Through the dreary winter days
they trudged on, and by April were all gathered on the Yohio-
geny, where boats had been built, and started for the Muskingum." A letter written late that year described the progress
of the new settlement. "We are continually erecting houses,
but arrivals are faster than we can possibly provide convenient
covering. Our first ball was opened about the middle of December, at which were fifteen ladies, as well accomplished in
the manners of polite circles as any I have ever seen in the old
States." The commandant at Fort Harmar, across the Muskingum from Marietta, reported that 4,500 persons had passed
that post between February and June, 1788, and that many of
them would have stopped on the lands of the Ohio Associates if
provision had been made for their reception.

On account of danger of Indian attack, settlements were
slow in spreading northward from the Ohio River. The ineffective campaign of General Joseph Harmar in 1790 and the
disastrous defeat of Governor Arthur St. Clair in 1791 tended
to check the advancing frontier. Following the decisive vic-

tory of General Anthony Wayne at the Battle of Fallen Timbers in 1794, however, there was a period of peace and settlers
took full advantage of the immunity. "All the great roads of
approach to the western country were crowded with adventurers directing their course towards the land of promise; and
fleets of boats were continually floating them down the Ohio."

When Francis Baily witnessed the founding of Waynes-
ville on the Little Miami in 1797 he was a spectator of scenes
such as were being enacted in many other places in the Ohio
Valley during this period. "After being here a few days," he
wrote, "I observed this wilderness begin to assume a very different appearance; for, after having built my friend a house,
the settlers set about their own plantations, and in a short time
I saw quite a little town rise from the desert." He thought
that in later years it would be pleasant to tell "how we raised
this flourishing settlement from the howling wilderness."

Largely through the activities of Oliver Phelps and Na-
thaniel Gorham and later of the Holland Land Company, the
lake region of western New York, so long the home of the fierce
Iroquois, was now opened to settlement. A writer in 1797 told
of the opening of a road from Fort Schuyler (Utica) to Geneva
and Canandaigua and of the running of regular stage coaches.
"This line of road having been established by law," he said, "not
less than fifty families settled on it in the space of four months
after it was opened. It now bids fair to be, in a few years, one
continued settlement." Three years later the English traveler,
John Maude, described the settlements around Bath, near the
Pennsylvania line. A few years earlier this had been a region
almost unexplored by white men. "Yet so rapidly," he wrote,
"has the spirit of improvement gone forth in this country—so
suddenly has plenty burst forth, where so late was famine—
and so quick the change of scene from dark-tangled forests
. . . to smiling fields, to flocks and herds, and the busy hum of
men; that instead of being indebted to others for their support,
they will henceforth annually supply the low country, Baltimore especially, with many hundred barrels of flour, and herds
of cattle." He wrote also of a bridge near Owasco Lake "the
longest in America—perhaps in the world! Yet five years ago
the Indians possessed the shores of this Lake embosomed in

almost impenetrable woods." The migration of New Englanders to central and western New York that began during this
period was of great significance in the history of that State.

Observers in the southwest reported similar progress in that
section. In 1792 Gilbert Imlay declared that the settlements
in western Georgia, on the Holston, French Broad, and Cumberland, and around Natchez were already of sufficient strength
to bid defiance to the Cherokee, Creek, and Choctaw tribes.
He predicted that the Spaniards in Florida would be obliged to
watch their manners or they would be forced to retire across
the Mississippi. "To a person who observes the migration to
this country," reads a letter written from Tennessee in 1795, "it
appears as if North and South Carolina, and Georgia, were
emptying themselves into it. It is not infrequent to see from
2 to 300 people in a body coming from those southern climates,
oppressed with diseases to revive and enjoy health in this
salubrious air." F. A. Michaux estimated in 1802 that there
were five thousand whites and three thousand negro slaves in
the Natchez district which, he declared, "daily acquires a fresh
degree of prosperity."

THE GREAT MIGRATION

Pictures like these might be multiplied indefinitely to show
how in the thirty years following the Revolution wilderness
regions west of the mountains were being transformed into
lands of prosperous farms and budding cities. The movement
was somewhat checked during the War of 1812. But immediately after its close, because of hard times in the East due to
the long-continued interruption of trade, there came what has
appropriately been called the "Great Migration," when all
America seemed on the move westward. The census of 1820
revealed a startling shift of population, although of course it
did not indicate the further spread of settlements into the
western portions of New York, Pennsylvania, and all the southern states. The census figures show the following populations
in western States and Territories in 1820: Alabama, 127,901;
Arkansas, 14,273; Illinois, 55,211; Indiana, 147,178; Kentucky, 564,317; Louisiana, 153,407; Michigan, 8,896; Missis-

sippi, 75,448; Missouri, 66,586; Ohio, 581,434; and Tennessee, 422,823. By comparing these figures with those for 1810 it will be found that there were nearly 1,140,000 more people living west of the mountains in 1820 than in 1810, without counting the increase in the western sections of the older States; while the population of the entire nation had increased about 2,230,000. The comparison also shows the geographical distribution of the westward migrants during the decade. Later we shall show how this movement was reflected in the admission of new States and the creation of new Territories.

Contemporaneous accounts of the "Great Migration" are exceedingly numerous, since the phenomena attracted widespread attention. *Niles' Weekly Register* for this period is a veritable mine of information. Its editor Hezekiah Niles, was ardently interested in the West and took delight in printing all the letters and items he could gather which described western settlement and progress. Journals of travelers again furnish us with many vivid pictures. Obviously only a few selections can here be made to illustrate and enliven the story summarized by the census figures of 1820.

A correspondent from Ohio wrote to Editor Niles in January, 1815, that the emigration to that State during the preceding summer had been "beyond all example, great. The main road through the state, I am told, has been almost literally covered with waggons moving out families." The missionaries, S. J. Mills and Daniel Smith, reported from the Wabash region in Indiana that "an immense number of settlers have been crowding out on that frontier during the last season." From Auburn, New York, in April, 1815, came the statement that "during the past winter our roads have been thronged with families moving westerly. It has been remarked by our oldest settlers, that they never before witnessed so great a number of teams passing, laden with women, children, furniture, &c. to people the fertile forests of New-York, Pennsylvania, and Ohio; they are mostly from the eastern states." About the same time a "New England Emigration Society" was formed in Boston to promote westward migration.

Timothy Flint tells us that "shoals of immigrants" were seen on all the great roads leading to the West, during the years

immediately following the second war with England. Towns
like Oleanne, Pittsburgh, Brownsville, Wheeling, Nashville,
Cincinnati, and St. Louis were overflowing with them. "Ohio
and Indiana," he continued, "beheld thousands of new cabins
spring up in their forests. On the borders of the solitary
prairies of Illinois and Missouri, smokes were seen streaming
aloft from the dwellings of recent settlers . . . Boon's-lick and
Salt River, in Missouri, were the grand points of immigration,
as were the Sangamon and the upper courses of the Kaskaskia,
in Illinois. In the south, Alabama filled with new habitations,
and the current, not arrested by the Mississippi, set over its
banks, to White river, Arkansas, and Louisiana. . . . Wagons,
servants, cattle, swine, horses, and dogs, were seen passing with
the settlers, bound to immense distances up the long rivers."
Of the moving settlers, Flint said "they drop, in noiseless
quietness, into their position, and the rapidity of their progress
in settling a country is only presented by the startling results
of the census."

A letter from Chillicothe, Ohio, in 1816, noted that newcomers were arriving in that town more rapidly than room
could be furnished for them. In a day's ride in southern Indiana, Timothy Flint was "continually coming in view of new
cabins, or wagons, the inmates of which had not yet sheltered
themselves in cabins." A communication from western New
York this same year told of farmers exchanging their log cabins
for "elegant framed or brick mansions." Auburn was now a
"place of wealth and business." Waterloo, further west, had
sprung into being as though obeying the "creative power of the
magician's wand. Here are, at least, 50 houses, most of them
of size and beauty—the work of a single summer." Even
Rochester contained "above 100 houses—two years ago it did
not exist." Out in Missouri it was reported that "Boon's settlement, which was a few scattered cabins the other year, in an
immense forest, has now become a country containing its courts
of justice and other municipal appendages." Fifty wagons
passed through Zanesville in a day carrying settlers westward.
Virginia, Kentucky, Tennessee, and the Carolinas seemed to
be pouring their people into Illinois and Missouri. "Every
ferry on the river is daily occupied in passing families, carri-

ages, wagons, negroes, carts, &c. &c." A traveler in the south estimated that in nine days he met 3,800 people on their way to the Alabama country.

For the year 1817 similar pictures present themselves. Morris Birkbeck, whose travel notes constitute an American classic, journeyed to Illinois this year. "Old America seems to be breaking up, and moving westward," he wrote while on the road to Pittsburgh. "We are seldom out of sight, as we travel on this grand track towards the Ohio, of family groups, behind and before us."

At Pittsburgh he "heard delightful music from a piano, made in this place, where a few years ago stood a fort, from which a white man durst not pass, without a military guard." During his stay at St. Clairsville, Ohio, he saw thirteen or fourteen emigrant wagons a day passing through the town. "The wagons swarm with children," he observed. "I heard to-day of three together which contain forty-two of these young citizens." One favorite route from New England to the Ohio Valley was across New York and down the Alleghany. In nine days 260 emigrant wagons passed a house on this route, besides many persons on horseback and on foot. A New York editor met "a cavalcade of upwards of twenty waggons containing one company of 116 persons, on their way to Indiana, and all from one town in the district of Maine."

In 1818 Timothy Flint was in Missouri where he counted one hundred persons a day, for many days in succession, passing through St. Charles. He saw a train of "nine wagons harnessed with from four to six horses. We may allow a hundred cattle, besides hogs, horses, and sheep, to each wagon; and from three or four to twenty slaves. The whole appearance of the train, the cattle with their hundred bells; the negroes with delight in their countenances, for their labours are suspended and their imaginations excited; the wagons, often carrying two or three tons, so loaded that the mistress and children are strolling carelessly along . . . the whole group occupies three quarters of a mile." The aged Daniel Boone, now nearing the end of his days at his home on the Missouri River, was reported to be very restless on account of the press of population and only detained from moving again beyond the frontier by his waning strength and failing eyesight.

The southern phase of the westward movement was reflected in the setting up of Alabama as a Territory separate from Mississippi and its admission as a State in 1819. These facts indicate a large influx of population. *Niles' Weekly Register* contained many items in 1818 and 1819 revealing the exuberance and typical western optimism of the inpouring settlers. Where only a single hut had stood two years earlier a town of 2,700 inhabitants was said to have arisen by 1818; and the Black Warrior River was designated as "the Nile of the West." Within one year another site covered with a heavy forest was described as having been transformed into a "city" of eighty houses, ten large warehouses "and the largest hotel in the territory." A printing press was on the way and a newspaper was to be launched. To this town, named Blakely, one hundred brickmakers and fifty ship carpenters had recently come from New York. "The emigration is wonderful," said one writer, "and seems daily to acquire new power."

From the River Raisin near Detroit came the report that that region, so well known for the humiliating defeat of General Hull in the late war, "now presents an aspect that forbids the prospect of another such scene in its neighborhood." A new village named Monroe had appeared and "large tracts of country . . . are now so well populated that a thousand men may be called together, as it were, by the beat of a drum."

The inclination of New Englanders to migrate in groups, or to settle where others from the same section had established themselves, was noted. "They established a new Connecticut in the Ohio territory," commented Hezekiah Niles, "and that not merely in name but in fact. The inhabitants of a township in the eastern states, who may be disposed to explore the western wilds, generally understand one another, concert their measures beforehand, and if they do not depart in a body, yet they eventually come together at a preconcerted rendezvous. School-fellows and companions in infancy, reunite in a far distant spot, remote from the scenes of their early pleasures: and it often happens that the grown up man meets there and marries the playmate of his childhood." This tendency on the part of New Englanders was a continuation of the practice of pre-arranged group migration established in the early days of colonial expansion. In the south, on the other hand, people more generally moved westward as individuals or single families without concerted action either in moving or in choosing a place for settlement.

Numerous religious colonies and social experiments were established in the West during the era of settlement. There was another type of group migration which was illustrated by an account in a New York newspaper in 1819 of a caravan "consisting of eleven covered waggons, drawn by two, three, or four horses each, two coaches, a number of outriding horses, and about 120 persons, composing the expedition under Captains Blackman and Allen, for the state of Illinois." These two men, having made fortunes as ship-masters in the China trade, had now determined to form a settlement on lands which they had purchased in Illinois, and this caravan was the first of two parties organized to carry out the plan. "In the company which passed here yesterday," ran the story, "there were farmers, carpenters, blacksmiths, wheelwrights, masons, coopers, &c, &c. with their families, mostly natives of the 'northern hive.' All their equipments were in fine order, and the emigrants in fine spirits."

One more quotation will serve as a summary of the "Great Migration" in the north. In 1819 Niles reviewed the progress made in western settlement since 1812. The western parts of New York and the northern portions of Pennsylvania and Ohio "then nearly in a state of nature . . . now teem with men, and abound with large towns, villages and *ports*. . . . Buffalo and Erie, and Sackett's Harbor, remote points beyond the 'back woods,' with Rochester and other places not then upon the map, are celebrated for their shipping and commerce! Detroit and Michilimackinac, then far distant posts, and rarely heard from, now seem close to us. . . . St. Louis, now a *port* on the Mississippi, then at about the extreme point of the emigrants voyage in that direction—is turned into a *starting-place*." There was now a town called Franklin, with one thousand inhabitants, located at Boon's Lick *"somewhere* on the Missouri."

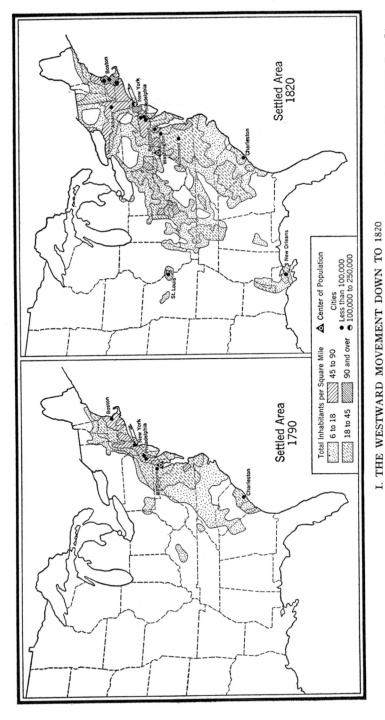

I. THE WESTWARD MOVEMENT DOWN TO 1820

(Population density of 6 or more per square mile. Based on maps in *Report of the Eleventh Census of the United States*, 1890, Part I.)

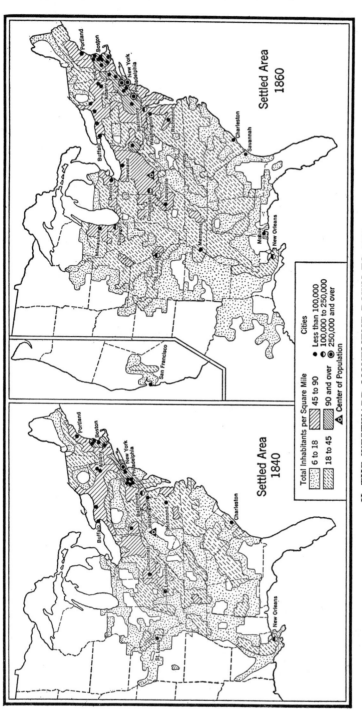

II. THE WESTWARD MOVEMENT DOWN TO 1860

(Population density of 6 or more per square mile. Based on maps in *Report of the Eleventh Census of the United States*, 1890, Part I.))

CHAPTER II

STILL THEY COME

"THEY come in crowds a mile long," said an Iowa editor in 1854, in describing the tide of new settlers pouring into that State, "they come with wagon-loads of household fixings, with droves of cattle and flocks of sheep—they come from every land that ever sent adventurers westward, and the cry is 'still they come.'" Words like these might truthfully have been written in many western States and Territories during almost any year of the four decades following 1820—the year to which the story of the westward movement was carried in the preceding chapter. The increase in population from 1820 to 1860 in the section now under discussion is indicated in the following figures from the census returns:

	1820	1830	1840	1850	1860
Alabama	127,901	309,527	590,756	771,623	964,201
Arkansas	14,273	30,388	97,574	209,897	435,450
Illinois	55,211	157,445	476,183	851,470	1,711,951
Indiana	147,178	348,031	685,866	988,416	1,350,428
Iowa			43,112	192,214	674,913
Kentucky	564,317	687,917	779,828	982,405	1,155,684
Louisiana	153,407	215,739	352,411	517,762	708,002
Michigan	8,896	31,639	212,267	397,654	749,113
Minnesota				6,077	172,023
Mississippi	75,448	136,621	375,651	606,526	791,305
Missouri	66,586	140,455	383,702	682,044	1,182,012
Ohio	581,434	937,903	1,519,467	1,980,329	2,339,511
Tennessee	422,823	681,904	829,210	1,002,717	1,109,801
Wisconsin			30,945	305,391	775,881

Florida is not included in this list, although there was a considerable migration to the western section of that State. Neither do these statistics reveal the continued settlement of the western portions of the eastern States, especially New York, Pennsylvania, and Virginia. With due allowance for the natural

14

increase in population in the longer settled States of the West, these figures are worthy of study as showing the volume and direction of the westward movement. This is especially true with regard to the newer Territories and States as they appeared in the census reports from decade to decade. On the other hand, these figures fail to tell us how many people, attracted by the lure of newly opened lands, moved to the more distant frontier from many of the older States of the West. For instance, in 1821 Hezekiah Niles estimated that during the preceding decade the outflow of people from Kentucky about equalled the inflow of new settlers. The greater profits of cotton-raising in Alabama, Mississippi, and Louisiana were attracting many to that region, while the "ravages of the 'independent banks,' together with the want of employment drove off tens of thousands of the laboring classes of white people into Ohio, Indiana and Illinois."

THE WESTWARD MOVEMENT DURING THE TWENTIES

Roads thronged with movers' wagons and the sight of large numbers of Ohio River flatboats bearing emigrants to the West had largely ceased to be items of news interest in States which had five or six hundred thousand inhabitants by 1820. Nevertheless, even in such States during the ensuing decade editors and travelers frequently expressed their wonderment at the unending movement and their appreciation of the rapid transformation it was achieving. Six months after Indianapolis was laid out, on unoccupied land, to be the seat of government of Indiana, it was noted that forty dwelling houses had already been erected, besides stores, workshops, and mills. In 1822 *Niles' Register* referred to the fact that Rufus Putnam, often called the father of Ohio, was still living in that State. "He has lived to see the wilderness in which he located himself divided into three independent states," said the editor. "If the good old gentleman shall live to the year 1830, he may expect to find a population in those parts of nearly a million and a half of busy, hustling, happy beings—though the soil 50 years before, was only trodden by wild animals and untutored Indians."

Western Indiana filled rapidly with settlers during the last half of the decade. From fifty to one hundred wagons a day were said to have passed through Indianapolis all during the fall of 1826, bound for the Wabash country. Three years later emigrants were passing through the same town bound for the same region at the rate of six thousand a week. The same period witnessed a large influx into previously unoccupied sections of Tennessee. "During the present week," wrote the editor of the *Jackson Gazette* in 1825, "we have observed an increased number of moving families, passing through this place and its vicinity, for the purpose of settling on the Forked Deer, Hatchie, &c . . . no parts of the country . . . are settling faster at this time than those adjacent to the south boundary of the state."

It was in the regions where settlers' cabins were appearing for the first time that the phenomena of the westward movement naturally received the most attention. Michigan was one of these regions. In the census of 1820 this Territory showed less than nine thousand inhabitants, most of whom were of French blood or half-breeds—descendants of the fur traders and villagers who lived there in the days when Cadillac and his successors ruled at Detroit. Americans had scarcely entered Michigan, except at Detroit or as traders in the western portion. The region was away from any practicable route of travel and transportation. It was also thought to be chiefly a country of swamps and pine forests. Acquaintance gradually proved the falsity of this impression. But the chief factor in turning settlers for the first time toward Michigan was the building of the Erie Canal. As work on this epoch-making project got under way not only western New York, but also northern Ohio and even Michigan assumed an attractiveness to settlers hitherto lacking. An all-important means of communication with eastern markets would be available with the completion of the canal.

The movement to Michigan did not become voluminous until after 1830, but it began to receive notice early in the twenties. It was characteristic of the cautious temperament of New Yorkers and New Englanders, who constituted the main element in this early emigration, that they frequently sent out parties to reconnoiter before they ventured to move their families to the new country. "So numerous have been the arrivals of emigrants to this territory since the opening of navigation," declared a Detroit editor in June, 1822, "that it is difficult, at this time, to ascertain, with any degree of certainty, their actual numbers. . . . The interest which is awakened in many parts of the Union, in relation to this territory, and above all, the arrival of numerous intelligent emigrants and gentlemen who come to 'see the country,' induce a conviction that the barriers to emigration are giving way, and that a 'tide' has begun to flow which nothing will retard." Then, as for many years afterward, the principal source of incoming settlers was New York, but Vermont, Massachusetts, Pennsylvania, and Ohio were liberally represented. A colony of Quakers on the River Rouge was mentioned the following year, when many foreigners were also noted.

From this time there were numerous references in the *Detroit Gazette* to the incoming emigrants. In 1824 there was mention of "Michigan companies" being formed in various parts of New York. The following spring saw the coming of nearly five hundred settlers in two days on steamboats and schooners. "To use the words of an emigrant," said the editor, " 'the people at the east are all alive for Michigan'— hundreds of families are determined to come even if they sell their farms and property at half price." In September steamboats and schooners, as well as taverns in town and country, were reported overflowing with prospective settlers. Complaint was made that the newspapers of Cleveland and Sandusky were disparaging Michigan in the effort to dissuade settlers from going thither. "It is not to be wondered at," averred the Detroit editor, "that the people of Ohio now that our lands are surveyed and in market, should feel a little bit waspish when they see every steam-boat and other vessel which happens to touch at their ports, filled with emigrants on their way to this fertile and healthy region."

By 1829 attention was called to the fact that many people from the southern States were coming to Michigan. The *Detroit Gazette* quoted a Charleston, Virginia, paper to the effect that "during the month of Sept. it was computed that not less than 8,000 individuals have passed through that place, bound for Indiana, Illinois and Michigan. They were principally from the lower part of Virginia and South-Carolina. They jog on, careless of the varying climate, and apparently without regret for friends and the country they leave behind, seeking 'forests to fell,' and 'a new country to settle.'"

Reference to the census figures will show that Illinois received a large accession of population during the decade of the twenties. Late in 1825 an Edwardsville editor called attention to the rush of settlers to the northern counties of the State, and wrote of "astonishing" numbers of people crossing the Wabash and of roads "thronged with movers." Arkansas likewise received some notice. Hezekiah Niles was a good prophet in 1822 when he predicted that Arkansas and Michigan would come into the Union together, although that event was delayed longer than he apparently expected. Just at the close of the decade the *Arkansas Gazette* was gratified to report the greatest emigration since the organization of the Territory in 1819. Several counties, and especially the region recently acquired from the Cherokee Indians, he said, "have increased astonishingly in population, during the last twelve months, and the influx of settlers from Alabama, Tennessee, Mississippi, and the other states east of the Mississippi, and from Missouri, on the north, appears to be daily increasing." Alabama and Mississippi each more than doubled in population between 1820 and 1830.

The Westward Movement During the Thirties

During the decade of the thirties the movement to Michigan and Arkansas reached large proportions, especially in the case of the former, and bore fruit in the admission of both States into the Union. Michigan had seven times and Arkansas more than three times as many inhabitants at the end of the ten-year period as at the beginning. During these years the newspapers of New York and Michigan contained frequent news items like that in the *Buffalo Republican* in 1830, which read: "Our steam boats, and other vessels, have for several days been literally crammed with passengers, and a great part of them emigrants from the East, intending to settle in the fertile parts of Michigan and Ohio. It is said that within the past week, as many as one thousand souls passed through this place for such destination. On board one of the canal boats that arrived the other day, we saw several families that numbered together fifty-nine persons." Soon the newly opened roads also became the avenues over which the wagons of settlers poured into Michigan.

In the spring of the same year an Arkansas newspaper reported that "not only is every Steam-boat crowded with cabin and deck passengers, but the roads are also lined with wagons, conveying families to the Eden of Arkansas—as it is considered abroad—the counties of Washington and Crawford." The people of Memphis were charged with disseminating "vile and false slanders" against the soil, climate and inhabitants of Arkansas in the effort to deter settlers from crossing the Mississippi. Thus at last Arkansas, which hitherto had been too far north for those moving up the Mississippi and too far south for those coming down the Ohio, began to receive favorable attention, and in the succeeding years its population increased steadily, although never as rapidly as that of Michigan and other northern regions.

Illinois also more than trebled in population during this decade. S. A. Ferrall, who traveled the roads of that State in 1831, met several large parties of settlers moving to the Illinois River section. They were mostly "Georgians, Virginians and Kentuckians, whose comparative poverty rendered their residence in slave states unpleasant." People from south of the Mason and Dixon Line and the Ohio were conspicuous in the early settlement of southern Illinois. Many of them were poor people, but Timothy Flint saw others who were persons of some note and with property, including slaves, "whose immigration was accompanied with a certain degree of éclat." On the other hand, it was said in 1835 that "the emigration from New-York city is immense; they come in companies of hundreds, and pitch their tents in some hitherto wild and uncultivated place, and in a few days make it one of the most considerable settlements in the country. The old inhabitants are amazed and overawed by the persevering enterprise of the 'Yankees.' " The emigration to Illinois for the spring of 1839 was estimated to exceed 40,000 by a Sangamon editor.

Across the river in Missouri similar scenes were observed. A Columbia editor in 1835 denied any exaggeration when he asserted that "for several weeks past, the number of wagons, with their usual appendages, which have daily passed through Columbia, must have averaged forty! Indeed, we do not recollect ever to have seen our streets and roads so thronged. Independent of the actual movers, the number of travellers on horseback, exploring the country, is prodigious. The emigration to Missouri the present season is immense." Most of the new settlers were said to be "from Virginia and Kentucky, with a sprinkling of Tennesseans and Carolinians—substantial farmers and enterprising merchants and mechanics, with here and there a young 'limb of the law,' or a disciple of Esculapius seeking in the 'Far West' a home for themselves and a patrimony for their children."

Two new Territories appeared in the census of 1840—Wisconsin, recently set off from Michigan; and Iowa, including an extensive area west of the Mississippi and north of the State of Missouri. There had for many years been an increasing population in the lead-mining region in southwestern Wisconsin and settlements had now begun to appear along Lake Michigan and in the interior.

Lead-mining around Dubuque had likewise been the attraction that first drew people to Iowa, even when it was still Indian territory. In 1832, however, a strip of land about fifty miles wide on the west bank of the Mississippi, known as the Black Hawk Purchase, was relinquished by the Indians. When this treaty went into effect on June 1, 1833, settlers began to cross the Mississippi and stake out claims as thousands of others had done in other western regions, without waiting for the surveys to be made. Booming towns soon appeared and the process of settlement was in full swing. "The great thoroughfares of Illinois and Indiana, in the years 1836-7," wrote John B. Newhall, "would be literally lined with the long blue wagons of the emigrants slowly wending their way over the broad prairies, the cattle and hogs, men and dogs, and frequently women and children, forming the rear of the van—often ten, twenty and thirty wagons in company. Ask them, when and where you would, their destination was the Black Hawk Purchase." In 1839 an Iowa editor declared that "whole neighborhoods in Illinois, Indiana and Ohio are 'organizing' for emigration, and will soon take up their line of march for Iowa; even the substantial yeomanry of the Keystone, the proud sons of the old Dominion, and the enterprising 'down easters' are turning their steps westward and looking to Iowa as their future home."

The Westward Movement During the Forties

The movement to Wisconsin and Iowa, thus begun, continued without abatement during the "roaring forties," and led to statehood in both cases before the decade closed. A Madison editor estimated in 1843 that two hundred new settlers for Wisconsin were landing daily at the lake ports. "Hundreds of emigrants," he said, "are daily and hourly pouring into the Territory from all parts of the country, by water and by land. The Lake and river counties and the mineral region are fast filling up with settlers, and first rate land is rising in price." Year after year the movement continued. In 1845 much attention was paid to the arrival of a group of more than a hundred people from Rochester, New York, sixty-two of whom were members of the Allen family. "The patriarch of the family," said a Rochester editor, "will be 88 years old in July. He is one of the venerable relics of the revolution. . . . He moved off, in his old chair, surrounded like Abraham, with his scores of descendants, anxious to die, as he has lived, amongst them."

In Iowa the settlements pushed rapidly westward, especially after Indian title to the New Purchase, embracing the fertile valley of the Des Moines was relinquished in 1843. "Emigrants rushed to the New Purchase by way of the Ohio and the Mississippi," says Jacob Van der Zee, "or they rolled overland in great, rumbling wagons. For weeks and months before this wonderful country was opened to settlement alluring prospects brought hundreds of persons to the frontier border and only military force could restrain them from building homes on the red man's soil."

The spread of settlements into Iowa and Wisconsin attracted special notice during this period because they were the cutting edge of the advancing frontier. Into all the other States between the Appalachians and the western border of the Mississippi Valley commonwealths a steady stream of people was pouring, adding to the population of the towns and filling up the farming lands. A glance at the census figures will show that this movement was quite evenly distributed, although there was greater relative gain in the States north of the Ohio as compared with those to the south. This, too, was the decade when "Manifest Destiny" became the watchword of western America. This was the decade which witnessed the romantic trek to Oregon, the march of the Mormons to their new home in the Rocky Mountains, and the gold rush to California—all of which will receive attention in later chapters.

The Westward Movement During the Fifties

The westward movement during the fifties was not only large in volume but also of great political and economic significance when viewed in connection with the great sectional struggle which followed. During the ten years from 1850 to 1860 the total population of the eight States of Ohio, Indiana, Illinois, Michigan, Wisconsin, Minnesota, Iowa, and Missouri increased by more than 3,350,000—an increase of more than 167 per cent, due partly to natural increase, partly to foreign immigration, and mainly to the westward migration of the American people. The increase in the six States of Kentucky, Tennessee, Alabama, Mississippi, Louisiana, and Arkansas during the same period was slightly less than 1,075,000, or only 26.2 per cent. It is evident, therefore, either that emigration into these southern States had largely ceased or that the outflow practically balanced the inflow. In other words, the westward shift of population during this period definitely established the numerical and economic superiority of the North, and filled the grain-producing States with people opposed to the further spread of slavery. Because of the much greater volume and importance of the northern phase, only the movement in that section will be described.

From the standpoint of actual numbers of new settlers Illinois had a notable growth. The population of that State, already large in 1850, more than doubled during the decade. Minnesota, which achieved statehood in 1858, had an increase of 2,730 per cent in population during the ten years. In 1850 Minnesota contained only a few scattered settlements with a total of 6,077 inhabitants; but in the years that followed such a stream of emigration set in that by 1860 there were 172,023 people in the State. Iowa had an increase of over 251 per cent during the same period. The census of 1860 shows that during the decade Iowa received more than 68,000 emigrants from Ohio, over 37,000 from each of the States of New York, Pennsylvania, and Indiana, and nearly 30,000 from Illinois.

Illinois was the favorite region for settlement for emigrants from the largest numbers of States. Missouri attracted settlers from the second largest number of commonwealths, while Ohio and Iowa stood third and fourth in this respect. On the other hand, the migrations of native-born citizens of the eight States under discussion exemplified the rule that emigration tended to follow parallels of latitude or to flow into adjoining jurisdictions. Again, it is to be noted that it was during the fifties that foreign immigrants began to come into the Mississippi Valley in large numbers. The foreign-born population of these eight States was increased by 881,000, or more than doubled.

Thus it is apparent that this decade witnessed a remarkable emigration into the upper Mississippi Valley, both of native American families and of home-seekers from foreign shores. Nearly 43,000,000 acres of public land were taken up in this region during these ten years, and, to quote a contemporary, "the energies thus called into action have, in a few years, made the States of the Northwest, the granary of Europe, and that section of our Union which, within the recollections of living men, was a wilderness, is now the chief source of supply in seasons of scarcity for the suffering millions of another continent."

But a more definite picture of the great wave of humanity which swept over this region may be gained by taking a cross-sectional view of the emigration into one particular State. For this purpose no better illustration can be found than the notable rush of settlers to Iowa during the two years from 1854 to 1856. The completion of railroads to the Mississippi, and the publicity given by land companies, scores of emigrant guide-books, and hundreds of articles in eastern newspapers all helped to facilitate travel and stimulate emigration by making the name "Iowa" a household word. Farmers in the eastern States and in Ohio and Indiana were discouraged because of drouth, a fatal epidemic of cholera, or hard times. Hence the prospect of acquiring a quarter section of cheap government land in healthful, productive Iowa was very attractive to them. And so in large numbers they sold out, packed their goods in wagons or on boats or trains, and turned their faces westward toward the land beyond the Mississippi.

"The immigration into Iowa the present season is astonishing and unprecedented," ran an account in an eastern journal in June, 1854. "For miles and miles, day after day, the prairies of Illinois are lined with cattle and wagons, pushing on toward this prosperous State. At a point beyond Peoria, during a single month, seventeen hundred and forty-three wagons had passed, and all for Iowa. Allowing five persons to a wagon, which is a fair average, would give 8,715 souls to the population." This was only the emigration of one month on one road out of many.

At all the principal points along the Mississippi River an almost continuous stream of emigrants was crossing over the ferries into Iowa during the fall and early winter of 1854. Beginning at the north with the three ferries in the vicinity of Prairie du Chien and Mac Gregor, it was reported that "each of these ferries employs a horse-boat, and is crowded all the time with emigrants for Iowa. Sometimes the emigrants have to encamp near the ferry two or three days to await their chance to cross in the order of their arrival." The same situation prevailed at Dubuque where emigrants were arriving daily and almost hourly, and at Davenport where the ferry was kept busy at "all hours in passing over the large canvas-backed wagons" filled with would-be Iowans. At Burlington it was declared that "20,000 immigrants have passed through the city within the last thirty days, and they are still crossing at the rate of 600 and 700 a day." Even at Keokuk such large numbers of settlers came in by boat that a journalist was led to say that "by the side of this exodus, that of the Israelites becomes an insignificant item, and the greater migrations of later times are scarcely to be mentioned." It was said that one thousand people from Richland County, Ohio, came to Iowa that fall.

The movement was checked temporarily during the coldest winter months, but with the opening of spring in 1855 it began again with full strength, if indeed it did not assume larger proportions than during the previous year. Throughout the summer the invasion continued. "Seek whatever thoroughfare you may," wrote a traveler in central Iowa in June, "and you will find it lined with emigrant wagons. In many instances large droves of stock of a superior quality are met with. On our last days drive . . . we met 69 covered wagons seeking a home in the valley of the Des Moines." The report of the General Land Office for the year ending June 30, 1855, indicated that there had been taken up in Iowa during that year more than three million and a quarter acres of public land.

The autumn of 1855 witnessed no appreciable diminishing of the stream of land-hungry settlers pouring into the newer counties of the State. The National Road in Ohio and Indiana was again lined with wagons on their way to Iowa and Wisconsin. "The Immigration to Iowa this season is immense," wrote an Iowa editor in November, "far exceeding the unprecedented immigration of last year, and only to be appreciated by one who travels through the country as we are doing, and finds the roads everywhere lined with movers." At Rock Island, although two steam ferry-boats made one hundred trips a day they were unable to handle all the business.

Illustrations of this character might be multiplied almost indefinitely to show how the great tide of emigration spread out over the valleys and prairies of Iowa during the two years from 1854 to 1856. Furthermore, what has been said in regard to Iowa during these two years was true, though perhaps in a less noticeable way, in the neighboring States throughout the entire decade of the fifties. By 1860 the commonwealths bordering the upper Mississippi had to a large extent passed the frontier stage, and were factors to be reckoned with in national affairs during the stirring years which followed.

In this and the preceding chapter, at the risk of tediousness, the purpose has been to leave a vivid impression of the continuity and volume of the great westward movement from the winning of independence to the outbreak of the war for the preservation of the Union. Thus far we have been concerned only with the settlement of the humid, tree-covered area extending to the western border of the first tier of States west of the Mississippi. We shall now see how these people traveled to their new western homes, how they acquired land, met Indian occupants, reacted toward the presence and policies of neighboring nations on the north and south, and in general how their economic, social, and political ideas and institutions were shaped by the frontier environment.

CHAPTER III

ON THE WAY TO THE WEST

"THE pioneer, no matter of what date or locality, was always a traveller before he was a producer or shipper of goods, and the common experience of the people, gained on their journeys, was—save in one instance—the basis on which future permanent routes and methods of travel were planned and created. The one exception to this manner of evolution lay in the memorable demonstration that steam could be successfully used for the propulsion of travel vehicles. It was an instance wherein genius and reason overshadowed experience and precedent." So writes Seymour Dunbar in the opening pages of his admirable *History of Travel in America*.[1]

The period covered by the westward migrations described in the two preceding chapters witnessed a transformation in the means and speed of travel that was more revolutionary than that caused by the aeroplane in our own day. It was a far cry from the crude flatboat to the palatial steamboat, and from the slow-moving pack-horse on uncertain trails to the speeding railway train. The first settlers who ventured into the West made their way as best they could along Indian trails or through the roadless forests; or they used the waterways as they found them, with all their obstructions and perils. The improvements to river navigation and the building of real roads were largely the results of the needs and demands for better means of transportation and communication, after the settlers had established themselves in their new western homes. To be sure, later emigrants were immensely benefited by these improvements as long as they remained in relatively settled regions. But those who moved to the edge of the frontier always came to a "jumping off place" beyond which the conditions of the unmodified wilderness prevailed. The story of internal

[1] Quoted by permission of The Bobbs-Merrill Company, publishers.

improvements—the building of roads, the improvement of river navigation, the growth of steamboat traffic, the digging of canals in the West itself, and the construction of railroads—belongs with the narrative of economic development after settlements had been made. This chapter is concerned with the experiences and the methods of travel of the first settlers on their way to various sections of the West.

EMIGRANT TRAVEL ON THE OHIO

The only real highways which white men found ready for their use as they pushed into the interior of America were the rivers. But the system of inland waterways seemed providentially designed to lure and facilitate the movement of people westward. The great Ohio River, springing from the union of two navigable streams, flowed westward with gentle current and beckoned invitingly to all who came to its headwaters. Thus, to use the words of Archer B. Hulbert, this river "is entitled to a most prominent place among Historic Highways of America which greatly influenced the early westward extension of the borders and the people of the United States." The tributaries flowing into the Ohio from the north and the south offered access to large areas. Then, when these lands were settled or ceased to be sufficiently attractive, settlers could float down the Ohio to its junction with the Mississippi, and descend that great stream at will, breast its current hundreds of miles to the northward, or make their way up one of that river's numerous affluents. It is not surprising, therefore, that the Ohio River was a highway used by thousands and no doubt hundreds of thousands of pioneers journeying to their new western homes.

Several types of river craft preceded the coming of the steamboat. The canoe and the pirogue were mainly used by the explorer, the hunter or Indian trader, and the individual adventurer. The keelboat, the barge, and the flatboat were crafts of commerce. The flatboat, or ark as it was sometimes called, was also the well-nigh universal river vehicle of the settler moving westward with his family and his possessions. These boats were cheap and easily constructed, and they were made of sawed lumber which the settler could use most advantageously in building his cabin upon arriving at his destination. They could be purchased at numerous "boat-yards" on the upper Ohio in 1811 for about thirty-five dollars. The description written by Francis Baily in 1796 was equally applicable to the flatboats in use thirty or forty years later. They were, he said, generally from thirty to forty feet in length and twelve feet wide. Their construction consisted of "a framework fastened together with wooden pins, which constitutes the bottom of the boat, and to this is fastened a flooring, which is well calked to prevent leaking; the sides are about breast high, and made of thin plank; and sometimes there is a rude kind of covering, *intended* to keep the rain out."

A covering over a portion of the boat was apparently the rule, especially on the type called the "Kentucky flat" or "broadhorn" because of the long oar on either side for use in steering. The equipment of oars was employed mainly in propelling the boat to and from the bank or in avoiding obstructions in the channel. The current of the river provided the only momentum under ordinary circumstances, and thus a flatboat journey down the Ohio was slow and of long duration. Timothy Flint declared that the typical flatboat had much the appearance of a New England pigstye when viewed externally. But he hastened to add that many of the "family-boats" were "large and roomy, and have comfortable and separate apartments, fitted up with chairs, beds, tables and stoves. It is no uncommon spectacle to see a large family, old and young, servants, cattle, hogs, horses, sheep, fowls, and animals of all kinds, bringing to recollection the cargo of the ancient ark, all embarked, and floating down on the same bottom."

Two or three additional quotations from the writings of contemporaries will furnish glimpses of these flatboats and their occupants as they floated down the Ohio. F. A. Michaux, writing of his western journey in 1802, told how he was traveling along the bank of the Monongahela when he saw five or six of these strange craft on the river. "I could not," he said, "conceive what these great square boxes were, which, left to the stream, presented alternately their ends, sides, and even their angles. As they advanced, I heard a confused noise, but without distinguishing anything, on account of their sides being so high. However, on ascending the banks of the river, I perceived in these barges several families, carrying with them their horses, cows, poultry, waggons, ploughs, harness, beds, instruments of agriculture, in fine, everything necessary to cultivate the soil, and also for domestic use."

A generation later, in 1828, James Hall wrote of similar sights and noted many variations of the typical flatboat party. For instance, he saw a man and a woman about sixty years of age floating and paddling down the Ohio River in a flat-bottomed boat, twelve feet long with high sides and a roof. They were seeking a new home further west. "Why, Sir," replied the old man when questioned as to their motives, "our boys are all married, and gone off, and bustling about for themselves; and our neighbors, a good many of 'em's gone *out back*, and so the old woman and me felt sort o' lonesome, and thought we'd go too, and try our luck."

Hall also described "two large rafts lashed together, by which simple conveyance several families from New England were transporting themselves and their property to the land of promise in the western woods. Each raft was eighty or ninety feet long, with a small house erected on it; and on each was a stack of hay, round which several horses and cows were feeding, while the paraphernalia of a farm-yard, the ploughs, waggons, pigs, children, and poultry, carelessly distributed, gave to the whole more the appearance of a permanent residence, than of a caravan of adventurers seeking a home. A respectable looking old lady, with spectacles on nose, was seated on a chair at the door of one of the cabins, employed in knitting; another female was at the wash-tub; the men were chewing their tobacco, with as much complacency as if they had been in 'the land of steady habits,' and the various family avocations seemed to go on like clock-work."

Steamboats did not by any means supplant flatboats as carriers of emigrating families. Those with some means patronized the more comfortable and expeditious vessels, but until the entire Ohio Valley was well settled the humbler craft continued to be used by the impecunious and the thrifty. It appears, however, that steamboats played a large role in transporting upstream emigrants to the lands along the Mississippi. This was true of those who came up from the south to settle in Arkansas and Missouri, and also of many whose destinations were the lands bordering the great river in Iowa, Illinois, and Wisconsin.

EMIGRANTS ON THE ERIE CANAL

The only other waterway in any degree comparable to the Ohio River as a highway of the westward movement was one which was partly man-made. The completion in 1825 of the Erie Canal, connecting the Hudson River with Lake Erie, was an achievement of far-reaching significance, not only in establishing the commercial supremacy of New York City, but also in facilitating the settlement and development of western New York and the lands on the shores of the Great Lakes. The greatest importance of "Clinton's Ditch" lay in its service as a link in a water highway of commerce. Nevertheless, in the early years of the canal's history it was used by many emigrants, who either settled in western New York or transferred their goods at Buffalo to schooners or steamboats and proceeded to a more distant destination in Michigan or Ohio, or later in Wisconsin. Travel by canal boat was cheap for deck passengers. For instance in 1822, before the completion of the canal, a Rochester paper noted the arrival of a boat filled with emigrants who had come a distance of 150 miles at a cost of one dollar and a half each.

The effect of the Erie Canal in accelerating the westward movement became more noticeable as it neared completion. "From some towns bordering upon the Canal, and which might therefore be expected to reap the most signal advantages from that great work," commented a New York editor in 1824, "we understand that not less than one hundred inhabitants have emigrated within the last year." The same year a Utica paper asserted that "Scarcely a boat from the east passes without a number of families on board, with their household goods and farming utensils, bound to the 'Genessee country,' 'Ohio,' or the 'Michigan Territory.' There is no method of ascertaining the number of this description of passengers on the canal, for they pay no toll, and are not reported at the collector's office;

but some estimation may be formed of the amount, when it is known that wagons with emigrants are literally swept from the roads, formerly the great thoroughfare of the west. It is not uncommon to see from thirty to forty women and children comfortably stowed away in one of the large covered canal boats, as chirp as a flock of blackbirds." More than a decade later it was remarked that "no one who does not witness it, can have any just idea of the 'immense and intermingling throng of people' who are wending their way, by the route of Lake Erie, to the West. The steam boats and schooners plying between the various ports on the Lake, are represented to be constantly crowded."

The Evolution of Roads

In spite of the ease and economy of travel by the Ohio River and the Erie Canal-Great Lakes route, it is safe to say that the settlement of the West was accomplished mainly by people who journeyed on land by pack-train, wagon, or on foot. The covered wagon became, and remains in retrospect, the pre-eminent visible symbol of the westward movement.

The story of the evolution of roads is full of interest and fascination. The first paths were Indian trails, many of which in turn followed buffalo traces. Some of these Indian trails were very long, especially those running north and south, like the one which followed the mountain ranges from New York and Pennsylvania to the Carolinas. They were narrow, blind paths, unblazed and only to be followed with certainty by experienced woodsmen. They ran along the highlands and thus were often much more circuitous than the modern roads which utilize valleys and water-level routes. Occasionally trails between Indian villages or leading to favorite hunting grounds were somewhat widened by the frequent and continued passage of travails and pack-horses.

The widening of the longer trails was begun by the pack-trains of white traders and settlers. The trampling of many horses gradually broadened the pathway and the bulky loads extending on either side of the horses wore away the overhanging branches and underbrush. With the exception of

Braddock's Road and Forbes' Road, there were few routes by which a journey across the mountains could be made before 1800 in any better manner than on horseback with accompanying pack-train.

The next step in the widening of the trails was taken when people determined to force their way through with wheeled vehicles—carts with huge wheels or wagons. Even then only the most primitive road-making was done, with results that would not be tolerated to-day in building a temporary logging road. The underbrush and trees were cut away, leaving many of the stumps; and logs were thrown down to form puncheon bridges across creeks and especially troublesome bogs. The succeeding improvements such as graded turnpikes, stone or gravel surfacing, plank roads and adequate bridges, to be described in a later chapter, came after the country was settled and there were commodities to be transported. The early settlers traveled roads that were such only in name. As Archer B. Hulbert points out, they might more properly be designated as "routes." The rock-strewn, precipitous roadway over the mountains was no worse than the rutted or muddy course through the lowlands, where the road often broadened out amazingly as each succeeding group of wagons sought a better and firmer track.

Emigrant Highways to the West

Even if it were possible, it would accomplish no useful purpose to enumerate and describe all the various roads that served as highways of emigration across the Appalachians and into the Mississippi Valley. From New York to the Carolinas and Georgia, Indian trails evolved into roads and white men laid out other paths to suit their desire to reach some particular land of promise. Most romantic in its early history, because linked with the name of Daniel Boone and the exciting years of Kentucky's first settlements, was the Wilderness Road through Cumberland Gap. This highway was soon joined by a well-traveled road from Philadelphia, through Richmond, and thus it became a great thoroughfare over which hordes of emigrants traveled to settle the region south of the Ohio River.

The main roads converging on the head-waters of the Ohio, however, rivaled if they did not surpass the Wilderness Road as thoroughfares of emigration. Whether settlers were planning to "take water" on reaching the Ohio or to proceed westward overland, they were obliged to make their way over the mountains by road. Braddock's Road, the route of which was later followed in a general way by the Cumberland Road, except that its western terminus was Wheeling instead of Pittsburgh, was the favorite highway for those coming from Maryland or Virginia. Forbes' Road through the central part of Pennsylvania to Pittsburgh was heavily traveled by emigrants from that State and from the region to the east and northeast. A few excerpts from the writings of contemporaries depicting emigrant travel over these roads will serve to illustrate the methods of travel everywhere.

One of the best descriptions is that given by Morris Birkbeck who traveled across Pennsylvania in 1817, when the Great Migration was in full swing. Writing of the typical emigrant party, he said: "A small waggon (so light you might almost carry it, yet strong enough to bear a good load of bedding, utensils and provisions, and a swarm of young citizens,—and to sustain marvellous shocks in its passage over these rocky heights), with two small horses; sometimes a cow or two, comprises their all. . . . The waggon has a tilt, or cover, made of a sheet, or perhaps a blanket. The family are seen before, behind, or within the vehicle, according to the road or weather, or perhaps the spirit of the party."

Birkbeck noted differences in the habits of people from the various eastern States. "The New Englanders," he said, "may be known by the cheerful air of the women advancing in front of the vehicle; the Jersey people by their being fixed steadily within it; whilst the Pennsylvanians creep lingeringly behind, as though regretting the homes they have left." He described also the travel methods of those not so fortunate as to own a team and wagon. "A cart and single horse frequently afford the means of transfer, sometimes a horse and pack-saddle. Often the back of the poor pilgrim bears all his effects, and his wife follows, naked-footed, bending under the hopes of the family."

A few years later James Hall journeyed through the same region and "found the roads crowded with emigrants of every description, but the majority were of the poorest class. Here I would meet a few lusty fellows, trudging it merrily along; and there a family, more embarrassed and less cheerful; now a gang of forty or fifty souls, men, women and children; and now a solitary pedestrian, with his oaken staff, his bottle, and his knapsack." Hall described one family in particular. "The senior of the party was a middle-aged man, hale, well built, and decently clad. He was guiding a pair of small, lean, active horses, harnessed to a light waggon, which contained the bedding and provisions of the party, and a few articles of household furniture; two well-grown, barefoot boys, in homespun shirts and trousers, held the tail of the waggon, laudably endeavoring to prevent an upset, by throwing their weight occasionally to that side which seemed to require ballast, while the father exerted his arms, voice, and whip, in urging forward his ponies. In the rear toiled the partner of his pilgrimage, conducting, like John Rodgers' wife, 'nine small children and one at the breast.' "

Variations from the methods of travel already mentioned were occasionally seen on western roads. Although not wholly unknown in other sections, the people of a Missouri community were surprised at the "novel method of flitting" of a man and his wife and four children, who arrived there in 1834 from Ohio. "The man and the woman walked, and the man drew a small hand wagon, in which the children and the clothing and some other articles were; this he dragged the whole distance of their journey." Several years later, near the Wabash River, Rev. James L. Scott passed a small family who "had one ox in the thills of a two wheeled cart, in which were one or two boxes, and a mat or bed. This was all we could see that they possessed. . . .This I thought, was traveling poverty indeed." And, believe it or not, a traveler passing through Tennessee in 1818, "met a travelling house, drawn by six horses, two stories high, and containing three families, or 29 persons in the whole. They reported themselves from the district of Maine, bound to Alabama."

Such a vehicle was no doubt unique, but what Timothy

Flint called the typical "southern wagon" was "strong, comfortable, commodious, containing not only a movable kitchen, but provisions and beds. Drawn by four or six horses, it subserves all the various intentions of house, shelter and transport; and is, in fact, the southern ship of the forests and prairies. The horses, that convey the wagon, are large and powerful animals, followed by servants, cattle, sheep, swine, dogs, the whole forming a primitive caravan not unworthy of ancient days. . . .The procession moves on with power in its dust, putting to shame and uncomfortable feelings of comparison the northern family with their slight wagons, jaded horses and subdued though jealous countenances."

CHAPTER IV

THE NATIONAL BOUNDARIES IN THE WEST

WHEN exuberant American settlers poured across the Appalachian Mountains after the winning of independence they no
doubt thought that now they would be entirely free from the
hampering restrictions of Old World politics.   In this they
were greatly mistaken.   For more than thirty-five years after
the signing of the Treaty of 1783 westerners were keenly conscious that they were bounded and limited by territories possessed by European powers.   During most of this period the
West seethed with international intrigues and western problems
occupied an important place in American diplomacy.   Jay's
treaty with England in 1794, Pinckney's treaty with Spain in
the following year, the purchase of Louisiana, Burr's conspiracy, the occupation of West Florida, the War of 1812, and
the acquisition of all of Florida—all these occurred or were
accomplished partly or largely because of western resentments,
demands, and pressures.   Volumes have been written in regard
to each of these episodes, but a brief survey will serve to show
both their significance in western development and the part
played by westerners.

THE SPANISH-AMERICAN FRONTIER

The refusal of the Spaniards to allow Americans the free
navigation of the Mississippi River was the first rude shock
received by the buoyant settlers in the Ohio Valley   It will be
remembered that the Treaty of 1783 stated that the citizens
of both England and the United States should have a right
of freely navigating the Mississippi.   It was also agreed that
the thirty-first parallel should be the southern boundary of
the new republic, although there was a secret understanding
that the boundary should be the line running through the

mouth of the Yazoo River in case England should reconquer West Florida from Spain before the final treaty was signed. Spain refused to acknowledge that England had the right to make an agreement concerning the navigation of a river over which she had no control. The Spaniards likewise declined to admit that the terms of the Treaty of 1783 regarding the southern boundary of the United States had any validity, since Spain had conquered West Florida which under England extended as far north as the Yazoo River, or 32 degrees 28 minutes.

The boundary controversy was largely conducted through diplomatic channels; although naturally Americans, and especially those living in the West, were not uninterested in the subject. In brief, during the early negotiations Spain advanced claims the most extreme of which would have left the United States very little territory south of the Ohio and west of the Appalachians. Spain's object was to interpose an Indian buffer territory between the United States and her possessions in Louisiana and the Floridas. As has been noted, the Spaniards never had any love for the Americans. On the contrary, they hated and feared the frontiersmen, and were far-sighted enough to know that unless some barrier could be interposed it would be only a question of time until the resolute, liberty-loving borderers would be invading Spanish territory.

The navigation of the Mississippi River was far from being a mere diplomatic question to the western settlers. It was a matter of intimate personal concern to every inhabitant of the West, for the Mississippi was the highway and New Orleans was the market or shipping point for all the produce of the "men of the western waters." The lack, at that early day, of roads across the mountains made the transportation of agricultural products to Atlantic coast markets virtually prohibitive. On the other hand, shipment by flatboats floating with the current of the Tennessee or the Ohio and the Mississippi was easy and inexpensive. Even though the river traffic was actually very small in volume during the first years following the Revolution, every farmer in the West looked to the rivers and New Orleans as the outlet that would ultimately make farming profitable for him.

Imagine then the consternation of these western farmers when they learned that the Spanish had closed the Mississippi to Americans except on payment of prohibitive duties, and their resentment when they discovered that the American government was disposed to aquiesce. Don Diego de Gardoqui, Spanish chargé d' affaires, and John Jay, Secretary for Foreign Affairs under the Congress of the Confederation, carried on a series of negotiations in 1785 and 1786. In the end Jay recommended that Americans forbear to use the Mississippi within Spanish territory for twenty or thirty years in return for a commercial treaty much desired by the merchants and shippers of the northern States. Only the stout resistance of the southern states prevented Congress from adopting this policy. Even men like Washington and Jefferson expressed the opinion that it would be wise to postpone a definite showdown on the Mississippi question until the western settlement had grown sufficiently to determine the question by force of numbers.

The settlers on the Holston, on the Cumberland, and in Kentucky received this news with bitter indignation. The ties which bound them to the Union were tenuous at best. They had for some time been protesting that the federal government was negligent in providing protection against the Indians, and now this apparent willingness to permit the closure of their only highway to market was regarded as an inexcusable sacrifice of their interest.

The Spanish were quick to take advantage of this situation. There followed a period of intrigues in which nearly all of the frontier leaders—men like John Sevier, James Robertson, William Blount, George Rogers Clark, Benjamin Sebastian, and others—were involved. The arch plotter of them all was James Wilkinson of Kentucky, a man whose name will always be associated with base perfidy, even though he later held high rank in the American army. Equally colorful but less successful was the adventurer, Dr. James O'Fallon, agent for the South Carolina Yazoo Company. Talk of setting up an independent government was rife in the West. There were plots to bring the western settlements under Spanish protection and control. On the other hand the Spanish officials at New Orleans were frequently thrown into a panic by reports of expeditions of American frontiersmen being organized to descend upon Louisiana and take possession of the Mississippi by force of arms. Efforts of the Spaniards to attract American settlers to locate around Natchez and at other points along the river were matched by proposals of American land companies and speculators to establish colonies with or without Spanish consent. In 1789 the seizure of a British vessel by the Spaniards in far-away Nootka Sound brought these two nations to the verge of war in 1790. Westerners saw in the situation visions of British aid against the Spanish in Louisiana, but this hope was short-lived. The crisis passed and war was averted.

It is doubtful whether any considerable number of American frontiersmen would at this time have really placed themselves under Spanish rule with all its restrictions upon individual activity. For a time the danger of a separation from the Union was imminent, but the moment passed, and the underlying attachment of westerners to their own American government reasserted itself. After he became President under the new Constitution, George Washington showed his wisdom by conciliating the disgruntled western settlers. Overlooking their lapses, he appointed many of the favorite spokesmen of the West to civil office in the newly created Southwest Territory or to high rank in the army. The admission of Kentucky into the Union in 1792 did much to allay discontent.

All these measures, however, did not prevent the people of the West from listening eagerly to Citizen Edmond Genêt, the first representative of the French Republic, when, in 1793 and 1794, he proposed the organization of an expedition to capture the Floridas and Louisiana from Spain. One of those enlisted in this scheme was George Rogers Clark, the hero of Vincennes, who had become embittered by the seeming ingratitude of Virginia and the American government as expressed in their continued failure to reimburse him for expenses incurred in the Illinois campaign during the Revolution. To him Genêt sent a provisional commission as "Commander-in-Chief of the Independent and Revolutionary Army of the Mississippi." Genêt's plan failed largely through lack of funds, and partly because his home government disavowed his actions. Enthusiasm for his expedition in the West also cooled somewhat when it became known that the federal government was making a determined effort through diplomacy to secure the right of navigation of the Mississippi.

These negotiations were terminated at San Lorenzo on October 27, 1795, when Manuel de Godoy and Thomas Pinckney signed a treaty between Spain and the United States. By this treaty the United States gained virtually everything she had been seeking: commercial agreements pleasing to easterners and the free navigation of the Mississippi for all American subjects. The southern boundary of the United States was fixed at the thirty-first parallel. Americans were given the right to deposit their goods at New Orleans, subject only to reasonable storage charges, for a period of three years. At the end of this time the privilege of deposit at New Orleans was either to be continued or an "equivalent establishment" was to be assigned at some other point on the Mississippi. As pointed out by Arthur P. Whitaker, one of the main reasons why the Spanish acceded to these terms was the fact that, after years of experience with efforts to hold back the steady western progress of the Americans, they now "preferred a treaty with the established government of the United States to an intrigue with its irresponsible frontiersmen." There was delay in executing the boundary provisions of the treaty and within a few years the shadow of Napoleon Bonaparte fell across the American West. For the time being, however, western settlers were satisfied, for their government had secured for them the free use of the Mississippi.

PROBLEMS OF THE NORTHERN BORDER

Another provision of the Treaty of 1783 affecting the West was one by which the British agreed to withdraw their troops from all posts in American territory with "all convenient speed." It was not until 1796 that this promise was fulfilled. At Pointe-au-Fer and Dutchman's Point in the Lake Champlain country, at Oswegatchie on the St. Lawrence, at Oswego and Niagara on Lake Ontario, at Erie on Lake Erie, at Detroit strategically located on the straits between Lakes Erie and Huron, and on the island of Michilimackinac between Lakes

Huron and Michigan, the British maintained their garrisons as though no treaty had been made. In vain did our representatives in London seek to hold England to her agreement. They were repeatedly informed that England did not propose to evacuate the western posts for the reasons that the American government had failed to carry out is promises in regard to the collection of British debts and the treatment of loyalists.

There were good grounds for this excuse, although it is an open question as to which nation first violated the provisions of the treaty. As a matter of fact, the excuse was only a convenient pretext. The real reason why the British refused to give up the frontier posts lay in the unwillingness of merchants to relinquish control of the lucrative fur trade of the Great Lakes region. Furthermore, many Englishmen confidently looked forward to the not distant time when the weak American Union would be dissolved—an expectation which seemed close to fulfillment as far as the West was concerned during the period of the Spanish intrigues just described. British officials in Canada and at the western forts, therefore, used every means to extend and strengthen their influence over the Indian tribes of the northwest. Like the Spanish, they had a project for an Indian buffer territory under British protection, and this territory was to include all the region north of the Ohio River, as well as a strip of country in what is now northern New York.

It was not difficult to convince the Indians that their interests lay with the British rather than with the Americans. The former were concerned only with trade, while the latter were seeking land for settlement. The evident weakness of the American government also served the English cause, especially after Arthur St. Clair's disastrous defeat by the Indians on November 4, 1791. Three years later, however, the situation was greatly changed and American prestige was enhanced among the Indians by the aggressive but cautious campaign under Anthony Wayne, culminating in his decisive victory at the Battle of Fallen Timbers on August 20, 1794. From the beginning of Wayne's expedition the British commanders at Detroit and at an outpost on the Maumee River were suspicious that these posts were the real objective, and they gave every possible aid to the Indians. For a time after the defeat of the redskins hostilities between Wayne's men and the British seemed inevitable, but after a few days the American commander wisely retired to Fort Defiance, which he had built the previous year further up the Maumee.

By this time the question of the western posts was in process of settlement. On November 19, 1794, John Jay and Lord Grenville signed the famous agreement known in American history as Jay's Treaty. While the provisions of this treaty with respect to commerce and the rights of the United States on the high seas were far from satisfactory to a majority of Americans, it did result in British withdrawal from the western posts by the date agreed upon—June 1, 1796. Grenville had come to the conclusion that the holding of posts within American territory was not essential to the continuance of British trade with the Indians of the northwest. Stations north of the boundary line would serve equally well. In this expectation he was entirely justified, for, as will be seen, British influence over the Indians, emanating from such points as Malden across the Canadian border, long remained a cause of complaint and indignation among the settlers in the Ohio Valley. Nevertheless, Jay's Treaty of 1794 and Pinckney's Treaty of 1795 finally led to the fulfillment of the Treaty of 1783 with respect to boundaries and the rights of Americans in the West.

THE LOUISIANA PURCHASE

The boundary line specified in Pinckney's Treaty was not run, nor did Americans come into possession of Natchez, until 1798, three years after the signing of the treaty. Westerners, however, were unhampered in their use of the Mississippi River and the right of depositing goods at New Orleans for reshipment was continued even after the three-year period mentioned in the treaty had expired. The prospect of free access to profitable markets for western produce seemed secure. Then, in the first years of the new century disturbing rumors gained currency in America—rumors that the great Corsican had looked with covetous eyes at Louisiana, the ancient possession of the French. These rumors were well-grounded, for on

October 1, 1800, at San Ildefonso, Spain had retroceded Louisiana to France in a secret treaty. With visions of a magnificent colonial empire in America, Napoleon soon made plans to take possession. Desiring a convenient naval base, he sent an army to the island of San Domingo, but disease and the resistance of the negroes led by the heroic Toussaint l'Ouverture, brought failure to this undertaking.

Meanwhile in the United States, and especially in the West, alarm was growing apace, for with France and Napoleon in control of the mouth of the Mississippi the safety and peace of America would be seriously threatened. In October, 1802, the worst fears were confirmed when the Spanish intendant at New Orleans closed the Mississippi River to Americans. Immediately the West was ablaze with excitement and with talk of an expedition to seize New Orleans and settle the Mississippi question forever by force of arms. In the words of Frederic L. Paxson, "the bad news rushed up the trail from Natchez, and reaching Washington apprised the President that either the West would act, or he; and that his action must be prompt or not at all."

President Jefferson now faced a difficult dilemma. He was an ardent friend of France and a passionate devotee of peace. On the other hand, he understood and sympathized with the westerners in their determination to use the Mississippi. He knew that unless something were done promptly a frontier army would be on the march against New Orleans and war with France would result. Even in Congress resolutions were introduced and discussed authorizing the raising of an army to seize New Orleans before Napoleon's troops could take possession. How fully Jefferson appreciated the gravity of the crisis is indicated by his statement to Robert R. Livingston. "From the moment that France takes New Orleans," he wrote, "we must marry ourselves to the British fleet and nation."

Jefferson realized that the only way to satisfy the belligerent frontiersmen and avoid war with France was, if possible, to purchase territory at the mouth of the Mississippi and thus gain a voice in the control of the river. Here again he found himself in difficulty. Being a leading exponent of the strict construction of the Constitution, he believed that he had no authority to purchase territory. Furthermore, he was opposed to an increase in the national debt, such as any substantial purchase would necessitate. Yet clearly something must be done. For what he did Thomas Jefferson well deserves the credit which history has bestowed upon him.

Early in March, 1803, Jefferson despatched James Monroe to Paris as a special envoy to join Robert R. Livingston, our minister to France. Monroe was instructed to employ every effort to purchase New Orleans, and if this concession were not obtainable then he was to seek a restoration of the right of deposit for American goods. When Monroe arrived in Paris he found Livingston already in the midst of preliminary negotiations with Barbé-Marbois. To the astonishment, not to say the consternation, of the two American commissioners, Napoleon had offered to sell the whole of Louisiana to the United States.

The offer was well-nigh overwhelming, far exceeding anything involved in Monroe's instructions. Nevertheless, the two men hastened to accept and signed a treaty bearing the date of April 30, 1803, by which the territorial area of the United States was more than doubled. They pledged their country to pay $15,000,000, agreed that French and Spanish ships should receive special privileges in Louisiana ports for a period of twelve years, and promised that the inhabitants of the ceded territory should "be incorporated in the Union of the United States, and admitted as soon as possible, according to the principles of the Federal Constitution, to the enjoyment of all the rights, advantages, and immunities, of citizens of the United States." The boundaries of Louisiana were not specified, but the ceded province was declared to have "the same extent that it now has in the hands of Spain, and that it had when France possessed it"; and the United States was to have all the rights which France had acquired from Spain under the Treaty of San Ildefonso.

Bonaparte's sudden decision to sell Louisiana was a violation of both the French constitution and of his promise to Spain. But he foresaw an approaching European struggle and he knew it would be impossible to defend Louisiana against England. His motive in selling it to the American nation is revealed in his statement that the treaty "assures forever the power of the United States, and I have given England a rival who, sooner or later, will humble her pride." The latter part of this prediction can hardly be said to have been fulfilled.

The Louisiana Purchase Treaty was ratified and the purchase money appropriated only after a bitter party wrangle in Congress, during which the Federalists reversed themselves and opposed the treaty as unwarranted by the Constitution. Westerners, however, were not troubled by constitutional scruples in such matters. To them the treaty was more than satisfactory. It opened a vast area for American expansion and it settled forever the question of the free use of the Mississippi River.

AARON BURR'S CONSPIRACY

What might have happened in the West without the Louisiana Purchase is suggested by the vague and enigmatic episode known as the Burr Conspiracy. The treaty quieted apprehensions and discontent and increased loyalty to the Union, but it did not destroy the ambition of restless frontier leaders or their willingness to engage in any sort of enterprise which promised personal glory or profit. To men of this type in 1805 there came Aaron Burr, disappointed because of his failure to achieve the supreme success in politics and smarting under the sting of public disapproval occasioned in the East by his killing of Alexander Hamilton in the famous duel at Weehawken in 1804. His personal charm won him ready access everywhere in the West. Here duelling was still the accepted method of settling quarrels and his killing of the great Federalist leader was regarded by many as a public service. Especially did he captivate Harman Blennerhassett, a man of considerable wealth living on an island in the Ohio River near Marietta, who opened his home as headquarters for Burr and contributed money to his enterprise. Here in 1805 and 1806 there was organized an expedition the objective of which is not known with certainty to the present day.

It is obvious that at least a few people must have known Burr's real designs, but they left no records. To others he told whatever he thought would interest them most. Anthony

Merry, British minister to the United States, was intrigued by a proposal to bring about the separation of the West from the Union with the aid of an English fleet at New Orleans. Spanish officials in Florida and Texas were alarmed by rumors that Burr contemplated an expedition against Spanish territory. Burr talked several times with such men as Andrew Jackson and Henry Clay, but their failure to denounce him is an indication that to them he did not reveal any plan for the dismemberment of the United States. One man who almost certainly believed he knew Burr's plan and at first gave him encouragement was James Wilkinson, now western commander of the army and at the same time the continued recipient of a Spanish pension. Before the project could be carried into effect Wilkinson characteristically sought credit by turning informer. The best judgment of historians is that Burr's immediate plan was for a filibustering foray against the Spanish, with the probable hope of setting up a separate empire with himself as ruler—an enterprise which certainly would find little opposition in the West.

Every student of American history knows that Aaron Burr's dream, whatever it may have been, was short-lived. He was hailed into court in Kentucky, under Jefferson's orders, and acquitted. Once more, in 1807, he was arrested on a charge of treason and tried before John Marshall, but there was not sufficient evidence to sustain the charge and he was set free. As is well known, the political antagonism between Marshall and Jefferson had an important bearing upon the outcome of the trial.

The War of 1812 in the West

With the exception of events in West Florida and the desire of the people of the southwest to acquire entire possession of the Floridas, to be described later, the northern border became the great subject of interest on the part of westerners within less than a decade after the purchase of Louisiana. In this instance the demands and aggressive spirit of the young, western "war-hawks" plunged the nation into a war with Great Britain, from which it emerged only by good fortune with undiminished territory and without achieving most of the objects for which the struggle was ostensibly waged.

The War of 1812 has been called our "second war for independence," a description which is appropriate only in the sense that it added somewhat to our prestige in spite of its indecisive outcome, and that it contributed powerfully to the growth of the spirit of nationality. Historians long accepted the impressment of American seamen and interference with American commerce by Great Britain as the causes of this conflict; and it is true that these grievances were assigned at the time war was declared. It is now generally agreed, however, that it is in the West that we must look for the real motivation. In other words, the War of 1812 was a westerners' war.

The people of the West were noted for their aggressive, chip-on-the-shoulder dispositions. Among large numbers of them personal honor was something to be defended at all odds and by any method. The code of the West sanctioned personal encounters and even duels on slight provocation. It was natural, therefore, that they should be peculiarly sensitive on the point of national honor in the trying period of the Napoleonic wars when this nation as a neutral was subjected to the insults of both France and England. To be sure, it had not been long since westerners had been flirting with proposals for separation from a Union which seemed indifferent to their needs. But that was their quarrel. They were indignant when outsiders slighted and insulted their government. After all the West was the most nationally-minded section of the Union even at this time, for it was to the federal government that most of the people of West were indebted for their land titles, for their mail service, for defense against the Indians, and for their territorial and state governments. But there was a more immediate and potent reason for this demand for a war against England.

We have already seen that when the British withdrew their garrisons from the western posts in 1796 in accordance with Jay's Treaty, they had no intention of relinquishing their remunerative fur trade with the Indians south of the Great Lakes. They simply moved over to the Canadian side of the boundary line and continued their activities. Malden, opposite Detroit, in particular, was the center from which British influence over the Indians was exerted.

For a decade after Wayne's campaign and after British evacuation of the western posts there was little trouble with the Indians. Then depredations began to occur among the scattered settlements along the northwestern frontier. When in 1810 and 1811 news of the progress of Tecumseh's Indian confederation spread throughout the West, there was virtually a panic in the Ohio Valley which was not quieted even after the Battle of Tippecanoe. It is of little value to say that the million white people then living west of the mountains really had no cause to fear a few thousand Indians. Neither does it help to point out the incontestable fact that it was the pressure of settlements on Indian lands which was largely responsible for the depredations by the red men. From first to last, rightly or wrongly, the frontiersmen hated and feared the Indians; and every tale of outrage sent a thrill of horror along the frontier that awakened memories accumulated through generations of brutal warfare.

In this case there was an added animus to the wrath of the western settlers. Ever since Revolutionary War days there had been a settled conviction, not wholly unfounded, in the Ohio Valley that the Indians were instigated and encouraged in their raids on the settlements by the British officials and traders along the Canadian border. Charges to this effect were now revived and when English guns and ammunition were found on Indians slain at Tippecanoe the cry for revenge rang throughout the West. John Rhea of Tennessee expressed the attitude of westerners when in Congress he declared that the United States must "put it out of the power of Great Britain, or of any British agent, trader, or factor, or company of British traders to supply Indian tribes with arms or ammunition; to instigate and incite Indians to disturb and harass our frontiers, and to murder and scalp helpless women and children."

Western leaders were now convinced that the only way to accomplish this purpose was to drive the British out of Canada. They were equally sure that this desirable result could be achieved with comparative ease and in a short time. Henry

Clay of Kentucky, then Speaker of the House of Representatives, outlined plans for the invasion of Canada. "I should not wish," declared Richard Johnson of the same State, "to extend the boundary of the United States by war if Great Britain would leave us to the quiet enjoyment of independence; but considering her deadly and implacable enmity, and her continued hostilities, I shall never die contented until I see her expulsion from North America, and the territories incorporated with the United States." Other western members of Congress spoke in language equally belligerent. And so the western "war-hawks" had their war, in spite of a reluctant President and a nation unprepared. Throughout the Ohio Valley after the declaration of war on June 18, 1812, editors and state legislatures expressed their joy and approval; and at public dinners the people drank to such toasts as: "May the Twelfth Congress no longer tamely submit to British outrages, but wrest from her every foot of possession she holds in North America."

With the general aspects of the War of 1812 we are not concerned. Nor need we dwell long on the pitiable campaigns in the northwest that fell so far short of the boastful predictions and confident anticipations of western leaders and people. General Henry Dearborn in the Niagara-Lake Champlain sector was kept in a state of harmless inactivity through incompetence at Washington. William Hull, instead of penetrating deep into Canada, ingloriously surrendered Detroit on August 16, 1812, without firing a shot, and was later tried and convicted of cowardice. On the preceding day the garrison at Fort Dearborn, where Chicago now stands, was treacherously massacred by the Indian members of an attacking party who violated pledges of safe conduct made by the British commander who received the capitulation of the fort. In January, 1813, a force under James Winchester was defeated on the River Raisin. By this time all hope of the conquest of Canada was gone. The only relief in the general gloom came in September and October, 1813, with Perry's victory on Lake Erie and the campaign under William Henry Harrison which resulted in the recapture of Detroit and the defeat of a British force at the Battle of the Thames on Canadian soil. Among the slain in the latter battle was the great Indian leader,

Tecumseh, whose death hastened the disorganization and pacification of his followers.

It was from the military operations in the southwest that the people of the West gained greatest satisfaction. The Creek Indians went on the war-path in 1813 and on August 30th killed nearly five hundred settlers at Fort Mims at the junction of the Tombigbee and Alabama Rivers. This massacre was avenged in March of the following year, when the Tennessee militia commanded by Andrew Jackson won a smashing victory over the Indians at the Horseshoe Bend of the Tallapoosa River. This exploit was the first of a series which established Jackson's fame as an Indian fighter and helped to make him the hero of the West. A little later Jackson proceeded southward into Florida and burned Pensacola, which, though neutral territory, had been used as a base of operations by the British, as had also other points in western Florida. The region, however, was soon restored to Spanish control.

Late in the year of 1814 it was learned that the British were planning an attack on New Orleans. Jackson, now major-general in the regular army, gathered a nondescript force of frontiersmen and pirates from the islands along the coast and went to the defense of the city. There on January 8, 1815, fifteen days after the signing of the Treaty of Ghent which officially closed the war, he won the greatest American victory of the entire struggle. The seasoned British troops under Sir Edward Pakenham were completely defeated, retiring after a loss of more than two thousand men killed or wounded. Andrew Jackson was now a man marked for high honors at the hands of an admiring nation.

During the peace negotiations the British commissioners again brought forward a proposal for an Indian buffer territory, but naturally it was not considered by the Americans. The northern boundary remained undisturbed by the events of the war. There was some gain for the westerners, however, because after 1815 the peace of the northern border was never again threatened. Furthermore, the Indian tribes north of the Ohio, bereft of the hope of British aid, never again gave serious trouble.

TROUBLE ALONG THE FLORIDA BORDER

The situation along the southern border was still unsettled and far from peaceful. For the beginning of the movement that culminated in 1819 in the acquisition of the Floridas by the United States we must go back to the period immediately following the purchase of Louisiana. With Spain still controlling the Floridas it required no gift of prophecy to forsee the early appearance of trouble along the boundary, scarcely less disturbing than that occasioned by the closing of the Mississippi. The settlers in the southwest were certain to demand access to the Gulf, and rivers, like the Flint, Chattahoochee, Coosa, and Tombigbee, which served as their avenues of transportation, had to cross Spanish territory before reaching the sea.

Soon after the Louisiana Purchase, through Monroe and Pinckney, Jefferson endeavored to secure the cession of the Floridas from Spain. France seemed for a time to lend encouragement to these efforts, but Napoleon finally lost interest and the project fell through. Nevertheless, within a few years the United States was in possession of the greater part of West Florida. This occupation was based upon a rather doubtful interpretation of the Louisiana Purchase Treaty in accordance with which it was contended that Louisiana as ceded by France extended as far east as the Perdido River, now a part of the eastern boundary of Alabama. Spain's objections to this interpretation were of little concern to the American frontiersmen. They moved into the western portion of West Florida, staged an insurrection, declared their independence of Spain, and appealed to the United States for annexation. In response President Madison issued a proclamation declaring that the region belonging to the United States extended to the Perdido River, and ordered the official occupation of a portion of it, asserting, however, that his government was ready to make a "fair and friendly negotiation and adjustment" with Spain. In 1812 the country as far east as the Pearl River was incorporated in the newly admitted state of Louisiana; and the region between the Pearl and the Perdido was added to Mississippi Territory.

Spanish possession of East Florida remained undisturbed, except for a short-lived "revolt" early in 1812, stimulated by United States military officers acting under instructions from President Madison. Nevertheless, the people of the southwest joined their brethren of the Ohio Valley in demanding war with Great Britain in 1812, partly at least, because they hoped for the conquest of all of Florida from Spain, then an ally of England as far as the European war was concerned. In this hope they were disappointed. We have already seen that the British made use of Florida posts during the War of 1812 and that the region was invaded by Andrew Jackson after he had defeated the Creek Indians.

After the close of the War of 1812 troubles along the Florida border speedily reached a climax. Smugglers and bandits infested Amelia Island at the mouth of St. Mary's River. Runaway slaves found a ready asylum among the Seminoles. Desparadoes of all sorts made various points below the boundary line their haunts. Indians made sorties from the same region to harass the frontier settlements in Georgia and Alabama. Little or no government was maintained by the Spanish. In view of this situation the United States decided to take a hand. The hero of New Orleans was placed in command of the expeditionary force and early in 1818 he entered East Florida. Proceeding in the belief that he had the approval of President Monroe for his proposal to pacify Florida (a point over which there was waged a vitriolic controversy), Jackson soon increased his popularity in the West by his vigorous actions. He captured and summarily executed two British traders whom he accused of instigating the Indians to attack American settlements. He also seized Spanish posts and deposed the governor. Of course such measures might easily have brought on a war with both England and Spain. Fortunately England chose to accept Secretary of State Adams' contention that the two traders deserved their fate. Spain protested, but confronted with the necessity of either maintaining order in Florida or making the cession desired by the Americans, she chose the latter alternative.

In 1819 there was signed a treaty by which Spain ceded claim to the Floridas to the United States, in consideration of the latter's agreement to assume the payment of claims for damages up to the amount of five million dollars. As will be described in more detail later, the same treaty defined the boundary between the United States and the remaining Spanish possessions in Texas and the farther west. When Florida was formally transferred to its new owner in July, 1821, the desires of the western expansionists were temporarily or at least partially satisfied. In the same year the Territory of Florida was established, with Andrew Jackson as its governor.

CHAPTER V

THE RECEDING RED MEN

THE PRECEDING CHAPTER indicated that the controversies and conflicts of the United States with the English along the Canadian border, and with the Spanish in Louisiana and the Floridas, were aggravated by troubles with the Indians. The native tribes of North America were often used as pawns by the French and the Spanish and the English in their struggles for the control of the continent. For the frontiersmen, however, these international complications were only intensifying factors in a situation of irrepressible antagonism wherever the two races came into contact. From the landing of the first English colonists on the Atlantic coast to the passing of the frontier, nearly three centuries later, there was always some region in which the long-standing hatreds were freshly in evidence.

THE FRONTIERSMEN AND THE INDIANS

"There are moralists," said John Quincy Adams in an oration delivered in 1802, "who have questioned the right of the Europeans to intrude upon the possessions of the aboriginals in any case, and under any limitations whatsoever. But have they maturely considered the whole subject? The Indian right of possession itself stands, with regard to the greatest part of the country, upon a questionable foundation. Their cultivated fields; their constructed habitations; a space of ample sufficiency for their subsistence, and whatever they had annexed to themselves by personal labor, was undoubtedly by the law of nature theirs. But what is the right of a huntsman to the forest of a thousand miles over which he has accidentally ranged in quest of prey? Shall the liberal bounties of Providence to the race of man be monopolized by one of ten thousand for whom they were created? Shall the exuberant bosom of the common mother, amply adequate to the nourishment of millions, be claimed exclusively by a few hundreds of her offspring? . . . No, generous philanthropists! Heaven has not been thus inconsistent in the work of its hands. Heaven has not thus placed at irreconcilable strife, its moral laws with its physical creation."

Such, in essence, has been the line of argument advanced by the most moderate spokesmen of the white race in justification of its actions wherever, throughout the world, it has taken possession of lands occupied by primitive peoples. Substantially this same attitude has been the basis of the Indian policy of the United States government. Concerning the basic morality of this attitude there have been relatively few protests. But there the general agreement has ended. From first to last our treatment of the Indians has been the subject of a wide range of views and opinions, from vigorous defense to caustic criticism.

This much can be said: the frontiersman living in daily contact with the Indians could scarcely be expected to view that race with the perspective that was possible to the person dwelling in safety in a settled community far removed from scenes of conflict and irritation. Felix Grundy of Tennessee in a speech in the United States Senate once expressed the attitude of the first generation of frontiersmen—those whose hatred of all Indians was based on ineradicable memories. "I can remember," he said, "when death was in almost every bush, and every thicket concealed an ambuscade. If I am asked to trace my memory back, and name the first indelible impression it received, it would be the sight of my oldest brother bleeding and dying under wounds inflicted by the tomahawk and the scalping knife. Another, and another, went the same way! I have seen a widowed mother plundered of her whole property in a single night. . . . Sir, the ancient sufferings of the West were great." Men living through such experiences were not qualified to give judicial consideration to the wrongs suffered by the Indians at the hands of white men.

On the other hand it is noticeable that when once the Indians had been removed from a given region and settlements had grown and prospered for a few years in complete security, many western spokesmen were ready to defend the receding natives against governmental approval of the demands of pioneers on a further western frontier, where the conflict was now in process. Thus, for instance, in 1827 Representative Vinton of Ohio apparently ran little risk of disfavor among his constituents when he said that, no matter to what distant district the Indians might be removed, "the pioneers would be there in advance of them; men of the most abandoned and desperate character, who hang upon the Indians to defraud them. You cannot run away from these men nor shut them out from access to Indians, scattered over the wilderness; for, with the pioneers, the law is a jest, and the woods their element."

Indian Policy of the United States

When the United States government took over the regulation of Indian affairs it followed the practice and adopted the policy in force during colonial days. Indian tribes were regarded as possessing at least some of the attributes of sovereignty, including the right of occupancy of their lands—a right which could be extinguished only by treaties negotiated by official representatives of the government and ratified by the United States Senate (after the adoption of the Constitution). The motives which led to the adoption of such a policy were doubtless honorable and represent a consideration for the rights of the natives not always exhibited by the white race in other parts of the world. And yet it is the judgment of history that the policy was a mistaken one and that in operation it produced results not much different from what might have been achieved by a program of frank and deliberate exploitation. Our first treaty was made with the Delaware Indians in 1778. Long before treaty-making was abandoned nearly a century later, in 1871, the veil of pretense had worn very thin, and the Indians had received treatment far different from that any nation would accord peoples whom it sincerely regarded as in any sense sovereign and independent.

There were several basic factors which made treaty-making with the Indians an unsatisfactory procedure. In the first place, with a few possible exceptions the Indians had no conception of either individual or tribal ownership of land corresponding to the ideas of white men. To the natives land was like air and water—something they needed and enjoyed but not something to be bought and sold. They only vaguely understood the meaning of a treaty ceding their right to a given region. Not until after repeated, bitter experiences did they finally learn that they could not return to hunt on land to which they had relinquished their title by making a few marks on a sheet of paper. Then again, chieftains and leaders did not have the power or authority to bind their fellow-tribesmen to an agreement such as resides in official representatives among civilized nations. Finally, numerous tribes frequently hunted over the same territory, and therefore a treaty made with one tribe did not extinguish titles held with equal validity by other tribes.

On the other hand, the United States government was virtually powerless to control the actions of its own citizens. To be sure there were stringent laws prohibiting trespassing on Indian lands, with severe penalties for offenders. Occasionally half-hearted attempts were made to drive settlers off forbidden territory, but even more determined efforts would have been fruitless. In fact, it is only fair to say that the government's good intentions with respect to the Indians were frustrated by irresponsible traders and aggressive settlers. Plans to establish the relationship between the two races on a peaceful basis were one after another brought to naught. "The story of one failure," to quote Ruth A. Gallaher's terse description of the oft-repeated cycle, "has been the story of all such attempts. A treaty was made; friendship was declared; the Indians ceded lands and received in return annuities and presents; a boundary line was marked off; and for a few years there was a peace that was only suspended hostility. Then the pioneers, driven westward by insatiable land-hunger, crossed the line and settled on the unceded lands of the Indians. There were protests, massacres, and retaliations, a campaign by the troops, and another treaty in which more land was ceded, more presents given, and another 'peace' was established." [1]

To this outline should be added the statement that there is good ground for suspicion that traders all too frequently helped to bring about situations leading to treaties, in order that they might claim the annuities in satisfaction of debts contracted by the Indians for goods and whiskey at greatly inflated prices. For instance, in 1839 an Illinois editor asserted that as much as $100,000 was thus secured by a single trading company.

It would be tedious and unprofitable to mention all the treaties made with the Indians before the principal tribes were removed to their new locations west of the Mississippi. Naturally the treaties negotiated at the close of Indian disturbances or so-called "wars" attracted the most attention and were hailed with the greatest satisfaction by the advancing settlers. A brief sketch of the most notable Indian campaigns, with the resulting land cessions, will illustrate the most spectacular phase of the process by which the tribesmen's title to large areas was extinguished and the land made available for white settlement.

EARLY INDIAN WARS AND TREATIES IN OLD NORTHWEST

In 1784 the Iroquois Indians signed a treaty at Fort Stanwix reaffirming the agreement made at the same place in 1768, relinquishing all right to the land north of the Ohio River which they had claimed on the basis of ancient conquests. The tribes occupying this region did not recognize the validity of this treaty as far as they were concerned. In 1785, however, a number of these tribes agreed at Fort McIntosh, below Pittsburgh, to remain north of a boundary line running in a general way along the watershed between the Ohio and Lake Erie. These treaties made little impression on the Miami, Wyandot, Delaware, Shawnee, Chippewa, Ottawa, and other tribes, who continued to roam at will over the region bordering on the Ohio. Thus when white settlements were planted at Marietta

---

[1] Ruth A. Gallaher, "The Indian Agent in the United States before 1850," in *The Iowa Journal of History and Politics*, January, 1916, pp. 4-5. Published by the State Historical Society of Iowa.

in 1788 and began to spread to other points on the north bank of the river, there was constant danger of attack by Indians.

At Fort Harmar on the Ohio a treaty was made in 1789 by which the tribes re-affirmed the agreements made at Fort Mc-Intosh. But even this did not result in the departure of the Indians from the region along the Ohio. In addition to their lack of understanding of the full meaning of treaties, it is evident that the Indians were encouraged in their resistance by the knowledge that the British were still in possession of the posts along the Great Lakes and by secret suggestions made by English officers and traders. Accordingly General Joseph Harmar was sent on an expedition to the northward to overawe the tribesmen. Harmar's troops were poorly equipped and without discipline. When attacked by the Indians they were not entirely routed, but retired in poor order and with severe losses to Fort Washington at Cincinnati.

Governor Arthur St. Clair of the Northwest Territory was now ordered by President Washington to lead an expedition to punish the Indians and bring peace to the settlements. The outcome was a disaster comparable to that suffered by General Braddock. In extenuation it is only fair to state that St. Clair was growing old, he was physically unfit for such an arduous campaign, and he lacked any adequate military experience. The army furnished him was of the most nondescript character, inexperienced, unruly, and poorly equipped. The plan of campaign was well conceived, namely to establish a chain of forts from Fort Washington to the Maumee River. The expedition, consisting of about two thousand fighting men, got under way early in October, 1791, and for a time proceeded according to plan. Fort Hamilton was erected about twenty-five miles above Cincinnati and Fort Jefferson near the present site of Greenville, Ohio. Then at daybreak on November 4th catastrophe befell the army encamped in the forest on the Wabash near the present Ohio-Indiana boundary line.

The sleeping troops were suddenly awakened by war-whoops and volleys of bullets and arrows from the encircling forest. A scene of the wildest confusion ensued as the half-clothed soldiers rushed to their arms and sought to return the fire of their hidden foes. Despite the fact that he was ill, St.

Clair exhibited the utmost bravery. Three horses fell beneath him and his clothing was repeatedly perforated by bullets. Nothing he could do, however, could prevent an utter rout. More than six hundred of his men were killed and nearly three hundred wounded—altogether nearly half of his entire force. The dispirited remnants straggled back to Cincinnati, leaving the Indians jubilant and confident. Over the frontier settlements hung a cloud of gloom and apprehension.

The man chosen to administer retribution to the Indians and restore the lost prestige of the United States army was "Mad Anthony" Wayne of Revolutionary War fame. In the campaign which he conducted he exhibited none of the apparent recklessness that had earned him his sobriquet. In the fall of 1792 at Pittsburgh he took command of an army of 2500 men of about the same type as had followed Harmar and St. Clair. Instead of moving at once into the Indian country he spent the winter a short distance below Pittsburgh drilling his men. Even the next year he proceeded with the greatest deliberation. Near Cincinnati he spent the summer and autumn of 1793, everlasting drilling and forging his units of infantry, cavalry, and artillery into a competent fighting machine. Still another winter was spent at Fort Greenville, where there was still more drilling. During this period a fort, significantly named Fort Recovery, was built on the site of St. Clair's debacle. All this preparation was trying to the impatient settlers, but it likewise kept the Indians in a state of nervous excitement.

Not until late in July, 1794, was the real advance into the Indian country begun. Every precaution was taken. There were scouts in advance and on the flanks and a protected line of communication with the rear was maintained. Fort Defiance was built on the Maumee River at the mouth of the Auglaize. Then as he was proceeding down the Maumee towards the head of Toledo Bay on August 20th, Wayne was confronted by the Indians under Little Turtle, arrayed behind natural breastworks of trees uprooted by a tornado at a place known as Fallen Timbers. The presence of Englishmen among the Indians was presumptively indicated by their very unusual readiness to fight a pitched battle. In the conflict which ensued the Indians were decisively defeated and their finest warriors slain. Wayne remained for a short time in the neighborhood, giving, as we have already seen, much worry to the British authorities in Detroit and vicinity. Then he proceeded westward, destroyed a number of Miami Indian towns, erected Fort Wayne near the source of the Maumee, and retired to Fort Defiance.

In the summer of 1795 Wayne gathered representatives of ten or eleven tribes at Fort Greenville. There on August 3rd, after nearly two months of feasting and speech-making, the thoroughly humbled Indians signed a treaty giving up all claim to the southern half of the present State of Ohio and the southeastern corner of Indiana. This time the treaty was observed, at least on the part of the Indians. For a period of fifteen years peace was unbroken on the northwestern frontier.

TECUMSEH'S CONFEDERATION

During these years, however, the resentment of Indian leaders smoldered and increased. Traders cheated the tribesmen and plied them with bad liquor until sturdy braves were degraded into slinking sneak-thieves. Social diseases spread rapidly as the baser element among the frontiersmen found easy access to Indian women, and thus the physical stamina of the natives was further weakened. During the early years of the nineteenth century various tribes were induced by prospects of annuities, or when their chiefs were under the influence of liquor, to sign treaties ceding land beyond the line established by the Treaty of Greenville. Thus the farming frontier pressed steadily into Indiana Territory. For the Indians the most disheartening feature of the situation was the fact that even the most respectable and law-abiding frontier farmers were inexorable in their demand for more and more lands for settlement. Added to all these festering grievances were the secret encouragements given by British traders and officials at Malden across the Canadian border, and the hope that some day the English would join the Indians in a war against the Americans.

The leader who became the spokesmen for the Indian tribes

north of the Ohio was the Shawnee brave, Tecumseh—a man still in his thirties when he began the plans which made him notable among Indian statesmen. He was not a chief, but he possessed the qualities of leadership which won him a wide influence among the tribes equal to that earlier exerted by Pontiac. Scarcely less influential among the superstitious natives, although less capable, was Tecumseh's brother, known as The Prophet and reputed to have powers of magic and divination. As Tecumseh brooded over the desperate situation of his race he saw only one hope. To his mind the Indians' right of occupancy was one which all enjoyed in common and which no tribe or tribes could alienate without the consent of all. Of course he could not fully realize that this view never could or would be accepted by the whites, because it would mean a permanent Indian barrier to further expansion. But with this principle as the basis of his statesmanship Tecumseh set about the task of winning the tribes over to a plan of passive resistance and of refusal to make any further land cessions. In 1808 Tecumseh and The Prophet established themselves at a place which became known as Prophet's Town, on the Wabash near the mouth of Tippecanoe Creek, and across from the site of the present city of Lafayette, Indiana. Here was the region of the densest Indian population and through it ran the great pathway traveled by the tribesmen from Malden, opposite Detroit, to Pensacola and the other Spanish settlements on the Gulf. From this point Tecumseh began preaching the gospel of a great Indian confederacy that would check white aggression and save the race from extinction.

The Governor of Indiana Territory was William Henry Harrison. When he took office in 1800 there was scarcely any land in the Territory to which the Indian title had been extinguished. In the succeeding years he took the lead and secured treaty after treaty opening lands in the southern part of the Territory, the most notable being the Treaty of Fort Wayne in 1809 by which three million acres were secured from the Indians. Naturally these activities made Harrison popular among the settlers, but among the Indians they caused growing alarm. The last named treaty, especially, was repudiated by Tecumseh and the chiefs who were not signatories.

Settlements were now approaching the Indian stronghold along the Wabash.

Harrison was particularly watchful of Tecumseh as his plans for an Indian confederacy began to develop. The two men held several conferences without any important result. It was noted that Tecumseh made frequent trips to Malden, and Harrison, like most of the frontiersmen, became convinced, and not without some justification, that the British were giving aid and encouragement to the Indian leader. Moreover, there was growing resentment along the frontier as people saw Indians returning from Malden with guns and scalping-knives which they had obtained in exchange for furs. In the early summer of 1811 the situation along the Indiana frontier became acute. Tecumseh set out on a tour of the southern Indian tribes. His young braves, who had been restrained with difficulty, now felt greater freedom. Soon there were complaints of depredations among the isolated settlements and there was widespread fear of an Indian war.

Harrison had apparently long been hoping for the time when he could make a name and win glory for himself as an Indian fighter. The opportunity seemed to present itself in the apparent need of decisive action to quiet the restless Indians. Late in the summer he gathered an army of about nine hundred men and marched up the Wabash. Fort Harrison was built on the site of Terre Haute and the army proceeded to Prophet's Town which was not destroyed in spite of the advice of some of Harrison's men. The night of November 6th found the army encamped in the rain on a ridge of ground south of Tippecanoe Creek. Before daylight the next morning the sentries gave the alarm and immediately a large number of Indians attacked the camp. Harrison and his men were able to hold their position, although with considerable loss, and at length the Indians withdrew. This was the famous Battle of Tippecanoe which was celebrated in song twenty-nine years later, when its hero was elected President of the United States. As has been indicated the struggle was virtually a draw, with neither side winning a decisive victory. Harrison retreated rapidly to Vincennes and the battle assumed more of the proportions of a great triumph with every mile traveled away from the scene of action and with every report sent to Washington. Nevertheless, although the battle was inconclusive it did discourage the Indians. When Tecumseh returned from his southern tour he found his influence weakened and all hope for his confederacy gone. As we have seen, Indians figured on the British side in most of the western engagements during the War of 1812. But after the close of that war the frontier north of the Ohio River was not again disturbed by anything approaching a real Indian scare for nearly another generation.

THE WINNEBAGO WAR

In 1827 there was a short-lived disturbance in southwestern Wisconsin where, in the lead-mining region, miners and settlers had encroached on the lands of the Winnebago Indians. The Indians complained ineffectually and a few members of the tribe murdered and scalped several white men, women, and children. Immediately there was wild excitement in the entire region as settlers and miners, fearing an Indian war, fled to Galena and to various forts. A strong body of regular troops and volunteers was soon in the field, however, and the terrified Winnebagoes hastened to surrender.

THE BLACK HAWK WAR

Five years later in this same region of southern Wisconsin and northern Illinois there occurred the so-called Black Hawk War. In 1804 representatives of the Sauk and Fox tribes, said to have been intoxicated at the time, signed a treaty at St. Louis by which those Indians ceded all their land between the Wisconsin and Illinois rivers to the United States, retaining the right to occupy the land until such time as the government decided to make it available for settlement. This treaty was confirmed in 1816 and again in 1825. In course of time two factions appeared among the Sauk and Fox Indians. One, following the lead of Chief Keokuk, moved across the Mississippi into the present State of Iowa. The other division, which remained in the tribal village on the Rock River in Illinois, was headed by the elderly Black Hawk, a man who at an earlier period when the odds were not so heavily against him might well have won for himself a place among Indian statesmen like Pontiac and Tecumseh. He and his followers continued to make annual pilgrimages to Malden and for this reason were often called the British band of the Sauk and Fox tribes.

By 1830 settlers without any legal right began to encroach on the Sauk and Fox lands along the Rock River, occupying their cornfields and plowing up their burying grounds. Black Hawk made frequent protests to no effect. In the summer of 1831 he became more threatening and destroyed some of the fields and houses of the settlers. Thereupon there arose a great outcry and urgent demand for protection. A strong force was raised under Edmund P. Gaines. At this show of force Black Hawk and his followers sued for peace and fled across the Mississippi.

In the spring of 1832, Black Hawk and from six to eight hundred warriors, with women and children, recrossed the river into their old haunts. Apparently he had conceived some visionary scheme of an Indian confederation with British aid, which would hold the white invaders at bay. Soon a number of white settlers and an Indian agent were murdered, as wandering groups of Indians visited their old homes. Among the settlers there was widespread fear. Volunteer companies were raised and from various directions regular troops were despatched to the scene of trouble. Ultimately as many as four thousand troups were in the field, under such leaders as General Henry Atkinson, General Winfield Scott, Colonel Zachary Taylor, and Colonel Henry Dodge.

The result of such an uneven contest, of course, was never in doubt, although the first meeting of a raw, undisciplined company of volunteers with a small group of warriors ended in the ignominious flight of the former. Black Hawk and his braves were pursued into the Four Lakes region of Wisconsin, where Madison now stands, and then back again to the Mississippi. There, as they were endeavoring to escape to the west bank, they were hopelessly overwhelmed and defeated, Black Hawk himself being captured. Even numbers of Indian women and children were victims of the bullets of the exultant victors. This was the famous Black Hawk War which enabled many a resident of Illinois and Wisconsin to tell his children and grand-children how he fought the redskins. As a result of the war the Sauk and Fox Indians signed a treaty in September, 1832, by which they relinquished title to a fifty-mile strip of land along the west bank of the Mississippi in what soon became the Territory of Iowa. Soon, also, Indian claims to most of the region between Lake Michigan and the Mississippi were ceded to the United States government, and settlers poured into the upper Mississippi Valley.

Jackson's Campaigns in the Old Southwest

In the Old Southwest the pressure of settlements on Indian lands did not begin as early as in the region north of the Ohio River. Consequently it was not until the War of 1812 that the United States government faced any Indian disturbance in the territory now included in Mississippi, Alabama, and western Georgia. In the fall of 1812 Georgia militia conducted a par-tially successful campaign against the troublesome Seminole Indians in Florida. During the following year one faction of the powerful Creek tribe took up the hatchet. Inflamed by the teachings of Tecumseh on his southern tour, and emboldened by the easy capture of Detroit by the British, these Indians seized the occasion to begin a war of extermination against the scattered settlements. On August 30, 1813, they attacked Fort Mims near the junction of the Alabama and Tombigbee, which the settlers had built as a place of refuge. Nearly five hundred settlers lost their lives in the massacre that ensued, and the entire frontier was panic-stricken.

Of several expeditions immediately organized to punish the Creeks only the one led by Andrew Jackson accomplished its purpose. Jackson's title to fame as a frontier hero rested not only on his victory over the Indians, but equally on the skill with which he handled his raw, undisciplined, mutinous Ten-nessee militia and their Choctaw and Cherokee allies. Mixing cajolery with severity, he won the obedience and confidence and even the affection of his men, and kept them in the field until his object had been achieved in spite of short-term enlist-ments. He met the Creeks in several minor engagements during the winter of 1813-1814. Then on March 27, 1814, at the Horseshoe Bend of the Tallapoosa River, he administered a crushing defeat to his foe. Fully two-thirds of the nine hundred Creek warriors participating in this battle were slain and the remainder fled for their lives.

Jackson then moved on down the Tallapoosa and erected Fort Jackson at the junction of that stream with the Coosa. Here in August, 1814, he concluded a treaty with the surviving Creeks, most of whom had been friendly to the whites, by which peace was pledged and a portion of the Creek lands were relinquished. Jackson was rewarded by being appointed Major-General in the United States Army.

Three years later, in 1817 and 1818, there occurred another so-called Seminole War. These Indians, who had their retreats in the fastnesses of the Florida everglades, were the cause of intermittent trouble for many years, and small bands, because of their inaccessibility, never were conquered. The difficulties at this time were those already described as a part of the conflicts and annoyances along the Florida border which hastened the negotiations culminating in the Florida Purchase Treaty of 1819. General Gaines led one expedition into the Seminole country and subdued a portion of the troublesome natives. It was during this disturbance that Andrew Jackson took possession of Spanish territory and hanged the two British traders, Arbuthnot and Ambrister.

THE UNPLEASANT STORY OF TREATY-MAKING

Military campaigns and "wars" constitute only the most spectacular and, on the whole, the most creditable part of the story of the dealings with the Indian tribes resulting in their dispossession of their homes and hunting grounds east of the Mississippi. The record of treaty-making with the aborigines is dreary and unpleasant reading even to one fully convinced of the inevitability of savagery giving way to civilization. North of the Ohio the process was accomplished with comparative ease, partly because of the successful campaigns of Wayne and Harrison, and partly because the tribes were relatively weak and poorly organized, except during the short period of Tecumseh's ascendancy. Even so, the methods employed in securing treaties were seldom above question.

It was in the Old Southwest and on the Georgia frontier, however, that the worst features appeared. Here were the powerful Creek, Cherokee, Chickasaw, Choctaw, and Seminole nations—the first two, especially displaying the traits which have given the whole group the appellation of the Five Civilized Tribes. For three decades these populous, intelligent tribesmen exhibited remarkable powers of resistance to every kind of pressure. The situation in Georgia was complicated by the compact made by the federal government in 1802 when that State relinquished her western land claims. At that time the United States had promised that title to Indian lands within the boundaries of Georgia should be extinguished as soon as it could be accomplished peaceably and on reasonable terms. At no time thereafter until the compact was finally fulfilled were the people of Georgia satisfied with the progress made by the federal government. Pressure of settlements on Indian lands in Alabama and Mississippi soon caused situations scarcely less troublesome. Every President from Jefferson to Jackson was forced to give much time and attention to the problems involved. Long and acrimonious debate occurred in almost every session of Congress.

Among the Indian tribes council after council was held, sometimes resulting in treaties, but as often ending in failure. In council and out of council, Andrew Jackson and a score of other equally determined agents and commissioners sought to bend the Indians to their wills by false promises, bribery, threats, and intimidation. It speaks volumes for the sturdy qualities of these southern tribes that they were able to resist so long and cling year after year to their ancient home lands. The pity of it all is revealed in the backward view, which indicates that Indians already so far along the path toward civilization as the Creeks and Cherokees might without serious difficulty have been absorbed in the citizenry of the States where they were living. But land-hungry settlers had no sympathy for such a solution, and in the end the Indians had to go.

It should not be thought that during all these years no voice was raised in behalf of the Indians. As a matter of fact numerous religious and philanthropic individuals and organizations were much concerned about the spiritual and temporal welfare of the natives. Private funds were raised for missionary and educational activities, and beginning about 1818 some aid was afforded by Congressional appropriations. Many devoted and capable men gave their lives to work among the Indians and, especially among the Cherokees, proved that noteworthy results could be achieved. In 1820 the Rev. Jedidiah Morse made an extended tour through the Indian country at the request of Secretary of War and later published an elaborate and valuable report on the condition of the various tribes, ending with the suggestion of a plan for the establishment of "education families" in various regions. During the debates in Congress numerous eastern Senators and Representatives sought earnestly to protect the Indians from the designs and practices of frontiersmen and from legislation drafted by their spokesmen.

THE INDIAN REMOVAL POLICY

Finally what seemed a happy solution for the perplexing Indian problem was formulated. Experience had shown only too clearly that the onrushing settlers would not tolerate the presence of any considerable body of red men in their vicinity. The haphazard and temporizing practice of securing land cessions and pushing the Indians further west in advance of the settlements was increasingly unsatisfactory to all concerned. A definite and practicable policy was badly needed. Such a policy, based on the suggestions of John C. Calhoun, Secretary of War, was recommended to Congress by President James Monroe in 1825 in his last annual message.

During the decade of the twenties the people of the United States as a whole were satisfied with their national boundaries and convinced that the Rocky Mountains would forever mark their western limit. Moreover, explorers and scientists had told them that the high, arid plains stretching eastward from the Rockies to the Missouri River were unsuited to white settlement. Here, then, was a region to which the Indian tribes east of the Mississippi might be removed and where they might be allowed to dwell permanently without further molestation by white men. This was the proposal which Secretary Calhoun made to President Monroe and which he in turn communicated to Congress in 1825.

The idea of removing the Indians west of the Mississippi did not originate with Calhoun. It had occurred to Thomas Jefferson and was embodied in the constitutional amendment which he drafted in 1803 but did not submit to Congress, for the purpose of satisfying his political scruples at the time of the purchase of Louisiana. Furthermore, the act establishing the Territory of Louisiana contained a clause authorizing the President to negotiate treaties with the Indians providing for the exchange of their lands east of the Mississippi for lands west of that river. In the succeeding years the plan of removal met with some favor, especially in the South. A few tribes, notably the Delawares, Kickapoos, and a portion of the Cherokees were induced to move to the western country, but no effort was made to secure a location for them there. They were left to find new homes as best they could.

The Calhoun-Monroe plan contemplated an elaborate series of treaties, first with the tribes already inhabiting the western plains securing room for the prospective newcomers, and next with the eastern tribes inviting and urging them to accept new lands in exchange for those they then occupied. Schools and other agencies of civilization were to be provided for them. The border of the Indian country was to be patrolled to protect the tribesmen from unscrupulous white traders and settlers. In short, the Indians were promised that if they would move to new western homes they could settle down secure in the assurance that they would never again be disturbed.

Congress did not immediately take action on Monroe's proposal, but treaty-making proceeded rapidly. With the accession of Andrew Jackson to the presidency in 1829 the removal policy became a party measure and in spite of strong opposition from religious and other organizations interested in the Indians, in 1830 Congress passed a law authorizing the President to exchange lands held by tribes within a State or Territory for lands beyond the Mississippi. There was no suggestion of compulsion in the law, but with a thorough-going westerner in the White House there could be little doubt of the outcome. The removal process was soon in full swing. The Cherokees and Creeks clung desperately to their southern homes and the years from 1835 to 1838 were marked by numerous disturbances. The Seminoles were even more unwilling to move, with the result that there was another "Seminole War" lasting from 1837 to 1842. The conditions under which the once-proud southern tribes were conducted to much less satisfactory lands west of Arkansas were difficult at best. These migrations attracted much attention at the time and they constitute a pathetic chapter in the story of the American Indians.

By 1840 the new Indian frontier was practically complete. In general the boundary ran west from Green Bay to the Mississippi, down that river to the lead-mining region near the mouth of the Wisconsin, in a southwestwardly direction into the Territory of Iowa, then south to the Missouri line and west on that line to the Missouri River, down that river and the western boundary of Missouri and Arkansas to the Texan line. The Commissioner of Indian Affairs in 1837 estimated that approximately 12,400 Indians remained in the States, more than 51,000 had already migrated, nearly 40,000 were under agreement to migrate, and that the tribes already resident in the western Indian country numbered nearly 232,000.

Thus was created the solid and supposedly permanent Indian frontier. It is reasonable to believe that the removal policy was conceived honestly and with the expectation that the promises made the Indians would not be broken. It can at least be said of the policy that, in view of all the factors involved, it was better than the ill-considered practices which it replaced. The policy was executed consistently and certainly without greater wrongs to the Indians themselves than they had previously suffered. The main cause for regret is that there did not exist the will and the wisdom to give some plan of assimilation a thorough and persistent trial.

CHAPTER VI

THE PUBLIC DOMAIN

MINGLED motives and varied compulsions actuated the millions of individuals who participated in the long-continued westward movement. Restlessness, yearning for new scenes, the contagious nature of the moving fever, dissatisfaction, distress, failure—all these had their effect. But land-hunger was the most potent of the impelling forces. Cheap and fertile land was the lure above all others which year after year filled the roads and waterways with emigrants to the West. Timothy Flint expressed the power of this attraction somewhat rhetorically, but none the less vividly, when in 1832 he wrote: "Sickness, solitude, mountains, the war-whoop, the merciless tomahawk, wolves, panthers, and bears, dear and distant homes, forsaken forever, will come over their waking thoughts, and revisit their dreams in vain, to prevent the young, florid and unportioned pair from scaling remote mountains, descending long rivers, and finally selecting their spot in the forests, consecrating their solitary cabin with the dear and sacred name of home."

The very earliest settlers throughout most of that portion of the West with which we are now dealing apparently were little concerned about land titles. They squatted where fancy or necessity dictated, built rude cabins, made small clearings, lived mostly by hunting, and after a few years moved on to some more distant frontiers, there to repeat the process. Those who followed them, however, were of different dispositions. They came with the intention at least of making permanent settlements. Land to them was something of great value and therefore the acquiring of valid title was of supreme importance. Out of this need and desire grew our public land policy. Because of the demand of westerners for a progressive liberalization of this policy thousands of pages were filled with Congressional debates and reports, political parties inserted planks in their platforms, and chief executives were compelled to express their views. In the history of the West and in that of the nation as a whole, therefore, the story of public land legislation and its operation constitutes a chapter of great significance.

THE CESSION OF THE WESTERN LANDS

When the thirteen American colonies threw off the English yoke the new state governments claimed jurisdiction in accordance with the boundaries established by the colonial charters and the subsequent adjustments made by Parliamentary legislation. Thus there were seven States—Massachusetts, Connecticut, New York, Virginia, North Carolina, South Carolina, and Georgia—which maintained title to lands west of the Appalachian Mountains. The Proclamation of 1763 had been interpreted in America as not abrogating the western land claims of the various colonies, but only as deferring their settlement. The Quebec Act of 1774, placing the region north of the Ohio River under the jurisdiction of the Canadian province, was cited as one of the grievances of the colonists, and it was not regarded as binding upon them, especially after the exploits of George Rogers Clark.

Beginning at the north, Massachusetts laid claim to a broad strip of territory extending across the southern part of the modern States of Michigan and Wisconsin and the northern edge of Illinois. Next was the claim of Connecticut to a narrower belt stretching across the northern border of the present Ohio, Indiana, continuing through Illinois and including the very southern fringe of Michigan. New York's claim to land west of Pennsylvania and reaching into Kentucky was of a more shadowy nature, since it rested on that colony's alleged suzerainty over the Iroquois Indians who, in turn, had asserted their jurisdiction over a vast region.

All three of these western land claims were disputed by Virginia, whose pretensions were the largest of all the States. That colony's second charter had specified that the colony should extend "all along the sea-coast" two hundred miles north and an equal distance south of Point Comfort, and that it should reach "up into the land throughout from sea to sea, west and northwest." The last statement was extremely indefinite and ambiguous. It is not surprising that the grantees chose to interpret this provision as meaning that the boundary lines should run west from the southern point on the sea-coast and northwest from the northern point. The southern boundary of Virginia was later modified and made definite when the Carolina grant was made. Consequently Virginia claimed not only modern Kentucky but all the land north of the Ohio and west of Pennsylvania, and for a time even the southwestern corner of that State. After the division of the Carolina grant, North Carolina included what is now Tennessee. South Carolina also extended indefinitely westward, but her claim was later limited by the creation of Georgia, at the most, to a narrow strip south of the present southern boundary of Tennessee. Georgia was given the land to the west of that colony, and there was some contention that this grant entirely obliterated South Carolina's claim.

There is every evidence that these seven States were planning to use their western land as a source of revenue. The six landless States (if we include Pennsylvania which had vast unoccupied areas in its western portion) naturally looked with envy upon the vast holdings of their more fortunate neighbors. This jealousy and ill will, as well as the prospect of quarrels between the States whose western claims overlapped, threatened to block the effort to secure unified action even in the midst of the war for independence. The Articles of Confederation, weak as they proved to be, were far better than no plan of union. But in 1780, three years after these articles of government were first submitted to the legislatures, they still lacked ratification by the requisite number of States. The question of the western land claims was the main stumbling-block.

Maryland was the spokesman for the small and landless States, refusing staunchly to ratify the Articles until the western land claims had been surrendered to the general government. The Maryland legislature asserted that this western land "if wrested from the common enemy by the blood and treasure of the thirteen States, should be considered as a common property." In November, 1779, Congress issued an appeal to the land-claiming States to yield in the interest of union. New York was the first to respond, when on February 1, 1781, she ceded her somewhat doubtful claims unreservedly to the federal government. A year later Maryland ratified the Articles of Confederation. There was considerable negotiation between Congress and Virginia before that State ceded her western lands on March 1, 1784, reserving Kentucky and such land between the Scioto and Little Miami Rivers as might be necessary to satisfy outstanding warrants.

Cessions by the remaining five States followed at intervals until 1802. Massachusetts surrendered her western lands

III. WESTERN LAND CLAIMS OF THE STATES

without reservation in 1785. Connecticut followed in 1786, retaining until 1800 what was known as the "Western Reserve" along the southern shore of Lake Erie in Ohio. South Carolina ceded whatever claim she possessed unconditionally in 1787. Three years later North Carolina yielded jurisdiction over the present State of Tennessee, but there were so many outstanding claims that very little land in that area was left for disposal by Congress. The last cession, that by Georgia, came in 1802 after long controversies between the State and the federal government, and after a notorious public scandal had grown out of the transactions of the Yazoo Land Companies.

These self-denying cessions created a public domain that proved a strong bond of union between the discordant States during the so-called "critical period" and the early years under the Constitution. Later accessions with each territorial acquisition by the United States, ending with the purchase of Alaska in 1867, greatly enlarged the area of the public domain. But in formulating a public land policy and a plan of territorial government the otherwise ineffective Congress of the Confederation won its chief title to remembrance. Both the Land Ordinance of 1785 and the Northwest Ordinance of 1787 setting up territorial government were of vital importance in the development of the West. Only the former ordinance will be discussed in this connection, since the latter did not deal with land policy.

The Establishment of a Public Land System

Scarcely had the Articles of Confederation gone into effect when Congress was called upon to decide what was to be done with the public domain. Revolutionary soldiers, still under arms, were clamoring for the lands that had been promised them at the time of their enlistments. They and others were also suggesting that the depreciated continental currency be accepted in payment for western land. Settlers were pouring into the West and many of them were squatting on lands north of the Ohio, causing discontent among the Indians. After his return from a western journey in 1784 George Washington wrote to R. H. Lee that "The spirit of emigration is great; people have got impatient; and though you cannot stop the road, it is yet in your power to mark the way." Clearly some policy must be established and some plan devised for the disposal of the western lands.

Two lines of colonial procedure furnished precedents for the study of Congress in seeking a solution for this problem. In New England the practice had been early established of permitting new settlements only in compact bodies and after prior government survey and marking of the lands to be occupied. The entire process was under the careful supervision of the colony, which made provision for adequate records and laid down the conditions under which settlements could be made. In the South, on the other hand, there was much less colonial oversight. New settlements were largely the work of individuals, who were permitted to locate on any unappropriated land that might suit them, mark their own boundaries, and record their claims accordingly. The New England system had the advantage of greater orderliness and compactness of settlement and greater certainty of boundaries and land titles. The southern procedure appealed more to the typical pioneer, but it led to endless disputes and litigation over poorly defined boundaries and titles. The plan which Congress finally adopted was a compromise between these two systems, although the New England procedure predominated.

A committee, of which Thomas Jefferson was a prominent member, reported a plan for a land system to Congress in 1784. Government survey into rectangular units prior to settlement was an outstanding feature of this report. The unit of the survey was to be the "hundred" ten miles square, divided into one hundred "lots" one mile square. This report was not acted upon at the time, but came up for discussion again the following year. In the course of the debate and committee action the plan was modified in many respects, including the reduction of the unit of survey to a "township" at first seven miles and later six miles square. On May 20, 1785, the ordinance was finally adopted.

The Land Ordinance of 1785, which laid the foundation of our public land system, contained the following important features, as well as many other details.   Indian title to the land must be extinguished before it could be opened to entry.   Surveys must be made prior to settlement, the rectangular plan being adopted, with townships six miles square divided into thirty-six lots or sections, as the subdivisions were soon called. The first meridian line was established and provision made for the survey of seven ranges of townships in southeastern Ohio. One-seventh of the land, selected by lot, was set aside for the Revolutionary soldiers and the remainder was to be put up for sale by auction in the various States at a minimum price of one dollar an acre.   Two plans of disposal were to be used in alternate townships.   One-half of the townships were to be sold entire and the other half in units of one section.   Another provision of far-reaching significance was the reservation of section sixteen in each township for the maintenance of public schools.

The Ohio Associates and the Scioto Associates

If Congress expected an immediate income from the sale of western lands it was largely disappointed.   Sales were slow and small.   Strong competition was offered by more favorably located land within the States.   The Indian menace in the region northwest of the Ohio was not conducive to settlement.   At the same time frontiersmen, especially those from Virginia and other southern States, were disinclined to abandon their habit of marking out "tomahawk claims" and making indiscriminate settlements to suit their own fancies, with little regard to the provisions of the Land Ordinance.   Thus it was that in 1787 the poor old Congress of the Confederation was ready to listen to proposals for large grants to land companies, and to nullify some of the important features of the plan it had adopted two years earlier.

In 1786 a group of Revolutionary soldiers in New England, led by Rufus Putnam, the Reverend Manasseh Cutler, Benjamin Tupper, Samuel Parsons, and others, organized the Ohio Associates or Ohio Company, which is not to be confused with the earlier Virginia company by the same name.   The purpose of this group was to obtain a large tract of land in Ohio primarily for the benefit of soldiers who, it was hoped, could in this way obtain some value for the virtually worthless government certificates paid them for their military service. Under the skillful management of Manasseh Cutler this proposal was presented in Congress in a manner that would do credit to the modern manipulator and lobbyist. Members of Congress were visited at their lodgings at the seat of government and even in their own homes in their respective States. The prospect of selling one million dollars worth of land, even in return for depreciated currency, was very attractive. Still more alluring and effective was the suggestion of Cutler that members of Congress and other interested individuals might indulge in promising speculation by joining in the organization of a similar company to be given similar privileges. The suggestion was followed and a group known as the Scioto Associates was formed. With this backing the request of the Ohio Company was granted in the summer of 1787.

The Ohio Associates were allowed to contract for the purchase of more than a million and a half acres of land on the Ohio River west of the seven ranges, upon making a down payment of $500,000 in continental currency worth about twelve cents on the dollar. They never were able to complete payment for the entire amount of land granted them. Nevertheless, they planted permanent and thriving settlements in Ohio, and it was their proposal that led to the adoption of the fundamental charter of territorial government in the United States—the Northwest Ordinance of 1787.

The Scioto Associates were given the right to purchase nearly five million acres. This group, however, did not affect any real organization and their only success was in duping some six hundred French artisans and peasants to come to America. By the time they arrived here the tenuous Scioto organization was virtually defunct. The unfortunate emigrés were sent to Ohio, where on lands of the Ohio Company they formed a settlement known as Gallipolis. Here they lived a miserable existence, relieved only in part by later Congressional donations of lands totalling 25,200 acres.

One other large land deal was made by the Congress of the Confederation in its last days. John Cleves Symmes of New

Jersey was permitted in 1788 to purchase one million acres of land north of the Ohio and between the Great Miami and the Little Miami rivers. He was never able to complete payment on the entire amount. Moreover, the affairs of his purchase gave much trouble to the territorial government and to Congress before they were finally adjusted.

THE LAND LAW OF 1796

This was the situation when the Constitution went into operation and the new Congress, with vastly increased powers and prestige, assumed the legislative function. As might be expected, the public land question soon demanded consideration. It was not until 1796, however, that anything in the nature of a general land law was enacted. In the meantime there were numerous reports and much debate, and it seemed for a time as though the sound and workable system outlined in the Land Ordinance of 1785 might be abandoned. Alexander Hamilton as Secretary of the Treasury made his well-known report of a uniform system for the disposition of the public lands. His object clearly was to use the lands primarily as a means of raising revenue for the federal government, although he recognized the rights of individual settlers. It is fortunate that his plan was not adopted, for it ignored many of the most beneficial features of the Ordinance of 1785. Equally fortunate was the failure of the efforts of members of Congress from the frontier section, like Thomas Scott of Pittsburgh, to return to a system of indiscriminate settlements, allowing the individual pioneer to settle virtually where he chose and on as much land as he wished. Other aspects of the land problem which were discussed were the respective merits of cash and credit sales, of sales in large or small amounts, and of a land office confined to the seat of government or branch offices situated in the regions where the land was to be offered for sale.

On May 18, 1796, a law was finally approved "providing for the sale of the lands of the United States in the territory northwest of the river Ohio, and above the mouth of the Kentucky river." Only lands to which the Indian title had been extinguished were to be surveyed. The system of survey prior to settlement and of townships six miles square was retained and established for all time. Half of the townships were left undivided to be sold in quarter-townships at Philadelphia. The other half of the townships were to be surveyed and sold in sections of 640 acres at land offices at Pittsburgh and Cincinnati. Sales were to be made at auction, with the minimum price at two dollars an acre. One-twentieth of this amount was to be deposited at the time of application, the remainder of one-half within thirty days and the balance within one year, with a discount of ten per cent for cash. Failure to make these payments caused forfeiture of both the land and any payments already made. The establishment of western land offices was a concession to the wishes and convenience of settlers. The increased minimum price was thought to serve as a discouragement to speculators.

The Harrison Land Law of 1800

The law of 1796 proved a discouragement not only to speculators but to actual settlers as well, and scarcely more than 120,000 acres were sold in the four years following its enactment. On December 2, 1799, William Henry Harrison took his seat in Congress as delegate from Northwest Territory. He was thoroughly imbued with the frontiersman's point of view and demands in connection with public land policy. Within three weeks he introduced a resolution calling for the appointment of a committee to consider necessary alterations in the land law. The result was the submission of a report, which, without material change, was adopted and incorporated in what is known as the Harrison Land Law, bearing the date of May 10, 1800.

In this law the argument of the settlers that a section was too large a tract for a poor man to buy was met by the reduction of the smallest purchasable unit to a half-section. The other contention of the westerners, that credit of one year was no credit at all for the farmer on new lands, was likewise accepted and a real credit system was provided, with installments over a period of four years. Four land offices were established at Cincinnati, Chillicothe, Marietta, and Steubenville, with a register and a receiver at each office. Land was to be offered at auction for a period of three weeks and afterwards sold at private sale, the minimum price at auction and the regular price at private sale still being two dollars an acre. Thus, to quote Frederic L. Paxson, "under the Harrison Law, the United States became the partner of every settler who wished to try his luck upon the public domain, required him to put up only fifty cents an acre in advance and took its chance with him as to the success or failure of the enterprise. In four years, if successful, the settler expected to earn his farm out of its produce. Whether it was a good system for the country, or a vicious inducement to speculation and evasion of obligations, remained to be seen as the law directed the flow of settlers into Ohio, Indiana, Illinois, Alabama, Mississippi, Louisiana, and Missouri." [1]

Mixed motives led to the passage of the Harrison Land Law. Those who looked to the western lands primarily as a source of revenue expected that their purpose would be served by the relatively high price prescribed, in combination with the credit system. The pioneers and their friends felt that they had gained a point in the adoption of the credit system and the smaller unit of sale. Both groups were certain that the two-dollar minimum price would discourage speculators from purchasing large tracts of land. The results failed to verify the accuracy of these predictions.

To be sure, much land was sold under the Harrison Law— over nineteen million acres by 1820—but it was not until after the close of the War of 1812 that the annual sales ran into the millions. The statistics of sales, however, are misleading, for nearly one-third of this land eventually reverted to the government because of the inability or unwillingness of the purchasers to complete payment, although a series of twelve relief laws had been passed in their behalf by Congress. In 1804 the smallest unit of sale was reduced to the now familiar quarter-section, and more favorable terms with respect to interest were granted. But even then to complete payment in four years on one hundred and sixty acres of land was in reality

[1] Frederic L. Paxson, *History of the American Frontier* (1924), p. 122. By permission of The Houghton Mifflin Company, publishers.

beyond the means of the poor men who constituted the large majority of the westward emigrants. There is no way of knowing how many thousands of wistful but prudent families were deterred from making the venture by the evident impossibility of getting together enough money to finance the migration, the eighty-dollar first payment, and sustenance until crops could be raised. There is ample evidence, however, that a great number of too optimistic families undertook the impossible.

The hope that the relatively high minimum price would discourage speculation was also vain. As the years passed and especially as the Great Migration following the War of 1812 got into full swing, Indian treaties were made and land offices were opened in rapid succession in the Old Northwest in Ohio, Indiana, Illinois, and Michigan; in the south in Alabama and Mississippi; and across the Mississippi in Louisiana and Missouri. Surveyors with line and chain were busy marking off the metes and bounds of millions of farms. Land fever was epidemic in America from 1814 to 1820, and in many regions it assumed the virulent form of wild speculation.

Town-booming was one of the favorite forms of speculation throughout the West. "When you hear about market-houses, and seminaries, and streets No. 1, 2, and 3, in the midst of a wilderness of fallen logs," wrote Timothy Flint concerning Vevay, Indiana, in 1816, "you will have some idea of the language appropriate to a kind of speculation, almost peculiar to this country, that is to say, town-making." In 1818 Hezekiah Niles wrote of "a town somewhere in the Alabama territory, to be called 'Florence'—52 lots in it were lately sold for eighty-two thousand dollars." Later reports from this new town showed that a townsite company paid from $150 to $251 per acre for a quarter-section and then sold 284 lots for $226,411. "The highest went at $3,500. The average was nearly $800 for half an acre of woods." These are illustrations of what was happening all over the West. Some of the towns grew and prospered and thus justified the great expectations of speculators and bona fide buyers alike, even at boom prices. Others never existed except on paper, while still others after promising beginnings, dwindled away and became "ghost towns," sad reminders of shattered hopes.

Speculation in agricultural land was less spectacular but nevertheless widespread. North of the Ohio it did not reveal itself in inflated prices at the auction sales. Statistics indicate that the actual receipts did not average much in excess of the minimum price of two dollars per acre, but these figures do not account for the large amount of land reverting to the government because of uncompleted payments. The original buyers, however, were not so modest in their confidence in the future of the region. Morris Birkbeck in 1817 found that fifty dollars an acre was frequently asked for improved land in Ohio. "I have," he wrote, "been asked thirty for a large tract, without improvements, on the Great Miami, fifty miles from Cincinnati, and similar prices in other quarters."

It was in Mississippi and Alabama that speculative fever was most in evidence in the bidding at the auctions. Even granting that the rich, black soil of that section justified the offering of relatively high bids by actual settlers and plantation operators planning to engage in cotton culture, many of the prices paid were clearly speculative and attracted national attention, besides inducing bona fide settlers to offer more than they could pay or the land was worth. Senator Walker of Alabama declared on the floor of the Senate that the sales were made "under a sort of delirium—the most prudent, calculating men in the country were swept away by the delusion." Newspaper reports of various land sales in that region in 1818, for instance, indicated that "very little land that was good went for less than thirty dollars an acre," that "some of the best lands sold at 73 dollars an acre," and that "the highest quarter section was bid off by a responsible planter at one hundred and seven dollars per acre." A St. Louis editor, contrasting these prices with the three-dollar average for the sales in Missouri, consoled himself by the reflection that "if the south belongs to the rich alone, the substantial yeomanry of the country will turn their attention to the Missouri."

A plan adopted by a company of speculators in Alabama may have had its counterparts in other regions. They agreed among themselves not to bid more than two dollars an acre for any land. At this price they succeeded in obtaining two valuable townships and were ready to bid for more, but the

Register of the land office had discovered the scheme and discontinued the sale. The speculators then sold their two townships at auction and netted profits amounting to $1980 for each of the forty members. "We presume," was the comment of an Alabama editor, "that the gentlemen speculators formed their plans on the commonly received principle, that the public is a goose, and that while its enchanting plumage offered so many temptations to pluck a few feathers, no other danger was to be apprehended than that of being hissed at!"

CHAPTER VII

THE FIGHT FOR FREE LAND

The Defects of the Credit System

The defects and the unfortunate results of the credit system in the disposition of the public lands were very apparent by 1820, not only among easterners but also in the West among those in whose supposed interest the Harrison Law had primarily been enacted. A writer in a Kentucky paper in 1819, signing himself "Franklin," sounded an ominous note of warning which no doubt found foreboding echoes in the minds of many thoughtful persons. "The debts which it has already produced," he said in commenting on the credit system, "will be a source of almost endless and infinite embarrassment to the general government. Year after year will indulgence be *entreated*, till our strength will enable us to *demand it*, in a voice of thunder. . . . Let numberless individuals of every description, from the most wealthy, intelligent, and influential, down to those who are the reverse, be deeply indebted to the government of the Union, and will they not be in some measure disinclined to support it? . . . No people are more patriotic and firmly attached to the government of the Union than those of the west; the idea of a separation has never been indulged; it is literally abhorred; but their patriotism and fidelity are not invincible."

"Let not, therefore," he continued, "the general government credit the people of the west to the amount of fifty or a hundred million dollars, if it would not foolishly drive them into a declaration of independence. . . . The Rubicon is not yet passed; but we now stand upon the shore, and it depends on the measures to be adopted by the next congress, whether we shall remain a peaceful, happy and united people, or advance, with a steady and certain pace, to civil war and a dissolution of the union."

Congress, indeed, found itself embarrassed by the problems arising out of the uncomfortable situation and for several years after 1820 was still engaged in passing laws for the relief of those who were in arrears in the deferred payments on their land. The extent to which land was over-bought under stimulus of the credit system was also revealed in the long lists of lands to be sold for taxes which began to appear in western newspapers. These lists indicate to what a surprising extent individuals had undertaken to pay for lands in amounts much in excess of the minimum unit of one hundred and sixty acres.

Inability to make the deferred payments was one thing. Unwillingness to make them was a natural outgrowth of the system and it spread by example. The government was in no position to take drastic measures against defaulters. Instead it was compelled to pass laws for their relief. The hard-working farmer who saw that nothing happened to his neighbor when he let installments go unpaid often decided to omit his own payments. Viewing the effects of this attitude from the perspective of time and a knowledge of later trends, Professor Paxson suggests that "the measurement of the injury done by the system to frontier standards of commercial honor would make an interesting study in group psychology." [1]

THE LAND LAW OF 1820

Altogether, the credit system was thoroughly in disfavor by 1820, and in that year Congress passed a new land law which provided for its abandonment. There was a strong and growing sentiment in the West in favor of free land, an objective partly in accord with the frontiersman's long-standing contention of right and justice and partly brought to the fore by the mental state of a debtor farming population. The time, however, was not ripe for the fulfillment of this desire. The revenue motive in land policy and the political strength of the Atlantic States, which feared and opposed any measure that would tend to further drain population from their borders, were still too strong to be overcome. The law of 1820 reduced

[1] Frederic L. Paxson, *History of the American Frontier* (1924), p. 223. By permission of The Houghton Mifflin Company, publishers.

the minimum price to $1.25 an acre to be paid in one cash payment. It also established eighty acres as the smallest unit of purchase. One hundred dollars would now secure the settler immediate title to at least a small farm, whereas under the credit system and the quarter-section unit eighty dollars would pay only one of four installments.

SPECULATION IN WESTERN LAND

A period of twenty years again elapsed before another general law affecting the basic principles of public land policy was passed. The question was far from being forgotten during this interval, however; on the contrary, it became one of the great topics of national concern. Congress enacted numerous laws dealing with various phases of the land problem, and spent much time at each session debating other proposals. The subject of the public lands became enmeshed in the sectional politics of the period and in the growing antagonism between the industrial East and the rapidly strengthening agricultural West.

The Land Law of 1820 went into operation while the effects of the Panic of 1819 were still strongly in evidence. It was probably for this reason, rather than primarily because of the cash payments required by the law, that the volume of sales of public lands fell off greatly. Not until 1829 did the total annual sales again exceed one million acres. During the early thirties the amount showed a steady increase as another great wave of migration got under way, and in 1835 and 1836 the sales reached astonishing proportions and constituted one of the causes of the severe Panic of 1837, as will be seen in a later chapter. In 1836 more than twenty million acres of public land were sold. There is ample evidence that much of this buying was speculative in nature.

Town boomers and others of what would now be called the "booster" type were inclined to regard the speculator as a useful citizen because of his loud advertising of various regions. More thoughtful and conservative people in 1836 both East and West, regarded the speculative rage as dangerous and detrimental. A Boston paper reported that "money is passing from the Atlantic to the Western States, almost as fast as steamboats and railroad cars can carry it, to be invested in lands. Are all these facts indications of real prosperity, or are they the projects of speculations, whose fruits will be as disastrous, and as much beyond parallel calamities as the present appearances are attractive and exhilarating?" A New York editor, in satirical vein, reported a recent conversation: " 'Well, how are the folks getting on in your country,' said we to a resident of the interior of this State. 'O, finely,' said he, 'Many of the people after three weeks absence, have returned from the far West—having purchased everything up to the Rocky Mountains, are now so rich, that they talk of casting every man in the poor house, who is not worth more than $100,000.' "

In western newspapers the widespread speculation also received disapproving attention. For instance a Galena, Illinois, editor stated that out of the total sales in the entire country in 1836, "eight millions of acres of public lands have this year passed into the hands of a few wealthy speculators, who will hold them up at an extravagant value. These lands, therefore, will remain unoccupied for many years, or occupied only by a dependent tenantry. The owner and cultivator of a single farm confers greater benefits upon the community than the monopolist of thousands of acres, permitted to lie waste and uncultivated." The same editor declared it was generally conceded that a number of members of Congress had joined with others in a company to speculate in public lands and had purchased millions of acres. The factual content of these statements may have been open to question, but the attitude expressed was typical of that of many western editors. A Dubuque, Iowa, editor pointed out that speculation was a "species of gambling" demoralizing to those who indulged in it. "Happy," he said, "is the man who escapes unscathed the enticing vortex." In any discussion of land speculation, however, it must be remembered that many of those who engaged in it lost heavily.

Cession, Graduation, and Distribution

During these years a large number of proposals in regard to land policy were being discussed persistently and eloquently both in and out of Congress. As will be seen later, the policy of making land grants in aid of internal improvements was firmly established during this period. Cession of unsold lands to the States in which they lay was ardently approved by westerners, and as vigorously opposed by the East. This idea was so at variance with the fundamental conception of a public domain belonging to the whole nation that it has never been adopted in full. Donation of land to actual settlers was, as has already been noted, warmly espoused on the frontier, and at this time had the general approval of the South. The industrial East, however, was violently hostile to a procedure that would greatly reduce the federal revenue received from land sales, and enhance the attractiveness of the West that was already depriving the eastern States of any excess population and thereby forcing a relatively high wage scale. Free land was not to be achieved for many years, after long-continued agitation.

Graduation was the name given to another proposal which failed of adoption during this period, but was put into operation later. In each of the land districts there was land that did not secure purchasers either at the auction sales or by private sale afterward. Sometimes this land was inferior in quality to that which was readily sold; sometimes its location away from avenues of transportation made it less desirable. Ever since the land system was established there had been supporters for a plan that would result in a progressive reduction of the price of such land according to the length of time it remained on the market. The suggestion was logical and during the thirties it was strongly advocated by such westerners as Thomas Hart Benton, who saw in it the next best thing to free land. But again the revenue argument and eastern opposition stood in the way of success. It was not until 1854 that a graduation law was passed.

The arguments in favor of using the public lands as a source of revenue were greatly weakened during the thirties by the fact that each year the income of the government exceeded the expenditures. In 1834 the national debt was entirely wiped out, and still the surplus continued to grow. Out of this situation there developed a formidable movement to distribute among all the States that portion of the surplus that was due to the sale of public lands. The sectional support of this measure was just the reverse of that given to the program already discussed. The eastern States were naturally heartily in favor of the distribution plan; while westerners were generally opposed to it, because it would give added strength to the sentiment against free land. Henry Clay was the most prominent sponsor of the distribution idea, which accorded nicely with his ambition to achieve a successful political combination of interest between the industrial East and the agricultural West.

In 1833 a distribution law passed Congress, giving one-eighth of the net receipts from the land sales to the States in which the land lay, and distributing the remainder among all the States on the basis of their representation in Congress. President Jackson vetoed the bill, on the grounds that it violated the original agreement in regard to the public domain and that it would weaken the position and dignity of the States by making them dependent on subventions from the federal government. He had another veto message all drafted in 1836, when the passage of another distribution bill seemed imminent, but was not obliged to use it. With curious inconsistency, he failed to disapprove another law passed the same year, directing that the greater part of the surplus in the treasury should be "deposited" with the States in four installments. The term "deposit" was pure camouflage, for there was no intention that the money should ever be returned by the States. Only three deposits were actually made. The Panic of 1837 prevented the payment of the fourth installment, and the law was repealed.

Preemption Legislation

Despite the fact that a surplus ceased to embarrass the federal government, the movement for a distribution law was too effective as political bait to be abandoned. In 1841 the advocates of this project won an empty victory by linking it in one bill with a favorite objective of westerners—namely, the right of preemption.

The right of preemption meant the right of the settler who had squatted without authority on Indian land or unsurveyed land to purchase that land after the survey at the minimum price in advance of the auction sale. Obviously such a right was directly contrary to the fundamental principles of public land policy. Nevertheless, the justice of such a privilege was firmly entrenched in frontier morality, and from the first session of Congress under the Constitution it was supported on the floor of the national legislature. In that session Thomas Scott from western Pennsylvania declared that "The emigrants who reach the Western country will not stop until they find a place where they can securely seat themselves . . . they must have a well grounded hope that the lands they cultivate may become their own." But Congress was not then or for many years in a mood to listen to such arguments. Instead, laws were enacted invoking forcible removable and dire penalties for intruders on the public domain before the date of legal entry. Year by year the futility of such laws became more and more evident.

There is no denying the fact that the advance guard of land-hungry pioneers paid little heed to Indian boundaries or to federal land laws. Hatred bred of brutal warfare had convinced the frontiersmen that the rights of the red men were no more entitled to respect than those of the wild beasts. The land laws were regarded as oppressive and out of accord with frontier needs. As the westward movement continued, and especially as it greatly increased in volume during the decade of the thirties, Indian treaties and government land surveys frequently lagged behind the pressure of land-seekers. In other cases many well-intentioned settlers found themselves illegally on lands which they had supposed to be within established land districts. Altogether, it is not difficult to understand how westerners could sincerely contend that the squatter who went ahead, even in technical or open violation of the law, and made improvements on his land had rendered a public service and merited a reward rather than punishment.

Time after time Congress was faced by the dilemma caused by the presence of large numbers of squatters on lands not open to entry. Nothing short of a determined campaign by the army could have dispossessed them, and such a drastic measure was wholly inexpedient. Eastern members of Congress might brand the western settlers as a brawling, lawless rabble. In the end they were obliged to listen to the petitions of these very intruders and to the memorials of western legislatures, and grant preemption rights. It was easier and far more comfortable to relieve the genuine or alleged distress of land law violators than it was to enforce the provisions of the law. Before 1841 sixteen special or temporary acts were passed giving preemption rights to squatters in particular regions or for limited periods.

When this right was denied or postponed the settlers frequently took matters into their own hands and provided their own means of protection. There was good ground for the warning issued by an Iowa editor in 1838. "Refuse to our hardy settlers the privileges heretofore granted and you create a necessity for combinations among them. They will combine to protect their fields and their homes." This is exactly what they did, by organizing claim clubs or claim associations. As has been stated, settlers who squatted on land, even though illegally, built cabins and put in crops, felt that they were entitled to the first right to the land and to protection against speculators or later purchasers whom they regarded as claim-jumpers. Accordingly when preemption rights were not granted they banded themselves together for mutual protection against outsiders when the land should be put up for sale. The spirit of these organizations is illustrated in the resolutions of a Wisconsin land club. They declared that "in case any person or persons shall purchase lands in this vicinity at the time occupied by claimants; that they be disregarded as neighbors, and that no dealings of any kind be had with them. That we will neither lend to them nor borrow from them, nor visit them, nor act with them in any capacity whatsoever, no upon any occasion." Further, they resolved, significantly that if any person should undertake to deprive any claimant of his rights, "we will not fail to rebuke his conduct with such sever ity as has been common in the settlement of this western country."

Although found in various western States the claim club reached its greatest perfection in the Territory of Iowa, where, according to Benjamin F. Shambaugh, "over one hundred of these extra-legal organizations existed." Many of these clubs adopted rather elaborate constitutions, by-laws, and resolutions, which prescribed the basis of membership, the officers and their duties, the amount of land which could be claimed, the method of keeping records, the action to be taken against claim-jumpers, and various other details. Each member marked off his claim as best he could with reference to natural features such as streams, trees, and large boulders; and these claims were recorded in the secretary's book. When the auction sale opened the club attended in a body, often with weapons freely displayed. As the various pieces of land were put up for sale the secretary bid for them at the minimum price of $1.25 an acre in the names of the respective claimants. Outsiders who had the temerity to bid higher were usually politely advised to desist. If this warning failed to discourage them more forceful means were frequently employed. In the main, the claim clubs served the same purpose for the settlers as a preemption law. They even went further and protected claimants who, for one reason or other, were unable to purchase their land during the progress of the auction sales.

In view of the effective operation of these organizations and after ample precedents set by a series of special acts, it is not surprising that a general preemption law was passed in 1841. Even then, however, it would doubtless have failed if it had not been linked with the distribution idea in one bill. In this form, after vigorous debate, it attracted both eastern and western voters, was passed, and received President Tyler's signature. The preemption provisions of the law gave the permanent right of preemption to heads of families, to men over twenty-one years of age, and to widows, providing they were citizens of the United States or had declared their intention of becoming citizens. Another limitation excluded all who were owners of more than 320 acres of land in addition to their preemption claim. All who met the provisions of the law could settle on

160 acres of land and later purchase it at the minimum price of $1.25 an acre, without submitting to competitive bidding at the auction sales. There were numerous other clauses dealing with the amount of improvement required and the method of establishing a claim.

An Iowa editor was entirely correct when he said that the Preemption Law of 1841 "legalizes a course which, although universally in vogue, was in fact unlawful," and that the bill had passed "under the influence of the argument that it is better to legalize what is incurable and inevitable, than to keep on the statute book a provision which is a dead letter." The law was also characterized contemporaneously as merely "declaratory of the custom of the common law of the settlers." On the whole it is perhaps fair to say that at the time of its adoption the law was the most practicable solution of a difficult problem. In the succeeding years numerous minor changes were made. Fifty years after its passage the defects of the law in actual operation were so apparent that it was repealed.

The distribution features of the Preemption-Distribution Law were not destined to be actually effective. The law provided that ten per cent of the net proceeds of the sale of public lands should be given to the States in which the land was sold and the balance distributed among all the States and Territories in proportion to their population. Southern Senators, however, succeeded in inserting an amendment in the bill stipulating that distribution should cease whenever customs duties in excess of twenty per cent were imposed. By 1843 the condition of the federal treasury was such that a tariff bill was passed with rates higher than twenty per cent. The distribution of funds was therefore suspended, and although nominally not repealed, the distribution features of the law were virtually inoperative. Thus the law of 1841 is generally known simply as the Preemption Law.

THE MOVEMENT FOR A HOMESTEAD LAW

The two decades following the passage of the Preemption Law witnessed the enactment of a number of laws on the subject of the public lands, but until 1862 no important change was made in underlying policy. In 1850 Stephen A. Douglas secured a liberal land grant for the Illinois Central Railroad which served as a precedent for later subsidies of a similar character and on a large scale. A law of 1854 put into operation the long-advocated plan of graduating the price of land according to the time it had remained on the market. The reduced prices ranged from one dollar per acre for land that remained unsold for ten years down to twelve and a half cents an acre for land still on the market after thirty years or more. Since there was no limit on the amount of such land one person could buy, it has been asserted, and probably with good reason, that non-resident speculators availed themselves generously of the provisions of this law. Nevertheless, it did result in the disposition of much land that otherwise would have been long in finding purchasers. Another law which unfortunately opened the door to speculation and fraudulent practices was one framed in 1850 and later amended, ceding to the States swamp and overflowed land with the intention that they would use the proceeds in reclamation work. As it turned out, an amount of land was selected and sworn to be swampy and overflowed that was many times the amount contemplated by the law.

All this time the West had by no means forgotten its ultimate objective—free land. The decade of the forties passed without any appreciable progress toward this goal, but during the fifties the section that was gaining political and economic power by leaps and bounds was increasingly able to make its voice heard and its wishes respected, especially among the politicians. In 1848 the Free Soil party declared in favor of free lands to actual settlers "in consideration of the expenses they incur in making settlements in the wilderness . . . and of the public benefits resulting therefrom." Four years later they renewed this support, but on different grounds. Now they asserted that "all men have a natural right to a portion of the soil; and that, as the use of the soil is indispensable to life, the right of all men to the soil is as sacred as their right to life itself." Therefore, they contended, "the public lands of the United States belong to the people, and should not be sold to individuals nor granted to corporations, but should be held as a sacred trust for the benefit of the people, and should be granted in limited quantities, free of cost, to landless settlers." From first to last these two arguments—reward for public service in developing the country, and natural right—were the chief lines of justification employed by advocates of the homestead or free land program.

Before achieving final success the homestead plan, as it was now called, was forced to run the gauntlet of all the interests, motives, and prejudices that were opposed to a measure that would inevitably hasten western development. Advocates of the maintenance of the time-honored revenue policy were naturally hostile. Easterners saw in free land only a further inducement to the draining of their labor supply and a corresponding increase in the political power of the West. As the fifties progressed the South, the old and the new States alike, became convinced that slavery could not spread further westward and that accordingly the chief beneficiaries of homestead legislation would be farmers bent on establishing free commonwealths. Adherents of the Know-Nothing or Native American movement were disinclined to countenance the granting of valuable privileges to alien immigrants. Moreover, it was charged that a homestead law would make people thriftless.

A homestead bill passed the House of Representatives in 1852, but failed in the Senate. From this time until 1860 the subject was constantly before Congress, but not until the latter year did a bill command enough votes to pass both houses. Even then a price of twenty-five cents an acre was retained. President Buchanan promptly vetoed the bill, basing his action on the principal arguments that had long been advanced by opponents of the measure. The advocates of the bill in Congress were not able to override the veto.

The very sectional conflict, however, which had raised the most formidable obstacle to homestead legislation, soon led to a situation which left the road to success entirely open. The new Republican party in 1860 achieved a successful combination of interests between the manufacturing East and the farming West by espousing both a protective tariff and free land. In their platform of that year the Republicans announced that "we protest against any sale or alienation to others of the Public Lands held by actual settlers, and against any view of the Free Homestead policy which regards the settlers as paupers or suppliants for public bounty; and we demand the passage by Congress of the complete and satisfactory Homestead measure." The victory of the Republicans in November, 1860, was followed by the secession of the southern States, leaving the triumphant party free to carry out its program. On May 20, 1862, Abraham Lincoln attached his signature to the Homestead Law and free land—the goal sought by generations of westerners since the inception of the public land policy—was attained.

The Homestead Law gave to "any person who is the head of a family, or who has arrived at the age of twenty-one years, and is a citizen of the United States, or who shall have filed his declaration of intention to become such," the privilege of acquiring 160 acres of land free of any charge except a small filing fee. The only requirement was that he must live on the land for five years and meet certain conditions in regard to cultivation. The Preemption Law was retained. Provision was likewise made for the commutation of homestead entries at any time by the payment of the regular price for the land. With numerous modifications, the basic features of the law are still in force to-day.

SUMMARY OF PUBLIC LAND POLICY

The Land Ordinance of 1785; the Harrison Law of 1800, experimenting with the credit system; the Land Law of 1820, recognizing the failure of the credit plan and reducing both the price of land and the minimum area that could be purchased; the general Preemption Law of 1841; and the Homestead Law of 1862—these are the high points in the development of our public land policy. Changes and additions were made as new problems arose when settlements spread into an environment of semi-arid plains, mountains, and coniferous forests.

We have seen how the public land question became entangled in political maneuverings and how its solution was affected by every form of personal and sectional interest and prejudice. We have seen, also, what a prominent place specu-lation, greed, fraud, and illegal actions have in the history of the occupation of the public lands. It must be remembered, however, that these phases of the story are those which are spectacular, the aspects which were most played up in the public prints and in Congressional debates. No records were left by the millions of law-abiding families, both native Ameri-cans and immigrants from foreign shores, for whom the public lands were synonymous with opportunity. We can obtain only occasional glimpses of the exaltation of spirit which came to hosts of individuals when they plowed the first furrow on land that was their own. Not often are we permitted to know the plans and hopes and sacrifices that centered in innumerable farms carved out of what was once wild government land. While not overlooking the mistakes or condoning the abuses, it is still possible to regard the public land policy of the United States down to the Civil War as substantially beneficent.

CHAPTER VIII

TRANSPORTATION—INLAND WATERWAYS

LAND was the first interest of the settlers as they moved west. After they had located themselves, built their cabins and begun to raise a surplus of agricultural produce their greatest need was for avenues and facilities of transportation to markets. Farmers and residents of the rapidly growing western towns were also soon clamoring for means of reducing the enormous freight costs on manufactured goods. Extension of mail service and the establishment of public conveyances for passengers were other demands which quickly followed. Private enterprise, state and local governments, and the federal government were all enlisted in the task of meeting the vital need for means of transportation and communication in the West. Out of these demands grew the great public question of internal improvements which became entangled in constitutional interpretations, caused embarrassment to Presidents, occasioned long debates in Congress, and became a leading issue between political parties. More than all other factors contributing to the improvement of transportation was the revolution caused by the application of steam power to the propulsion of water craft and land vehicles.

FLATBOATS AND KEELBOATS

Rivers were the first highways of inland commerce and, with a few exceptions, they were accepted and used in their natural state. The era of river improvement, with its "pork barrel" politics, did not dawn until after the frontier stage had passed. The importance of the Mississippi River system to all the settlers on its waters was clearly shown during the period of the Spanish intrigues from 1783 to 1795 and just preceding the purchase of Louisiana. New Orleans had no important rival for the trade of the Mississippi Valley until the building of the Erie Canal and the coming of the railroads.

The earliest and simplest craft for the transportation of agricultural products, aside from canoes, pirogues and row-boats, was the "Kentucky flat" or "broadhorn" or "ark," as it was variously called. This was a flat-bottomed craft, oblong in shape, ordinarily about fifteen feet wide and fifty feet long, although the size varied. There were high sides and at least a part of the boat was covered. Obviously such a craft was designed almost entirely for downstream use. Little or no attempt was made to propel it, the main activities of the boat-men being confined to keeping it in the current and avoiding snags and obstructions by means of long oars. A crew of three or four men was sufficient to handle the boat, but their labors were prodigious when, as often happened, they ran upon a sandbar. Great quantities of farm produce and large numbers of cattle and hogs were floated down the Ohio and Mississippi in these flatboats, but there was no thought of a return trip. At New Orleans, before the days of the steamboat, the boat-men abandoned their craft and returned either overland by the Natchez Trace or by ocean to the Atlantic Coast and then across the mountains.

A great improvement as compared with the flatboat was accomplished by the introduction of the keelboat. As its name indicates, this boat was not flat-bottomed, but was built upon a keel. It was long and narrow, pointed at both ends, and was well roofed for the protection of cargo or passengers. It pos-sessed the special advantage that by the expenditure of great labor it could be propelled upstream. Thus this type of boat made it possible to supply the settlements along the Mississippi and Ohio with manufactured goods purchased in New Orleans. The larger keelboats, sometimes called barges, were confined to the Mississippi and its principal tributaries. Smaller craft could be used on the smaller streams, such as the Alleghany and Monongahela, the Tennessee and Cumberland and the rivers flowing into the Gulf. They were even carried across portages from one stream to another. For instance, in 1821 an Alabama newspaper reported the arrival at Montgomery of a loaded keelboat which hailed from eastern Tennessee, whence it had come one thousand miles by way of the Tennessee River and its tributaries, a land carriage of ten miles, and then down the Coosa and the Alabama. Going downstream the keelboat drifted with the current or its speed was accelerated by the use of oars and poles. Various means of propulsion were employed on the upstream trip: square sails, oars, poles, and the cordelle. It was seldom that a favorable wind made it worth while to put up the sail. Oars were used in deep water and wide channels. Poling was the method most practiced. On each side of the boat was a running-board along which the members of the crew walked with their poles. Starting at the front of the boat they "set" the poles on the river bottom and with their shoulders against the upper end walked toward the stern until, at the command of "lift" from the steersmen, they raised the poles and hastened again to the front to repeat the process. The cordelle was a rope or cable by which, when shore conditions permitted, the men towed the boat. At other times the cordelle was used in "warping," which consisted of fastening one end of the rope to a tree some distance along the bank and pulling the boat up to that point and repeating the operation as long as trees were available. "Bushwhacking," or pulling on the bushes and overhanging trees along the bank, was another means of locomotion frequently employed.

Obviously the labor of propelling a loaded keelboat against the swift current of the Mississippi or lower Ohio was prodigious. Fifteen miles a day was considered good progress. Usually it took three months to make the trip from New Orleans to the Falls of the Ohio. The men who performed this labor were a rough lot and helped to give travelers their impression of the wild character of western people. When at work these boatmen were prompt, cheerful, and uncomplaining. Their periods of leisure were occupied with carousing, fighting, and boasting. They liked to refer to themselves as "half horse, half alligator." It was the favorite boast of the celebrated Mike Fink that "I can out run, out hop, out jump, throw down, drag out, and lick any man in the country. I'm a Salt River roarer, I love the wimmen, and I'm chock full of fight."

Some idea of the volume of traffic by flatboat, keelboat and barge is indicated by the fact that in 1807 a total of more than 1800 of these craft arrived in New Orleans, although only eleven set out upstream. Even after the coming of the steamboats these more primitive vessels were long used for downstream transportation. In 1818 a passenger on an up-river steamboat counted 643 flatboats descending the Mississippi and Ohio. Timothy Flint, writing in 1826, told of walking along the river bank at New Madrid, Missouri, and seeing these boats arriving in fleets. He was especially impressed, he wrote, by "the immense distances which they have already come, and those which they have still to go. . . . You can name no point from the numerous rivers of the Ohio and the Mississippi, from which some of these boats have not come. In one place there are boats loaded with planks, from the pine forests of the southwest of New York. . . . From Kentucky, pork, flour, whiskey, hemp, tobacco, bagging, and bale-rope. From Tennessee there are the same articles, together with great quantities of cotton. From Missouri and Illinois, cattle and horses . . . together with peltry and lead from Missouri. . . . They have come from regions thousands of miles apart."

Ship-Building on the Upper Ohio

Henry Clay once related an anecdote concerning a port official at Leghorn, Italy, who at first refused to accept the papers presented by the captain of a sailing vessel indicating that he had cleared from Pittsburgh. The official insisted that there was no such port. Whereupon the ship captain produced a map of the United States, "pointed out the mouth of the Mississippi, led him a thousand miles up to the mouth of the Ohio, and thence another thousand up to Pittsburg. . . . The astonished officer, before he had seen the map, would as readily have believed that this vessel had been navigated from the moon."

The background of this incident was furnished by the enterprise of Tarascon, Berthoud and Company, and others, beginning in 1792, in building sailing vessels on the upper Ohio and loading them with produce for export to ports on the Atlantic coast, in the West Indies, and in Europe. Two such ships, one of 120 tons and the other of 250 tons, were built in 1792, and sent down the river the following year, with St. Thomas and Philadelphia as their destinations. Presumably the ships were sold, for of course they did not return up the rivers. The experiment was apparently successful, for by 1800 there were ship-yards at Pittsburgh, Wheeling, Marietta, Louisville, and possibly at other points on the upper Ohio. F. A. Michaux reported that when he was in Marietta in 1802 "they were building three brigs, one of which was of two hundred and twenty tons burthen."

T. M. Harris who visited Marietta the following year witnessed the departure or passage of several vessels. "The second week after our arrival, in consequence of three or four rainy days, the water of the Ohio rose fifteen feet, and gave opportunity for several vessels, which were waiting for a flood, to set sail. Accordingly on May 4th the schooner 'Dorcas and Sally,' of 70 tons, built at Wheeling and rigged at Marietta, dropped down the river. The following day there passed down the schooner 'Amity,' of 103 tons, from Pittsburg, and the ship 'Pittsburg,' of 275 tons burden, from the same place, laden with seventeen hundred barrels of flour, with the rest of the cargo in flat-bottomed boats. In the evening the brig 'Mary Avery,' of 130 tons, built at Marietta, set sail."

There are no records to indicate how many ocean-going vessels were turned out by the Ohio River ship-yards in succeeding years. It is certain that the business disappeared with the introduction of steamboats. The industry gives a colorful touch to river transportation probably never duplicated elsewhere in the world at an equal distance from the ocean. It is not difficult to imagine that the passage of these ships down the stream gave the dwellers along the Ohio a peculiar satisfaction because of the direct contact thus afforded with the markets of the world.

STEAMBOATING ON THE OHIO AND THE MISSISSIPPI

A new and brighter era for transportation on western waterways, and especially for up-river traffic, dawned when Nicholas J. Roosevelt launched his steamboat "New Orleans" at

Pittsburgh in the autumn of 1811. "There is now on foot a new mode of navigating our western waters, particularly the Ohio and Mississippi rivers," exultingly wrote Zadock Cramer in his little publication *The Navigator*, earlier that same year. "This is with boats propelled by the power of steam. . . . A Mr. Rosewalt, a gentleman of enterprise, and who is acting it is said in conjunction with Messrs. Fulton and Livingston of New York, has a boat of this kind now on the stocks at Pittsburgh, of 138 feet keel, calculated for 300 or 400 tons burden [100 tons was nearer the truth]. . . . It will be a novel sight, and as pleasing as novel to see a huge boat working her way up the windings of the Ohio, without the appearance of sail, oar, pole, or any manual labour about her—moving within the secrets of her own wonderful mechanism, and propelled by power undiscoverable!— This plan if it succeeds must open to view flattering prospects to an immense country, an interior of not less than two thousand miles."

The *New Orleans* arrived at Louisville on October 28th, after a voyage of sixty-four hours from Pittsburgh. "Frequent experiments of her performance," it was reported, "have been made against the current, since her arrival, in the presence of a number of respectable gentlemen, who have ascertained with certainty she runs thirteen miles in two hours and one half."

If the people of Louisville and vicinity had visions of the immediate establishment of steamboat service to and from New Orleans they were destined to disappointment. The *New Orleans* served as a Natchez packet for two years until it struck a snag and sank. The vicissitudes of early steamboating are illustrated in the brief history of the *Vesuvius*, which was built on the upper Ohio and descended to New Orleans in the spring of 1814. During the summer of the same year she attempted the ascent of the river, reached a point about seven miles up the Mississippi and was grounded on a sandbar, where she remained until floated by high water early in the winter. Thereafter for a year she made trips between New Orleans and Natchez. In 1816 she burned to the water's edge. Later her hull was salvaged and refitted and she engaged in the Louisville service until condemned in 1819.

Apparently the first steamboat to reach Louisville from New Orleans was the *Enterprise,* which made the trip in 1815 in twenty-five days. "How do the rivers and canals of the old world dwindle to insignificance compared with this," was Hezekiah Niles' comment in connection with the exploit, "and what a prospect of commerce is held out to the immense regions of the west, by the use of these boats!" The Ohio must have been sufficiently high that summer to permit the steamboat to ascend the rapids at Louisville. Late in July a newspaper published at Brownsville on the Monongahela in Pennsylvania announced the arrival of "the steamboat Enterprise, *Shrieve,* of Bridgeport, from New Orleans, in ballast, having discharged her cargo at Pittsburg. . . . She made the voyage from New Orleans to this port in 54 days, 20 days of which were employed in loading and unloading freight at different towns on the Mississippi and Ohio, so that she was only 34 days in active service, in making her voyage, which our readers will remember must be performed against powerful currents, and is upwards of 2200 miles in length."

The number of steamboats on the Ohio and Mississippi now increased steadily. By 1817 there were twenty; two years later the number had nearly doubled; by 1825 there were 75; and thereafter the number increased until there were more than a thousand by 1860. Improvements in the design and machinery of the boats made greater speed possible. For instance, in 1822 it was reported that the steamboat *Paragon* made the round trip from New Orleans to Louisville in twenty-five days. Fares decreased with competition and the growth of traffic. In 1818 it cost $30.00 to travel first class by steamboat from New Orleans to Natchez, $90.00 from New Orleans to New Madrid, and $125.00 from New Orleans to the Falls of the Ohio. Fares downstream from the Falls were lower; $22.50 to New Madrid, $60.00 to Natchez, and $75.00 to New Orleans. By 1835 fares were much lower. "The number of passengers which these boats carry is very considerable," wrote Michael Chevalier, "they are almost always crowded, although there are some which have two hundred beds. . . . The rate of fare is low; you go from Pittsburg to New Orleans for 50 dollars, all found, and from Louisville to New Orleans for 25 dollars." Flatboat men and others who were satisfied with scanty accommodations could return from New Orleans to Louisville as deck passenger for a fare of five or six dollars.

In the course of years the river steamboats assumed the appearance with which succeeding generations were long familiar. Usually there were two main decks and a "hurricane" deck. The first deck contained the boilers, the engine, and the wood used for fuel. On the second deck were the cabins, the dining room, a bar and social hall for men, and a ladies' parlor. The pilot house and the officers quarters were on the "hurricane" deck. Freight was stored in the hold and frequently on portions of the decks.

Many of these boats were fitted out in fine style. "A stranger to this mode of travelling," wrote Timothy Flint, "would find it difficult to describe his impressions upon first descending the Mississippi in one of the better steam-boats. He contemplates the prodigious establishment, with all its fitting of deck common, and ladies' cabin apartments. Over head, about him and below him, all is life and movement. He sees its splendid cabin, richly carpeted, its finishings of mahogany, its mirrors and fine furniture, its bar-room and sliding-tables, to which eighty passengers can sit down with comfort. The fare is sumptuous, and every thing in a style of splendour, order, quiet, and regularity, far exceeding that of taverns in general." Not all travelers were so favorably impressed. Michael Chevalier, writing in 1835, referred to the steamboats as "floating barracks." "Excellent as these boats are," he said, "great as is the service they render America, when the first feeling of curiosity is once satisfied, a long confinement in one of them has little that is attractive for a person of a cultivated mind and refined manners."

It is of course true that all sorts of people were thrown into close contact on a long steamboat trip. Gamblers infested many of the boats and reaped such rich harvests from the unwary that passengers were warned, both by notices on the boats and in the newspapers, to be on their guard against these suave, quiet-mannered sharpers. Liquor of course was abundant and intoxicated passengers troublesome. But the travelers as a whole were just a cross-section of the population of the West, with an admixture of easterners and foreigners apt to look askance at the numerous departures from the manners and practices of "polite" society.

Accidents to steamboats causing loss of life and property were of frequent occurrence. Part of these were due to snags or "sawyers" and floating logs in the river which crushed holes in the wooden hulls of the boats. For instance, in the spring of 1823 the *Tennessee,* with sixteen cabin passengers and 180 deck passengers, struck a log during the night in the Mississippi above Natchez and went down in five minutes. Thirty passengers lost their lives. The bursting of boilers was the cause of other disasters. "A steam boat called the Constitution (late the Oliver Evans) burst her boiler nearly opposite St. Francisville, on the Mississippi, by which every person in the cabin, 11 in number, at breakfast, were scalded to death." This newspaper item is typical of many during the succeeding years, and often the loss was much greater. Defective materials and workmanship in the boilers were sometimes responsible. It was also charged that new boats were frequently equipped with worn-out boilers taken from condemned or wrecked vessels in order to save expense.

Fires were other cause of disasters. In 1832 the *Brandywine* was burned near Memphis and all the 110 persons on board lost their lives. The following year an Arkansas newspaper reported six river accidents, three of which were the result of fires, two of snags, and one of a bursted boiler. In four cases there was loss of life, varying from one to sixty or seventy. "The Americans show a singular indifference in regard to fires," was Chevalier's comment, "they smoke without the least concern in the midst of the half open cotton-bales, with which a boat is loaded; they ship gunpowder with no more precaution than if it were so much maize or salt pork, and leave objects packed up in straw right in the torrent of sparks that issue from the chimneys." In fact he gained the impression that "the essential point is not to save some individuals or even some hundreds; but, in respect to steamers, that they should be numerous; staunch or not, well commanded or not, it matters little, if they move at a rapid rate, and are navigated at little expense."

There is no doubt that efforts to attain excessive speed were the frequent cause of fires and exploding boilers. Competition with boats of rival lines and the ambition to make records impelled the captains not only to fill the fire-boxes to the limit with wood, but to add turpentine or pitch or oil; and to cover the safety-valve in order to increase the steam pressure. Especially were all these means of increasing the speed employed during the numerous steamboat races which became a spectacular feature of the old days on the rivers. Racing so often ended in catastrophe that efforts were made to discourage it. In 1836 a Kentucky editor remarked that the practice of racing was sometimes condoned on the ground that it gave pleasure to the passengers. "That is natural," he said, "There is more than one mode of *intoxication*—and if a steamboat captain were to get his company mad with wine, and then put daggers in their hands to use upon each other, it would be just as good an excuse for him, that they were pleased with the debauch, whatever murders might flow from it, as it is for scalding them to death with hot steam, that they are childishly and irrationally desirous that he should outrun a competitor by a mile or two. Banters are made for bets of $20,000 dollars. Such bets should be punished by high fines."

Lloyd's Steamboat Directory for 1856 contained descriptions of eighty-seven "major disasters" to steamboats on western rivers up to that time, due to explosions, fire, snags, and collisions. In numerous instances the names of those losing their lives totalled more than one hundred. Then there followed accounts of 220 "minor disasters," in a majority of which there was loss of life, running in some cases as high as forty or fifty.

During the thirties the War Department superintended the work of improving the navigability of the Ohio and Mississippi by removing snags, sawyers, and other obstructions. By 1839 nearly ten thousand such hazards had been removed. Efforts were also made by riprapping to confine the stream to narrower channels at certain points to improve navigation in periods of low water. Appropriations for such enterprises ceased in 1844 and the work was not resumed until after the Civil War.

Previously the most important obstacle to steamboat traffic

on the Ohio had been overcome. The business of portaging cargoes around the Falls of the Ohio had long given employment to considerable numbers of men at Louisville. The coming of the steamboats, however, soon inspired a determined movement looking toward the building of a canal around the rapids. In 1825 the Louisville and Portland Canal Company was organized. The federal government aided the enterprise by taking more than half of the four thousand shares of stock. The canal, two and one-half miles in length, was completed late in 1830. The following year steamboats made more than four hundred passages through the canal, to say nothing of keelboats and flatboats, and the number increased rapidly in succeeding years in spite of the high toll rates which were characterized as highway robbery.

Steamboating on Other Western Rivers

Steamboating was early extended to all the navigable tributaries of the Mississippi and the Ohio. In 1818 the first steamboat reached Kaskaskia on the Mississippi. In May, 1823, the *Virginia* reached Fort Snelling far to the northward. J. C. Beltrami, an Italian refugee who was a passenger on this boat, noted the astonishment of the Indians. "I know not," he wrote, "what impression the first sight of the Phoenician vessels might make on the inhabitants of the coast of Greece, or the Triremi of the Romans on the natives of Iberia, Gaul, or Britain; but I am sure it could not be stronger than that I saw on the countenances of these savages at the arrival of our steam-boat."

Within a few years the Missouri, the Arkansas, and the Red rivers were teeming with steamboats. The expansion of the fur trade and the transportation of supplies for distant military posts furnished the initial stimulus for the rapid extension of steamboating on the first named stream. Supplying frontier forts also afforded business for these craft on the Arkansas and Red, which rivers witnessed the carriage by steamboat of thousands of Choctaw and Creek Indians to their new homes west of the Mississippi. The spread of settlements provided increasing traffic with each passing year. A peculiar obstruction to the navigation of the Red River was what was known as the Great Raft in northern Louisiana. This consisted of great masses of tangled logs, snags and tree-trunks that extended for a distance of more than 160 miles and at certain points bridged the river completely. Beginning in 1833 the federal government, through the War Department, undertook the removal of this raft. Captain Henry M. Shreve was placed in charge of the work, and with a large force of men and several snag-boats he began loosening the logs and floating them downstream. It was five years before the work was entirely completed. Even after that time it required constant activity to keep the raft from re-forming.

THE ERIE CANAL

The Mississippi River system constituted a network of navigable inland waterways admirably suited to the transportation requirements of the West during the early periods of settlement, and as long as New Orleans served the needs of all concerned as an outlet for produce and a source of supplies of merchandise. But with the growth of towns and the increasing taste and requirements of the people of the West for manufactured goods and luxuries there arose a demand for commercial connection with Atlantic coast cities. Similarly the merchants and manufacturers of New York, Philadelphia, Baltimore, and Charleston viewed with covetous eyes the expanding markets beyond the mountains and sought for means to break the virtual monopoly enjoyed by New Orleans. The building of the Cumberland Road, as will be seen in the next chapter, promised at first to solve the problem for Philadelphia and Baltimore, and it was an achievement of great significance in facilitating travel and communication between the coast and the trans-mountain region. Even on an improved roadway, however, freighting by wagon over a mountain range was laborious and exceedingly expensive. Thus it was that easterners and westerners alike centered their hopes on canals connecting eastward-flowing rivers with the waterways of the west.

Canal-building was not an innovation in America when the first projects to carry these hopes into the realm of reality were inaugurated. Several canals had been put into successful operation or begun in New Hampshire, Massachusetts, Pennsylvania, Virginia, and South Carolina between 1785 and 1812. The disappointing results achieved by the Potomac Company, in which George Washington was the prime mover, had demonstrated the futility of attempting the canalization of rivers. "Locks in Rivers are subject to many more Accidents than those in still water canals," wrote Benjamin Franklin. "Rivers are ungovernable things especially in Hilly Countries. Canals are quiet and very manageable." It had been demonstrated that it was advantageous to construct artificial waterways along the courses of rivers from which the necessary supply of water could be secured.

As early as 1788 Elkanah Watson and others in New York were preaching the desirability and practicability of making a connection between the Hudson River and Lake Ontario by the use of the Mohawk River and the streams flowing into the lake. In 1792 the Western Inland Lock Navigation Company was chartered by the New York legislature. Four years later this company had completed a canal nearly a mile long and containing five locks, around the Little Falls in the Mohawk, which had hitherto proved an effective obstacle to navigation. It was now possible for small boats to ascend the river as far as Rome, near the site of Fort Stanwix. There was enthusiastic talk of continuing the project westward, but the funds were not forthcoming. There was little to stimulate investments in an enterprise of this nature in a region still almost devoid of settlements.

Interest in the proposal did not entirely disappear and it revived after Albert Gallatin's comprehensive report on internal improvements in 1808, and especially after the authorization of the building of the Cumberland Road which would provide a trade route between Pennsylvania and Maryland and the Ohio Valley. Gouverneur Morris was continuously active in promoting the idea of a canal, but the man who was most responsible for the success of the plan was DeWitt Clinton. Lake Erie, rather than Lake Ontario, was now selected as the western terminus, and a canal extending the entire distance to the Hudson at Albany was substituted for the earlier project to use the Mohawk and other rivers. Congress refused to give

financial aid and efforts to interest Ohio and Indiana were without result. The War of 1812 caused the temporary suspension
of all agitation, but immediately after the close of that struggle
the promoters resumed their activities. In 1817 an elaborate
memorial drafted by DeWitt Clinton was presented to the New
York legislature, in consequence of which an act was passed
pledging the credit of the State to finance the undertaking.

The canal was to be built in three sections: from Albany
to Rome, from Rome to the Seneca River, and from the Seneca
River to Lake Erie. It was to be four feet in depth, forty
feet in width at the surface and twenty-eight feet at the bottom.
Clinton, now governor of New York, broke ground on the eastern section at Rome at a great celebration held on July 4, 1817.
Soon rows of stakes stretched across the State, up hill and
down, through forests and swamps, following the course of
the Mohawk to Rome, then in a general westwardly direction
through a region where Syracuse, Palmyra, Rochester, and
Lockport soon became thriving villages, and along the Tona-
wanda and Niagara Rivers to Buffalo on Lake Erie. The
skeptical still ridiculed the plan as visionary and impractical.
But when workmen, horses, wagons, plows, scrapers, and large
quantities of materials began to appear and work actually
began, scoffing gave way to enthusiasm and pride in the steady
progress of achievement. There were periods of despondency
as during the Panic of 1819, when there seemed no more money
to be spent on the canal, but the courage and determination of
Governor Clinton found the necessary funds and kept the
legislature and people to the task they had undertaken.

Section after section of the canal was opened and put into
use as rapidly as it was completed. Then on October 26, 1825,
came the day of triumph when cannon stationed along the
entire length of the canal boomed the message that the work
was finished. On that day the *Seneca Chief,* on which were
Governor Clinton and a party of notables, led a small flotilla of
boats out of Buffalo headed for Albany and New York City.
At each town along the canal stops were made for processions,
banquets, and other festivities. On November 4th the fleet,
now greatly augmented, arrived in New York City. Well out
in the harbor there was held a ceremony of wedding Lake Erie

with the Atlantic, when Governor Clinton poured two kegs of lake water into the ocean. "This solemnity, at this place, on the first arrival of vessels from Lake Erie," said Clinton, "is intended to indicate and commemorate the navigable communication, which has been accomplished between our Mediterranean Seas and the Atlantic Ocean, in about eight years, . . . by the wisdom, public spirit, and energy of the people of the state of New York; and may the God of the Heavens and the Earth smile most propitiously on this work, and render it subservient to the best interests of the human race."

As the work on the Erie Canal progressed newspapers throughout the nation, and especially in New York and in the West, were filled with glowing predictions of the benefits to flow from the achievement. The reality actually exceeded the predictions. In the course of a few years New York City outdistanced all her rivals as a commercial and shipping center. Western New York, hitherto largely an unbroken forest, rapidly filled with prosperous farms, and Rochester and Buffalo became thriving cities. Thousands of settlers now poured into Michigan Territory which had previously been far removed from the stream of the westward movement. Northern Ohio, Indiana, and Illinois received large accessions of emigrants from New York and New England who laid out farms, built towns and cities, and changed the political and social complexion of these States in which people from south of Mason and Dixon's line had predominated. The great inland lakes now began to teem with an ever-increasing volume of traffic, borne in sailing vessels and steamers, after the *Walk-in-the-Water* made its first voyage on Lake Erie in 1817. It is not too much to say that no other single man-made highway of transportation in the United States ever produced such far-reaching results as did "Clinton's Ditch."

The Era of Canal-Building

As might be expected the building and the success of the Erie Canal spurred other eastern States to emulation in the hope of preventing New York from getting the lion's share of the western trade. Pennsylvania, disappointed in the effects of the

Cumberland Road, in 1826 began the building of the famous Pennsylvania System—a transportation project that was unique and picturesque, but remunerative chiefly to the contractors and workmen who constructed it. This consisted of a combination of canals, tramways, and a series of inclined planes over the mountains, with a tunnel at the summit. The tramway ran from Philadelphia to Columbia on the Susquehanna. Here the horse-cars were at first unloaded onto canal boats. Later cars in the form of boats were devised that could be removed from their trucks and lowered into the canal without disturbing their cargoes. The canal extended along the Susquehanna and the Juniata Rivers to Hollidaysburg. Here the boats were once more placed on cars and by means of stationary engines and cables hauled by a series of inclined planes up the mountains nearly 1400 feet and lowered in a similar manner down the western slope more than 1100 feet to Johnstown on the Conemaugh River. Another canal ran along the Conemaugh and the Alleghany to Pittsburgh. A trip over this route was one long to be remembered, but the financial returns were disappointing and the entire system was later sold to the Pennsylvania Railroad Company and dismantled.

Maryland and Virginia, not to be outdone by Pennsylvania and New York, revived the early plan of Washington's Potomac Company to connect the waters of Chesapeake Bay with the Ohio River. The Chesapeake and Ohio Canal was the name given to the new project, launched in 1828, which was to extend along the Potomac to Cumberland and thence across the mountains to the Youghiogheny River. The canal was never completed further than Cumberland and even this point was not reached until 1850, when more than $11,000,000 had been expended. The canal was well constructed and serviceable, but it had the misfortune to meet bitter competition from the Baltimore and Ohio Railroad which was begun in 1828 and built along the same route.

The canal fever now spread into the West. The completion of the Erie Canal opened up alluring prospects to the people of Ohio, Indiana, and Illinois if only they could establish water connection with the Great Lakes. The numerous points at which the headwaters of streams flowing into the lakes interlaced with those of rivers flowing into the Ohio suggested the feasibility of constructing canals along these routes. The middle twenties saw all three States busy with plans for artificial waterways to give them connections with the eastern markets by way of the northern lakes. Four of these canals were eventually completed, in addition to other minor undertakings.

In Ohio what was known as the Ohio Canal was begun in 1825 at a ceremony which Governor Clinton of New York honored with his presence. The year 1832 witnessed the completion of the canal from Portsmouth on the Ohio along the Scioto, Muskingum, Tuscarawas, and Cuyahoga to Cleveland on Lake Erie. DeWitt Clinton also participated in the dedicatory ceremonies of another Ohio canal in the summer of 1825. This one, known as the Miami Canal, extended along the Miami and Maumee rivers from Cincinnati to Toledo. Financial difficulties delayed the construction of this waterway and operations were suspended during the period of the Panic of 1837, so that it was not finished until 1845. In Indiana the Wabash and Erie Canal was begun in 1832, opened from Toledo to Lafayette on the Wabash in 1843, and was later extended to Evansville on the Ohio. The Illinois project was known as the Illinois and Michigan Canal and as its name indicates, connected the lake with the navigable waters of the Illinois River. It was begun in 1836 and completed in 1848, by which time interest in canal-building had largely been swallowed up in the new enthusiasm for railroads.

To finance the building of these canals the States pledged their resources, but were obliged to market the canal stocks and bonds in the East, where they found buyers to the extent of millions of dollars. The Miami, Wabash and Erie, and Illinois and Michigan canals also received federal aid in the form of land grants. Congress not only gave rights of way through the public lands for the canals, but also donated to the States alternate sections of land for five miles on either side of the canals to be used in financing construction. In support of the land grant policy it was argued that the federal government would lose nothing, since the value of the alternate sections which it retained would be greatly enhanced by the building of the canals. In adopting this practice, as we shall see, they established a precedent for the later policy of making land grants in aid of railroads.

The canals in Indiana and Illinois proved somewhat disappointing, especially since railroad-building had made artificial waterways rather old-fashioned by the time of their completion. The reckless abandon with which the people of all three States had thrown themselves into the canal projects contributed to the severity of the Panic of 1837. Nevertheless, these western canals rendered an important service in the development of the northern portions of the States through which they ran. Prosperous farming sections rapidly appeared along their routes. The growth of Cleveland and Toledo and the beginnings of Chicago date from the period of their building. These waterways also helped, along with the Cumberland Road and later the railroads, to bind the Ohio Valley to the East by ties of commerce and to loosen the connection with New Orleans and the South.

CHAPTER IX

TRANSPORTATION—FROM TRAIL TO RAIL

WATERWAYS served the transportation needs of western settlers as long as they lived along rivers and were satisfied with such commerce as could be carried on through New Orleans. As soon, however, as the settlements began to spread away from the banks of navigable streams and as soon as the need was felt for direct communication between the West and the cities of the Atlantic coast a system of roads became a vital necessity. The most conspicuous outcome of this need was the building of the Cumberland Road linking the trans-montane region with the East. But for a half-century after the launching of the national government interest in the laying out and improvement of long-distance highways was widespread. Then the building of railroads claimed public attention and roads were left largely to the uncertain care of local authorities until the day of the automobile.

EARLY WESTERN ROADS

Road improvement in America showed little progress until the last decade of the eighteenth century. Information concerning the success of Macadam and Telford in England in constructing drained highways with a surface of crushed rock suggested the use of the new process in this country. The first macadamized road in America was the Lancaster Turnpike, built by a private company and extending from Philadelphia westward a distance of about sixty-six miles to Lancaster. This road, completed in 1794, was not only such a marvel of smoothness and all-year-around usability, but the prospect of profits to be made from tolls by similar enterprises was so attractive, that a large number of turnpikes were built in eastern States during the succeeding years.

The so-called roads across the mountains were little better than trails, such as the earliest settlers had followed in making their way into Kentucky and Tennessee or into western Pennsylvania and Ohio. To be sure the Wilderness Road through Cumberland Gap and Braddock's Road and Forbes' Road to the headwaters of the Ohio were well-worn highways. But as late as 1800 even these roads were traversed with great difficulty by wheeled vehicles, and elsewhere the packtrain was the only means of transportation across the mountains. The cost of such traffic was prohibitive for all bulky commodities and extremely burdensome for even the most necessary articles. Even when wagons could be used the cost of freighting by land from Philadelphia to Pittsburgh was $125 a ton, due to tolls on the turnpikes and bad roads the rest of the distance.

West of the mountains the first roads were merely Indian trails or paths made by the successive passage of packtrains and occasional wagons. They were free from the troublesome rocks and the dangerous declivities of the mountain roads, but throughout much of the year they were virtually impassable on the account of mud. Two of these roads early became well known, because they served as important post-routes and were used on the return trip by persons who had descended the Ohio and the Mississippi on flatboats or keelboats. In 1796 Congress authorized Ebenezer Zane of Wheeling to open a road from Wheeling to Limestone, Kentucky, later named Maysville. He was granted three sections of land as compensation for his labor. Zane's Trace, which was the result, was far from being a real highway in its early years, for the road-making done by Ebenezer Zane and his assistants consisted of cutting down the small trees and opening a path that could be followed by horsemen.

Although Zane's Trace officially terminated at Limestone (Maysville), it was continued by a road at least equally good to Lexington and the interior of Kentucky. This stretch later played a noted role as the Maysville Pike in the controversy over the question of internal improvements. From Lexington there was a path to Nashville, Tennessee, where it joined another famous trail leading to Natchez on the Mississippi and known as the Natchez Trace. "Notwithstanding the fact that it traversed for a great distance a most inhospitable region," says Julian P. Bretz, "the Natchez Trace was already one of the best known routes in the old Southwest. It possesses, for the historical student the fascination peculiar to an ancient line of travel. As an Indian path of great antiquity it connected the Gulf and the Great Lakes and in recent times it had been adopted by the boatmen returning overland from Natchez and New Orleans to their homes in the Ohio Valley." [1] The Natchez Trace became a post-route in accordance with an act of Congress in 1800.

THE CUMBERLAND ROAD

The vital importance of roads in the West was recognized in 1802 in the enabling act for the State of Ohio, by a provision that later bore fruit in the Cumberland Road. Five per cent of the net proceeds of the sale of public lands within the State were to be "applied to the laying out and making public roads leading from the navigable waters emptying into the Atlantic, to the Ohio, to the said state, and through the same, such roads to be laid out under the authority of Congress, with the consent of the several States through which the road shall pass." Another Congressional act passed the following year specified that three-fifths of this five per cent fund should be devoted to roads within Ohio and the remaining two-fifths, or two per cent, to a road connecting the Ohio with waters flowing into the Atlantic. Similar provisions were later included in the enabling acts of Indiana, Illinois, and Missouri.

In 1805 a Congressional committee recommended the laying out of a road from Cumberland on the Potomac to some convenient point on the Ohio between Steubenville and Wheeling. A law passed the following year authorized President Jefferson to appoint three commissioners to select and mark the route of the proposed road and make an estimate of the cost of construction. The route was to be cleared of trees to the width of four rods and in the center there was to be a raised

---

[1] Julian P. Bretz, "Early Land Communication with the Lower Mississippi Valley," in *The Mississippi Valley Historical Review*, June, 1926, pp. 6-7. By permission of publisher.

carriage-way of stone, earth, or gravel, with drainage ditches on either side. The President was requested to take the necessary steps to secure the consent of the States through which the road would be run.

Maryland and Virginia readily acquiesced, but Pennsylvania, largely through the influence of Albert Gallatin, made her consent conditional upon the routing of the road through Uniontown and Washington. Wheeling was finally chosen as the Ohio River terminus, partly because a connection would thereby be made with Zane's Trace, and partly because of the influence of Virginia and Kentucky—the latter represented by Henry Clay. Thus the route selected for the Cumberland Road extended from Cumberland, Maryland, to Uniontown, Pennsylvania, thence westward through Brownsville on the Monongahela and Washington to Wheeling.

The first contracts for the building of the road were let in 1811 and work began west of Cumberland. Construction was practically suspended during the War of 1812, but was resumed afterward and by 1818 the road was completed to Wheeling. Immediately a great stream of traffic flowed over the road, amply proving that it served a most useful purpose. In fact, each section of the highway had been opened to travel as rapidly as it was finished, with the result that by the time the western portion was ready for use the eastern sections were nearly worn out.

No provision for maintenance and repair had been made by Congress, and the prospect was not good for the passage of such a law. The question of internal improvements had become one of the great political issues involving views of constitutional interpretation, which in turn hinged on sectional and economic interests. Henry Clay had launched his idea of an American System to make Americans self-sufficient by means of a protective tariff, for the benefit of eastern manufacturers, and projects of internal improvement to open home markets both for manufactured goods and for the produce of western farms. The American System had strong support in the West and in the middle States on the Atlantic coast, but it made little appeal to New Englanders who saw no profit in it for themselves, and it met with opposition in the South. Here the protective tariff was opposed for economic reasons, and federal aid in internal improvements was viewed with growing dislike, because it meant the enhancement of the power of the central government and ran counter to the doctrine of states' rights which the South was more and more coming to regard as essential to the defense of its economic system.

In 1822 a bill passed Congress providing for the repair of the Cumberland Road by means of funds to be raised by a series of toll-gates to be established and operated by the federal government. President Monroe, strong in the tradition of his Republican predecessors, promptly vetoed this bill. He rejected the doctrine of implied powers recently enunciated by John Marshall, and declared the law unconstitutional on the ground that it violated the sovereignty of the States. Two years later, however, Clay's American System was obviously gaining in popular favor, not only in the West but in the eastern States as well. Monroe now found it possible to satisfy his scruples by agreeing that the power given Congress by the Constitution to maintain an army and establish military and post roads warranted federal aid in laying out and maintaining roads. An appropriation was made for the repair of the Cumberland Road and it was planned that it should then be turned over to the States through which it passed for future care and maintenance, as was later done.

The repair work was thorough-going. A macademized surface consisting of several layers of crushed rock was laid throughout the entire distance, the drainage was improved by means of spillways and permanent culverts, and massive stone bridges were built across streams. Altogether the Cumberland Road was an excellent piece of road-building. The work was so well done that some portions of the roadbed and many of the bridges and culverts are still in use.

In 1825 Congress approved of the extension of the road to Zanesville, Ohio, and authorized surveys of a route as far west as Missouri through the capitals of Ohio, Indiana, and Illinois. Successive acts provided for construction westward. Columbus, Ohio, was reached in 1833. Work was pushed in both directions from Indianapolis at the same time and the Indiana section completed by 1850. Grading was carried as far west as Vandalia, Illinois, but here it ended. Interest in the road had by this time been overshadowed by enthusiasm first for canals and then for railroads. West of Wheeling the highway was known as the National Road or National Pike, although the names Cumberland or National have been applied inter-

IV. PRINCIPAL ROADS TO THE WEST

changeably to the entire extent. All told, Congress appropriated nearly $6,825,000 for the construction and repair of the road.

The Cumberland or National Road was a highway the like of which was never again built in America until the automobile worked a revolution in the character of roads. It stretched like a ribbon from the Potomac through the forests and over the mountains of Maryland and Pennsylvania. "Leaping the Ohio at Wheeling," to use the words of Archer B. Hulbert, it extended across Ohio and Indiana, "straight as an arrow, like an ancient elevated pathway of the gods, choping hills in twain at a blow, traversing the lowlands on high grades like a railroad bed, vaulting rivers and streams on massive bridges of unparalleled size. . . . It is doubtful if there are on this continent such monumental relics of the old stone bridge builders' art."

After the road was turned over to the States, laws were immediately passed prescribing heavy penalties for damage to the roadway, milestones, culverts, or bridges. In Ohio, for instance, a person convicted of vandalism might be fined five hundred dollars or "imprisoned in a dungeon of the jail of the county, and be fed on bread and water only, not exceeding thirty days." Each commonwealth through which the highway passed took a real pride in seeing that its portion received proper care. In order to provide funds for repair and maintenance toll-gates were established. In Pennsylvania there were six gates and in Ohio one at least every twenty miles. Detailed schedules of toll rates were posted at each gate, the charges being determined by the wear on the road. Thus, Pennsylvania charged six cents for a score of sheep or hogs, twelve cents for a score of cattle, and four cents for a horse and rider. Rates for vehicles depended on the width of the wheels.

A retrospective view of the Cumberland Road enables us to recognize it as a significant bond of unity between the Ohio Valley and the eastern States. It was a visible symbol of the power and fostering care of the national government. While, as has previously been mentioned, it did not fulfill all the anticipations of its eastern advocates as an avenue of commerce, because the transportation costs were still necessarily high, it did greatly accelerate communication between the West and the federal capital. The possibilities of increased speed of travel received much comment. Hezekiah Niles noted that Senator Richard M. Johnson of Kentucky traveled from Washington to his home, a distance of 600 miles in seven days, and intimated that if anyone had predicted such a journey twenty-five years before he would have been thought extremely visionary. A Cincinnati newspaper told of a steamboat passenger who had made the trip from Baltimore in five and one-half days. James Veech was not exaggerating, therefore, when he wrote that the Cumberland Road, "served to harmonize and strengthen, if not to save, the Union."

FREIGHTING OVER THE CUMBERLAND ROAD

No doubt many of the contemporaries of the road's early years realized some of these effects. Whether or not they were conscious of intangible values, they were fully awake to the practical uses of the great highway. A great freighting business sprang up immediately, using the huge six-horse Conestoga wagons, or "mountain ships," as they were sometimes called on account of their boat-like bodies and their canvas covers. In 1822, four years after the road reached Wheeling, one of five commission houses at that place paid $90,000 for hauling charges on freight unloaded from 1081 wagons carrying loads averaging 3500 pounds. Wagoning became a lucrative occupation, employing a large number of regular teamsters, as well as farmers, dubbed "sharpshooters," who thus supplemented their incomes in slack seasons. The rates paid for freighting explain why teamsters occasionally undertook to haul prodigious loads. In 1838 one teamster hauled 3800 pounds of merchandise from Baltimore to Mt. Vernon, Ohio, a distance of 400 miles for $4.25 a hundred, making the trip in thirty days. He returned with a load of 7200 pounds of tobacco at $2.72 a hundred. About the same time a wagoner was reported to have hauled a load of tobacco weighing 10,375 pounds net from St. Clairsville, Ohio, into Wheeling. A little later a load almost equally heavy was hauled over the mountains.

As the traffic grew wagon houses were erected every few miles along the road for the accommodation of teamsters. Here at modest prices the wagoners could procure food or prepare their own meals, and make their beds on the floor of a large room before a great fireplace on winter nights, while outside there was a yard for the horses. It is not difficult to imagine the story-telling, the merriment, the quarreling, and fighting that took place in these wagon houses during the years when the wagon freight business was at its height.

In addition to the regular freight lines the road was thronged during portions of the year with the wagons of western farmers hauling their produce to market and returning with needed merchandise. About the only way in which western grain could be profitably marketed in the eastern cities was in the form of livestock, which could furnish its own transportation. Large herds of hogs and cattle were frequently driven over the mountains. Timothy Flint, while traveling through Pennsylvania encountered "a drove of one thousand cattle and swine" from Ohio on their way to market in Philadelphia. Morris Birkbeck met near Zanesville "a drove of very fat oxen on their way from the banks of the Miami to Philadelphia. They might, on the average, weigh six hundred pounds, cost about thirty dollars, and sell at Philadelphia at about fifty or fifty-five dollars per head."

Stage-Coach Lines and Taverns

More interesting and glamorous than the freighters, though economically not so important, were the stage lines which began operating over the Cumberland Road as rapidly as it was completed, section by section. "The great western mail and stages, . . . from Washington City to Wheeling, on the national turnpike, arrived in Brownsville—for the first time—on Wednesday last," reported a Brownsville newspaper in August, 1818. "It will pass three times a week. A regular line of stages is, also, established, by which the passenger will be enabled to reach either extreme—a distance of 270 miles—in five days." The first stage-coaches were little better than wagons, without springs and with seats running crosswise and with the door in front, making it necessary to crawl over the front seats to get to those in the rear. Before long, however, the familiar Concord type of coach came into use. These were slung on leather straps, which served as springs to absorb the worst shocks. The doors were at the sides and there were usually three seats inside, each capable of accommodating three passengers. There was a driver's boot on top in front and a baggage boot in the rear. Many of these coaches were handsomely painted and decorated and richly upholstered. Some of them were named, after the fashion of the modern Pullman cars.

Large stage line companies came into existence. The two greatest rivals on the Cumberland Road were the National Road Stage Company and the Good Intent Line, but there were other lesser concerns such as the Mail Pilot Line and the Defiance Fast Line. Time tables were printed somewhat like modern railroad schedules, showing distances between towns, time of arrival, and connections with other lines. Fares apparently varied at different times and on different runs from as low as four cents a mile to as high as six cents. For instance, at one time the fare from Cumberland to Wheeling was about eight dollars. The coaches ran day and night. About every twelve miles there was a sudden and brief halt at a stagehouse, the steaming horses were unhooked, a fresh relay was substituted, and with a crack of the whip they were off again.

The speed of the stage-coaches varied with the season of the year, the nature and condition of the road, and the character of the service being rendered by the particular coach, whether it was a local passenger or an express mail coach. In 1837, for example, the time of the ordinary passenger coaches from Washington, D. C. was indicated by the following illustrations: to Wheeling in 59 hours; to Columbus, Ohio, in 88 hours; to Indianapolis in 164 hours; and to St. Louis in 244 hours. The contract for the Great Western Express Mail called for the following time: to Wheeling in 30 hours; to Columbus in 45½ hours; to Indianapolis in 65½ hours; and to St. Louis in 94 hours.

Just as small boys today hope, when they grow up, to be air-mail pilots or drivers of racing cars, so many of the lads of the twenties and thirties of the last century nursed ambitions to become drivers of stage-coaches and especially of the mail coaches. Names like those of Redding Bunting, Jim Reynolds, Billy Armor, David Gordon, and James Burr were widely known and each had his admirers because of his exploits or his particular style of driving. These men and others like them also enjoyed a wide acquaintance among the noted men and women of the period before the Civil War who traveled by stage-coach over the Cumberland Road: Andrew Jackson, James K. Polk, William Henry Harrison, Henry Clay, and other Presidents and statesmen, to say nothing of Jenny Lind, General Lafayette, Black Hawk, and P. T. Barnum.

Thomas B. Searight is authority for the statement that the excellence of the taverns along the Cumberland Road, even in the isolated mountain sections, was a constant surprise to travelers. "That they were equal to the best on the road is conceded," he says, "and that the old taverns of the National Road have never been surpassed for bounteous entertainment and good cheer, is likewise conceded; in fact, has never been disputed." Most of these western taverns were named for their proprietors or their geographical location, but some of them bore more colorful appellations, such as the Sign of the Indian Queen, the Temple of Juno, the Sign of the Rising Sun, or the Sign of the Red Lion. Many of the tavern-keepers were men of social grace and administered with distinction as hosts to the comfort of the travelers whose names adorned their registers. Altogether a lengthy stage-coach journey, with stops overnight at some of the better taverns, must have been an experience long to be remembered.

Road-Building in the South

The Cumberland Road was the de luxe highway to the West in its day. It was the only real road built at federal expense and under federal supervision. Elsewhere the roads were only such as local funds and local initiative produced, and in the main they were rough, unimproved pathways difficult to traverse at any time and impassable on account of mud in the spring of the year. The stage-coaches were less luxurious or dependable and the inns meaner and less comfortable on these side roads, except on routes enjoying heavy traffic on account of growing centers of population.

The region south of the Ohio River never enjoyed a highway comparable to the Cumberland Road. Such road work as was done by the federal government was motivated by the need of facilitating the carrying of the mails. In 1801 and 1802 troops stationed in the southwest were employed in clearing and widening the Natchez Trace from Nashville to Natchez and in building rude bridges and causeways. Other appropriations were made for the improvement of this road, which for several years was the main post route from Washington, D. C., through Richmond, Knoxville, Nashville, and Natchez to New Orleans. For many years the mail was carried on horseback, indicating that the road was far from being a real highway.

After the close of the War of 1812 Congress made an appropriation for the opening of another road in the southwest. The result was what was known as Jackson's Military Road, extending from Florence, on the Tennessee River in northwestern Alabama, across Mississippi to a point not far from New Orleans. There was rejoicing at both ends of this road when the work, done by troops under Jackson's supervision, was completed in 1820. "The whole road was cut out, and bridges, and ferries, and houses of entertainment established, at the last advices," reported a New Orleans editor. "It is understood, this road will shorten the distance to New Orleans by land from three to four hundred miles." A Florence newspaper exulted in the prospect that "the day is not far distant when a line of stages will be established from Nashville to New Orleans, which must necessarily render the military road the most important of any other on the continent." He reported that the Postmaster General had been instructed "to run the southern mail through this route instead of sending via Natchez; and as this regulation, when put in operation will furnish New Orleans with dates several days earlier than usual, we hope that it will take effect without further delay." This hope was soon gratified.

Other appropriations resulted in some improvement of a route of travel from Georgia westward through Alabama and Mississippi and a portion of the mail from all the Atlantic coast points was eventually carried by this route. But one of the greatest ambitions of the South—for a great national highway running southward through the coast States—was destined to disappointment. Such a highway was suggested in Albert Gallatin's elaborate report on internal improvements in 1808. Hope for the project was revived in 1816 at the time of the establishment of the Second United States Bank. The law contained provision that the Bank should pay into the national treasury one and one-half million dollars. A bonus, in return for its franchise and as interest on the stock owned by the government.

In Congress the friends of internal improvements at national expense seized the opportunity to pass a bill specifying that this bonus should be expended on such projects. Among others John C. Calhoun supported the bill and urged that provision be made to facilitate communication from Maine to New Orleans. President Madison's veto of the Bonus Bill in 1817 dashed all these hopes. In 1826 a board of engineers reported on three routes from Washington through the southern States and westward to New Orleans, and in 1830 Congress debated a project for a highway connecting Buffalo, Washington and New Orleans. By this time, however, the southerners were set in their opposition to internal improvements at federal expense and proved their sincerity by discountenancing even projects designed for the benefit of their own section.

It was in 1830 that the advocates of internal improvements received their most discouraging set-back, when to their surprise and consternation President Jackson vetoed the Maysville Road Bill, authorizing a government subscription of stock in the "Maysville, Washington, Paris, and Lexington Turnpike Company." The citizens of Maysville were reported to have burned Senator Bibb of Kentucky in effigy because he voted against the bill. Southern strict constructionists, however, heartily approved the veto. "The great number of petitions which are annually urged upon the nation, calling for the aid of the general government in the construction of works, all of which are claimed to be of a national character, would," declared a Tennessee editor, "if sanctioned and adopted, in a short time exhaust the pecuniary resources of the government. . . . This cannot escape the observation of the people. They will no longer fold their arms and vainly look to the general government for the exertion of a power which does not legitimately belong to it, but with new energy and spirit put into requisition that individual enterprize, which will eventually lead to an efficient prosecution of their labours."

Aside from a considerable number of military roads laid out by the federal government, the story of road-making in the West is to be found in the histories of the various Territories and States. Legislatures enacted a large volume of road legislation, most of which, no doubt, was designed to meet a real need, but some of which was the result of log-rolling and pork-barrel politics. A number of excellent turnpike roads were built either by the States themselves or by private companies. In general, however, the tendency was toward turning the making and care of roads over to the local units of government—counties and townships. The practice of allowing people to work out their taxes on the roads produced results that varied with the industry and community pride of the workmen and the judgment and skill of the overseers.

The First Railways

The decade of the thirties witnessed the appearance of widespread enthusiasm for a new means and method of transportation which in the succeeding generation largely took the place of highways, canals, and rivers for long-distance hauling both of freight and of passengers. There had been talk about railroads almost from the beginning of the eighteenth century. The early proposals looked mainly to the providing of smooth tracks over which wagons could be drawn with greater ease and speed than over the ordinary roads. It was the thought that anyone might use these tracks who was willing to provide vehicles that would fit them. In 1808 Benjamin H. Latrobe made such a suggestion in a letter to Secretary Albert Gallatin.

Four years later John Stevens of Hoboken wrote a pamphlet in which he endeavored to prove the superiority of railroads, with carriages drawn by steam power, over canals. In the same year Oliver Evans, who had long been experimenting with "steam wagons," came to the support of Stevens, and became an outright prophet of steam railways. "When we reflect," he wrote in an article which appeared in *Niles' Register*, "upon the obstinate opposition that has been made by a great majority to every step toward improvement, . . . it is too much to expect the monstrous leap from bad roads to railways for steam carriages, at once. One step in a generation is all we can hope for. If the present shall adopt canals, the next may try the railways with horses, and the third generation use the steam carriage. . . . I do verily believe the time will come when carriages propelled by steam will be in general use, as well for the transportation of passengers as goods, traveling at the rate of fifteen miles an hour, or 300 miles per day." Evans and Stevens and others continued their propaganda in favor of railroads during the succeeding years, but the idea took hold slowly.

Naturally advocates of canals and improved highways were not likely to espouse the new movement. Besides, the conservatism of people stood in the way of the ready acceptance of an idea so revolutionary. Speed was one of the merits claimed for railroads. There were those who shook their heads and said that human beings could not stand the strain of travel at the rate of fifteen miles or more than an hour: serious nervous and mental disorders would result. Some said it would be sacrilegious to attempt to devise a method of traveling more rapidly than by the means which Providence had provided. As late as the early thirties the promoters of the Boston and Worcester Railroad were called "fools" and "idiots" and "knaves" and efforts were made to prevent them from launching their project.

Gradually, however, apathy and opposition gave way to interest in railroads, especially as news was disseminated concerning the growing success of the new method of transportation in England. There George Stephenson and others were experimenting with steam locomotives. By 1825 steam was being used as motive power on the Stockton and Darlington Railroad, and in 1829 Stephenson's *Rocket* hauled a loaded train over the Liverpool and Manchester Railroad at an average rate of fifteen miles an hour and attained nearly twice that speed at times.

The year 1827 may be said to mark the beginning of railroads in America. About that time two short railroads, using horse power, were constructed and attracted wide attention. One was a short road extending from Quincy to the Neponset River in Massachusetts and built for the purpose of hauling the granite used in constructing the Bunker Hill Monument.

The other was the Mauch Chunk Railroad, nine miles in length, running from a coal mine near Carbondale to the Lehigh River in Pennsylvania. It was in this year 1827, however, that charters were granted for the first real railroads in the United States: the Charleston and Hamburg in South Carolina, and the Baltimore and Ohio.

The Charleston and Hamburg Railroad, one hundred and thirty-six miles in length, was built to the falls of the Savannah River, in the hope that it might insure for Charleston a share in the cotton trade of the interior. It was started in 1830 and from the beginning was constructed with a view to the use of steam locomotives. It was on this road that the *Best Friend of Charleston*, the first locomotive built in America, was employed.

The Baltimore and Ohio Railroad had its origin in the desire of the citizens of Baltimore to check the growing ascendancy of New York City in the trade of the West, resulting from the opening of the Erie Canal. The plan to build a railroad over the mountains to the Ohio River was indeed a bold one for that early day. After the company had been organized and a charter secured the promoters were still so ill-informed that they appointed committees of investigation to find out what railroads really were and how they were operated. But enthusiasm ran high and stock in the road was over-subscribed. On July 4, 1828, ground was broken at a huge public celebration in Baltimore, at which time Charles Carroll, a signer of the Declaration of Independence, turned the first spadeful of earth. It was the original intention to use horse-drawn cars. Experiments were also made with vehicles propelled by sails and by horses operating a sort of tread-mill. But when in 1830 Peter Cooper ran his steam engine, the *Tom Thumb*, over the thirteen miles from Baltimore to Ellicott's Mills in one hour and fifteen minutes, the decision for steam power was finally made.

RAILROAD-BUILDING IN THE WEST

The story of how the region between the Alleghanies and the Mississippi gained its network of railways before the opening of the Civil War is too long and too full of details for inclusion here. The Baltimore and Ohio did not reach the Ohio River until more than twenty years after it was begun. By 1857 it was possible to make a railway journey from Baltimore to St. Louis by changing cars five times, crossing rivers twice on ferries, and making two short trips on steamboats. In 1854 the Pennsylvania Railroad reached Pittsburgh, after having purchased and scrapped the famous Pennsylvania System of canals, railways, and inclined planes upon which the people of the State had centered such high hopes. Travel from Albany to Buffalo was possible as early as 1842 by patronizing six different short railway lines which were later consolidated by the New York Central. The Erie Railroad was completed from the Hudson River opposite New York City to Dunkirk on Lake Erie in 1851. In the South railway construction faced greater handicaps, especially in the comparative absence of free capital for investment. Charleston long nursed the hope of railway connection with Cincinnati, but without realization. Before the Civil War, however, the Charleston and Memphis Railroad was in operation. By means of several short lines there was also a connection between Richmond and Chattanooga.

In the region north of the Ohio River enthusiasm for railroads was widespread during the thirties and by 1837 a short line from Toledo, Ohio, to Adrian, Michigan, was in operation, with at least one steam locomotive in use. The Panic of 1837 put an end to actual building of railroads until the latter part of the next decade. After this time, however, there was great activity, and the movement continued unabated until the outbreak of the Civil War. In 1860 of the total railway mileage in the United States (30,000 miles) nearly one-third was in the Old Northwest. Chicago by this time was the hub of a railway system that shortly enabled that rapidly growing city to become the metropolis of the West, displacing St. Louis which had pinned its faith on the control of the river trade. Railroads from the east, particularly the Michigan Central and the Michigan Southern, raced to enter Chicago. Lines reached out to the Mississippi at several points and Chicago also had connections with St. Louis and Indianapolis. Elsewhere in the

States of the Old Northwest lines were being built, north and south and east and west, so that by 1860 there was no region south and east of Lake Michigan not fairly well served by railroads.

THE CHARACTER OF EARLY RAILROADS

As has been suggested this railway network was made up mainly of a large number of short, independent lines.   This fact alone would have compelled passengers to make frequent changes of cars on long journeys and necessitated the unloading and reloading of much freight.   In addition the tracks varied in width from three to six feet.   Only a few lines at first adopted the now familiar standard gauge of four feet, eight and one-half inches between the rails.   The rails themselves at first were of hard wood topped by a thin strip of iron.   This plan soon proved unsatisfactory, especially since the iron strips showed a tendency to loosen and cause accidents, and solid iron rails were introduced.   The earliest railway passenger cars closely resembled the stage-coaches, giving way after a time to the American type of car with doors at the ends and an aisle down the center.   Certainly when compared with modern conditions a long railway journey over these early lines was a trying experience.   There were vexatious delays at junction points or when the engine broke down; the cars were poorly heated and ventilated; burning cinders from the engine were a constant menace both to passengers and adjoining fields in the summer time; and disastrous wrecks were not infrequent.   But railway trains made much greater speed than any other mode of travel or transportation, and railroads were accepted as one of the great improvements of the age.

THE FINANCING OF RAILROAD-BUILDING

The financing of railway-building in the Old Northwest taxed the resources of the region to the limit.   There were huge conventions at Memphis in 1845, at Chicago in 1847, and at St. Louis in 1849, and innumerable smaller gatherings at other places throughout the West, for the purpose of arousing enthusiasm for the building of railways. Enthusiasm was aroused without difficulty, but enthusiasm would not build railroads. Money was needed and in amounts far greater than those required for any previous American enterprises. In the Old Northwest the States pledged their credit and authorized local units of government, such as counties and towns, to do likewise by issuing bonds and using the proceeds to aid in railroad building. Joint stock corporations were organized and charters were granted. Experience with such companies was very limited and laws for their control were wholly experimental and inadequate. Irresponsible groups, as well as legitimate promoters with definite plans for railroads, were allowed to print bonds and stock certificates and sell them wherever they could, with little or no restraint. As a matter of fact, most of the capital secured by the sale of stocks and bonds, whether by the state and local governments or by the joint stock companies, was obtained in the East and in Europe. Later when some of these stocks proved fraudulent or when local governments defaulted the payment of their obligations because no railways were forthcoming, the antagonism between the East and the West was decidedly increased.

THE ILLINOIS CENTRAL LAND GRANT

Throughout the period of railroad promotion persistent efforts were made to secure direct aid from Congress, but with very little success until 1850. Rights of way through the public lands were readily granted. In 1852 a general law was enacted providing that whenever a railroad met certain conditions as to actual construction it should receive a right of way one hundred feet wide, with additional space for stations and the privilege of cutting necessary timber. Long before this time westerners, accustomed to receive land grants for various enterprises, had been urging Congress to grant lands in aid of railroads. The Senate was willing, but the House of Representatives, in which eastern and southern influence strongly predominated, repeatedly rejected the proposal. It remained for Stephen A. Douglas to achieve success in this method of railway finance, thereby establishing a precedent that was eagerly followed later when millions of acres of public lands were granted to railroads in the Far West.

Ever since 1836 there had been a project for an Illinois Central Railroad from Galena, in the lead-mining region of northwestern Illinois, through the fertile but isolated and relatively unsettled interior of the State to Cairo, at the junction of the Ohio with the Mississippi. In spite of active support, the plan for such a railroad remained only a plan. The State had no funds with which to build the road, nor could they be secured. Congress was importuned for land grants but to no avail. And yet, through the efforts of the State's young Democratic Senator, Stephen A. Douglas, such a law passed Congress in 1850 and received the executive approval. The victory was achieved through a masterful process of log-rolling and manipulation of sectional interests. The original plan for a line entirely within Illinois was not one to attract the votes of Senators and Congressmen from other sections. Douglas now added a proposal for a railroad known as the Mobile and Ohio from Cairo to Mobile, thus transforming the plan into one of national proportions and winning southern votes. Eastern support was gained by provision for a branch connection with Chicago which indirectly offered connection with the East.

The law gave the Illinois Central and the Mobile and Ohio a generous right of way through the public domain. In addition six sections of land for each mile of railway, arranged alternately in six-mile strips on either side of the right of way, were granted to the States through which the roads should run to be used by them in aiding railroad construction. The alternate sections retained by the federal government were to be sold at a minimum of $2.50 an acre, or double the usual minimum price. In this way the national treasury would not be the loser on the account of the land grants. If any of the sections allotted for the railroads were already occupied, substitute selections might be made within a distance of fifteen miles on either side of the railroad. Curiously enough, southerners including John C. Calhoun were willing to approve this method of investing a portion of the public domain, although they were still opposed to internal improvements at federal expense.

The brief outline here presented indicates some of the main

features of railroad-building between the East and the West and in the western region itself before the Civil War. It is difficult to exaggerate the significance of this progress to the western States and especially in its bearing on the destinies of the nation. The transportation facilities enjoyed by the region north of the Ohio River, as compared with those in the South, were of immense advantage to the North in the four-year conflict between the sections. Moreover, the railroads, as they pushed west from Chicago, played a large part in facilitating and encouraging the phenomenal rush of emigration into the grain-growing regions of the upper Mississippi Valley during the decade of the fifties—a movement of population which not only helped to change the political complexion of that section but greatly increased the economic superiority of the North.

CHAPTER X

ECONOMIC DEVELOPMENT OF THE MIDDLE
WESTERN FRONTIER

THE STAGES OF WESTERN DEVELOPMENT

No MORE graphic summary of the economic evolution of the
American frontier has ever been presented than that contained
in *A New Guide for Emigrants to the West,* written by J. M.
Peck and published in 1837. "Generally, in all the western
settlements," wrote Peck, "three classes, like the waves of the
ocean, have rolled one after the other. First comes the pioneer, who depends for the subsistence of his family chiefly
upon the natural growth of vegetation, called the 'range,' and
the proceeds of hunting. His implements of agriculture are
rude, chiefly of his own make, and his efforts directed mainly
to a crop of corn and a 'truck patch'. . . . A log cabin, and,
occasionally, a stable and corn-crib, and a field of a dozen
acres, the timber girdled or 'deadened' and fenced, are enough
for his occupancy. . . . With a horse, cow, and one or two
breeders of swine, he strikes into the woods with his family,
and becomes the founder of a new county, or perhaps state."
He was the type of pioneer or backwoodsman of whom Kipling
wrote: "His neighbors' smoke shall vex his eyes, their voices
break his rest." When hunting became less productive, when
neighbors of a different disposition began to appear, he generally sold his holdings and moved on to some new frontier,
there to repeat the process.

"The next class of emigrants," wrote Peck, "purchase the
lands, add field to field, clear out the roads, throw rough
bridges over the streams, put up hewn log houses with glass
windows and brick or stone chimneys, occasionally plant
orchards, build mills, schoolhouses, court-houses, etc., and
exhibit the picture and forms of plain, frugal, civilized life."

This class was made up of those whom we are accustomed to call settlers. They came with the intention of making real farms, and so, with prodigious labor they extended the clearings and opened up fields for grain, erected dwellings offering rude comfort, and, as Peck indicated, effected striking improvements in the habitability of the region. Frequently, the lure of lands further west was too strong to be resisted by these pioneer farmers. Many of them disposed of their farms and improvements after a few years and joined the procession of those moving to some newly opened region.

"Another wave rolls on. The men of capital and enterprise come. The settler is ready to sell out and take the advantage of the rise in property, push farther into the interior and become, himself, a man of capital and enterprise in turn. The small village rises to a spacious town or city; substantial edifices of brick, extensive fields, orchards, gardens, colleges, and churches are seen. Broadcloths, silks, leghorns, crapes, and all the refinements, luxuries, elegancies, frivolities and fashions are in vogue. . . . A portion of the two first classes remain stationary amidst the general movement, improve their habits and condition, and rise in the scale of society." When any given region had reached this third stage of progress the frontier was a thing of the past in that section. The wilderness had been transformed into a land enjoying a material civilization comparable in most respects to that of the longer settled areas further east; and each succeeding generation witnessed continued progress and increasing wealth and resources.

Practically all portions of the Ohio and upper Mississippi valleys passed through these or similar stages of development. It was not so in the plantation region of the Old Southwest. Here the backwoods pioneer came and went as in other sections of the West, and the clearings were enlarged by the small farmers. But here the similarity ended. The cotton planters appeared upon the scene. They needed large areas for cotton culture and for the employment of large numbers of slaves. Negro labor proved very inefficient when set to such tasks as clearing land. Consequently the planters found it most advantageous to purchase the cleared holdings of settlers; and as this trend became evident many enterprising individuals took up land and cleared it with the definite expectation of selling it for a good price to some cotton planter. When plantations covered the area progress had reached its highest point. For a number of years there was prosperity. Then the soil began to show the effects of single-cropping, of raising cotton year after year. Instead of a steady advance, there was gradual decline as debts piled up and productiveness decreased. Whenever possible the owners sold their plantations before diminishing returns became too evident and sought fresh land, where the process was repeated. Thus the concentration on cotton production, with its accompaniment of slave labor, halted the progress of frontier development that was normal in other sections with free labor and wide diversification of products and activities.

The present summary of western economic history is confined mainly to the Old Northwest and the upper Mississippi Valley. Kentucky and Tennessee, being border States, exhibited some of the characteristics of the free farming section as well as some of those of the plantation area.

Pioneer Homes

The first concern of the settler as he moved with his family onto the land he had chosen was the building of a cabin. Until this task could be completed the family lived in the open or in the wagon, or a rude shelter was made. Senator James Harlan, in his autobiography, told how his father constructed such a shelter by using the trunk of a huge, fallen tree as one side. Forked sapling poles were placed in the ground a short distance from the tree and across these a beam was laid. Other poles extended from this beam to the tree trunk and a covering of bark was laid on. Bed clothing and pieces of canvas formed the other sides. While the family camped in some such way the men and older boys cut logs from the forest, and hewed out rafters, joist and puncheon flooring. Then when all was in readiness the neighbors gathered for the cabin-raising. The logs, notched at the ends, were put in place alternately on the sides and ends. When the desired height had been reached the roof poles were added and a covering made of bark or "shakes," often held in place by saplings fastened at the ends with wooden pegs. All this was done to the accompaniment of jovial badinage, with frequent swigs at the whiskey jug and such feasting as resources permitted.

Later the finishing touches were added, by cutting a door and a window or two, filling in the chinks between the logs with moss or mud or clay, building a fireplace, laying the puncheon floor if there was to be any floor, building the bunks along the wall, and perhaps constructing a ladder to the loft. James Harlan wrote that their cabin was completed and ready for occupancy "in about six or eight days from the date of our arrival, with no tools other than a common chopping ax, an auger, frow and hand-saw, and without a single nail or screw, or metalic material of any description."

Inside these first cabins all was crude and lacking in what would to-day be regarded as the barest necessities. The fireplace furnished heat and most of the light in the evenings, for the making of tallow candles was costly in time and labor. Here the food was boiled in iron pots, suspended from cranes, fried in skillets, or baked in "Dutch ovens" thrust into the coals. The beds were springless bunks, with "ticks" filled with straw or corn-husks. All the furniture was home-made, unless perchance some prized chair or chest or dresser had survived the westward journey. Food was served in wooden bowls and eaten with iron knives and forks and wooden spoons. Windows were covered with blankets or oiled paper, since window glass was too expensive. Unusual was the cabin-roof which did not leak copiously in times of heavy rain.

PIONEER LIFE AND LABOR

The cabin was the realm of the pioneer wife and mother. Here she prepared the daily food, of which there was generally an abundance—wild game, meat of domestic animals but mostly pork, wild and later cultivated fruits, and vegetables in wide variety. Here she made hominy, salted and dried meat for the warm months, made woolen and linen cloth and fashioned linsey-woolsey garments for the family, raised a swarm of children, and too often went to an early grave. The annals of pioneering have never given full justice to the heroism of the women pioneers. Their labors were arduous and unceasing. In addition, they suffered more than the men from the psychological hardships of frontier life—loneliness, fear of Indian attacks, longing for loved relatives and friends left behind, worry and anguish in times of sickness without the possibility of even the poor medical care of the period.

If the men were less affected by these mental stresses, their toil was no less strenuous. The clearing of land covered with hardwood trees was a task for the strong and the persevering. First the small trees were cut and the underbrush grubbed out, raked into piles along with the accumulated debris of ages, and burned, the ashes serving as excellent fertilizer. Then the standing trees were "girdled" or "deadened" by cutting a ring deep through the bark so the sap could not flow and the trees would die. A garden patch was made in some open spot the first year and a small field of corn was planted among the deadened trees and left to mature as best it could with very little cultivation. In succeeding years the trees were cut down, some of the more suitable logs saved for making fence rails and the remainder rolled into piles and burned, unless a sawmill had made its appearance in the neighborhood and logs for lumber were in demand. There still remained the tenacious stumps to be dug, chopped or burned out, or left to rot if the energy requisite to their eradication was lacking. Needless to say, it was usually many years before a farm of as much as one hundred and sixty acres was completely cleared.

James Harlan pictured what was doubtless the normal situation in these frontier settlements. "Each of these settlers was the owner of a team of horses, a few cattle, hogs, sheep and poultry," he wrote in describing his boyhood environment. "Their livestock lived with but little care from the owners on the spontaneous products of the country. The women converted the fleeces from the sheep into clothing. . . . The country was alive with game, such as deer, elk, bear, turkey, and grouse. So that these settlers had from the first year onward an abundance of excellent food and comfortable raiment, the fruits of their own industry, frugality and skill." In the course of years large fields, enclosed by stake-and-rider or worm fences, extended where once forests had covered the land.   Cabins were enlarged and improved or replaced by frame dwellings, either by the original owners or newcomers. Window glass became available.   Tinware, "China" dishes and numerous other articles of utility and comfort found their way into the farm homes.   In short, advancing material civilization eventually brought life in each frontier region up to the standard of sections further east.

FRONTIER FAILURES

Just as every community had a few families who, because of wealth or good fortune or excess of energy, rose above the common average in their style of living and evidences of prosperity, so also it had others who failed to keep step with the march of progress.   In periods when the westward movement was in full swing and easterners were alarmed by the drain of their labor supply and by the rising political power of the West, it was often alleged that the western settlers were lawless, indolent, profligate, and, to use the words of Timothy Dwight, "too shiftless to acquire either property or character."   Some recent writers, in the reaction against the over-idealization of the pioneer and the influence of frontier life, have asserted that the westward migrations were largely composed of the failures, the misfits and the unfit, if not worse.   Such a characterization is, of course, as unwarranted as one which assigns superior qualities and motives to all pioneers.

Nevertheless, there was a closer relationship between the frontier and thriftlessness, failure, and deterioration, even in the economic realm, than we have been willing to admit.   Making due allowances for the prejudices of their writers, the journals and letters of travelers leave no ground for doubt that in every western community families were living under conditions implying either confirmed indolence and thriftlessness, maladjustment to environment, or the slackening of standards formerly observed in their previous homes.

Thomas Chapman, on a journey made in 1795, found a family of eight living on the Ohio River a short distance below Pittsburgh in "a Log Cabin not bigger than a good Hog Sty in

England, nor half so comfortable in appearance." He noted that they had "Plenty of fine rich Land, if they would but take the Pains to cultivate it." Francis Baily was shocked at the filthy, unkempt appearance of a doctor's cabin in Cincinnati in 1797. "It seemed to me very strange," he wrote, "that one who appeared to be a man of information should not take more pains about his habitation, and endeavor to render things about him more comfortable, particularly as it might be so easily done; but such is the force of example, that very few of the emigrants who come into this kind of half-savage, half-civilized state of life, however neat and cleanly they might have been before, can have resolution to prevent themselves from falling into that slovenly practice which everywhere surrounds them." Forty years later J. M. Peck gave similar testimony. "Many persons," he said, "on moving into the *back woods*, who have been accustomed to the decencies of life, think it little matter how they live, because *no one sees them*." Statements of this nature might be quoted indefinitely.

Similarly, numerous writers described the reverse side of the westward movement—the return eastward of people who had failed or were dissatisfied on the frontier. For example, Zerah Hawley, writing from Ohio in 1821, reported that families "are continually returning to the East, and many more designed to do the same, and still greater numbers desired to do so, but have it not in their power. There are many reasons for these returns, viz. the indifferent society, the want of market, where they may dispose of their produce, the impossibility of procuring many articles, which by habit have become necessaries of life, and the very great want of many other articles which are indispensably necessary to comfortable existence." The editor of the *Detroit Gazette* wrote of "instances in which the disappointment of too sanguine expectations and the partiality for home, has turned back with disgust a portion of the emigrants from situations possessing every advantage which could be reasonably looked for." A year or two later the same paper cited the case of a family from Connecticut who had moved to Illinois and purchased land costing five hundred dollars. After living for five years on this land the man became dissatisfied and homesick, wrote to friends in Connecticut for money, sold his land *"for an old horse and cart,* crammed his wife and children into his cart, and started for 'the land of steady habits.'"

Agricultural Progress

Agricultural progress is the central theme in the story of the transformation of the middle western frontier into a land of great productivity in the period before the Civil War. Diversity of crops, together with an increasing output of live-stock, early enabled the region to supply its own needs and to produce a surplus. While there was a tendency for settlers to take more land than they could afford or farm, especially under the Harrison Land Law of 1800, there were several influences which helped to keep down the size of the farms. The difficulty of meeting deferred payments under this law convinced the more prudent of the undesirability of taking too much public land. The land taxes imposed by western States operated in the same direction. The rising price of lands adjacent to growing towns and transportation routes lim-ited the purchases of the later emigrants. Finally, the absence of slaves or other adequate labor supply compelled the settlers to depend largely upon themselves in clearing the land and in planting and harvesting their crops; and this fact had an im-ortant bearing on the size of the farms.

New Orleans was the natural outlet for the products of the western country. We have already noted the urgent demand of the westerners for the opening of the Mississippi preceding Pinckney's Treaty with Spain in 1795. This demand was stimulated more by the prospective need for the Mississippi as a free highway of commerce than by current use. During this period Ohio Valley farmers found markets for their surplus in supplying the needs of the newly arriving settlers and of the army in the Indian campaigns. By the opening of the nine-teenth century, however, traffic on the Ohio and Mississippi began to assume a volume that steadily increased in the suc-ceeding years. A few figures will reveal this growth as well as the variety of products exported from the region.

An estimate in *Niles' Register* for the seven months from October 5, 1810, to May 5, 1811, said to represent only about three-fourths of the total, indicated that 743 flatboats and keel-boats had passed the Falls of the Ohio. Their total cargoes included, among a long list of enumerated items, 129,483 barrels of flour, 604,810 pounds of bacon, 9,477 barrels of whiskey, 47,795 barrels of corn, 24,691 pounds of butter, 465,-402 pounds of lard, 630,562 pounds of hemp, 113,015 pounds of yard and cordage, 2,311 hogsheads of tobacco, and 1,207,338 fowls. A similar estimate for the entire year 1820 offers a basis for comparison in regard to a number of commodities, "The whole number of boats which passed the Falls of the Ohio last year," according to this statement, "is estimated to be 2,400, wafting the rich produce of the western world to the markets on the seaboard; the principal part of which consisted of 1,804,810 lbs. of bacon, 200,000 bbls. of flour, 20,000 bbls. pork, 62,000 bushels oats, 100,000 bushels corn, 10,000 bbls. cheese, 160,000 lbs. butter, 11,207,333 fowls and 466,412 lbs. of lard." Lumber from western Pennsylvania and New York also became an important part of the cargoes which came down from the Alleghany and Monongahela. By 1830 a considerable amount of fruit, principally apples, was shipped from the Old Northwest.

After the opening of the Erie Canal and especially after the building of the canals in Ohio and Indiana, the Great Lakes-Erie Canal route carried much of the produce directly to the markets on the eastern seaboard. An excellent illustration is found in the export of flour and wheat by this route. In 1835 it was reported to be the equivalent of 543,815 bushels of wheat, in 1840 of 3,300,000 bushels, and in 1851 of 12,193,-202 bushels.

Even after the building of the Cumberland Road the hauling of grain over the mountains by wagons was prohibitive. Such traffic was limited to the less bulky and more condensed products, such as maple sugar, whiskey, cured tobacco, potash linen, and hemp. For many years cattle and hogs were also driven over the mountains from Kentucky, Ohio, and Indiana to Philadelphia and Baltimore, but the profits were uncertain because of the competition of livestock raised in the western sections of the eastern States. With the coming of the railroads direct access to the markets on the Atlantic seaboard was gained for all the products of western farms and the traffic down the rivers to New Orleans rapidly diminished. As Robert R. Russel has pointed out, the railroads not only "caused self-sufficing rural economy to give way to commercial agriculture with distant markets," and thus "brought prosperity to countless rural communities, but they caused countless others, sometimes century old, to die out, unable to withstand the new competition with more naturally favored districts far away." [1]

MERCHANDISE AND SUPPLIES FOR THE WEST

Another chapter in the story of the economic transformation of the frontier is concerned with the manner in which westerners were supplied with merchandise and manufactured articles. While cheap and fertile land was the West's primary attraction, it must be borne in mind that with the development of the country more and more people moved westward to take advantage of the constantly increasing opportunities in trade, commerce, and transportation. Zadock Cramer, in *The Navigator* for 1811, held out alluring prospects. He described how the ambitious merchant secured "a small square ark boat, which he loads at the head waters with various wares, liquors, fruits, dry goods and small groceries, and starts his bark for the river traffic, stopping at every town and village to accommodate the inhabitants with the best of his cargo—This voyage performed, which generally occupies three months, and the ark sold for half its first cost, the trader returns doubly invigorated, and enabled to enlarge his vessel and cargo." After several trips of this kind he might set himself up as a merchant or in some other occupation and live "amidst wealth and comforts the remainder of his days."

On account of the scarcity of specie in the West most of the trade in the early years was conducted by means of barter. For instance, when Thomas Ashe traveled west of the mountains in 1806 he decided to sell his horse at the headwaters of the Ohio. "I was offered in exchange for him," he wrote,

[1] Robert R. Russel, "A Revaluation of the Period before the Civil War: Railroads," in *The Mississippi Valley Historical Review,* December, 1928, p. 443. By permission of the publishers.

"salt, flour, hogs, land, cast iron salt pans, Indian corn, whiskey—in short, every thing but what I wanted, which was money. The highest offer made was cast iron salt pans to the amount of a hundred and thirty dollars. I asked the proprietor of this heavy commodity, how much cash he would allow me instead of such an encumbrance; his answer was, without any shame or hesitation, *forty dollars* at most. I preferred the pans; although they are to be exchanged again for glass bottles at Pittsburg, tobacco or hemp in Kentucky, and dollars in New Orleans."

Before the coming of steamboats on the western rivers practically all the merchandise had to be hauled over the mountains, and prices were accordingly high. A good illustration of the way in which business was conducted under these circumstances is to be seen in the case of Pittsburgh, which became a center for the trade not only of the surrounding country but also for the whole Ohio Valley. "The merchants here, as well as those of the western country," wrote T. M. Harris in 1803, "receive their goods from Philadelphia and Baltimore. . . . The terms of credit are generally nine to twelve months. The produce which they receive of the farmers is sent to New Orleans, the proceeds of which are remitted to the Atlantic States, to meet their payments." Payment at New Orleans was made either in credit on eastern firms or in Spanish dollars, which were especially prized throughout the West. Similar procedures were followed by the merchants of Steubenville, Wheeling, Louisville, Cincinnati, and other towns along the Ohio.

In a surprisingly short time, in spite of all the handicaps, local merchants in the larger frontier towns were able to supply their customers with a wide variety of merchandise. Thus, before the settlements in Ohio had advanced into the second decade the newspapers were advertising not only the common necessities of life but some of the luxuries. Tea, coffee and chocolate were on sale, as were also figs, raisins, almonds, pickled fish and oysters from the Atlantic coast, and choice wines from abroad. Ladies might purchase perfumery, madras handkerchiefs, kid shoes, silk umbrellas, hair powder, shawls, and many other articles. Queensware for the table, glass for windows, scythes, and various iron implements were listed.

Supplies of merchandise were more limited in the small villages and in isolated farming regions. Even there the cross-roads store soon brought the necessities within reach, and itinerant peddlers, tinkers, and shoemakers were welcome visi-tors. Floating shops and stores conducted a brisk trade in the settlements along the Ohio and Mississippi. "While I was at New Madrid," wrote Timothy Flint, "a large tinner's estab-lishment floated there in a boat. In it all the different articles of tin-ware were manufactured and sold by wholesale and retail. . . . A still more extraordinary manufactory, we were told, was floating down the Ohio, and shortly expected at New Madrid. Aboard this were manufactured axes, scythes, and all other iron tools of this description, and in it horses were shod. . . . I have frequently seen in this region a dry goods shop in a boat, with its articles very handsomely arranged on shelves."

Early Manufacturing in the West

The middle western frontier was not long dependent en-tirely upon the East for its manufactured goods. The presence of raw materials and the high freight charges stimulated the early establishment of local manufacturing along various lines. Grist-mills and saw-mills became abundant, and not only sup-plied local needs but produced a surplus for shipment. Salt wells were developed in Ohio, and especially in the "Wabash Saline" in southern Illinois. Domestic manufacture of woolen and linen cloth likewise provided clothing for the immediate family or community and an increasing amount for export. Breweries, distilleries, tanneries, flour mills, and paper mills transformed the products of field and forest into commodities of commerce. Early in the nineteenth century people began to speak of Pittsburgh as the Birmingham of America, and before many years Cincinnati was noted for the smoke pouring from its factory chimneys. By 1810 it was estimated that the value of goods manufactured annually in Ohio was nearly three million dollars.

As early as 1800 Kentucky newspapers advertised locally-manufactured leather, paper, spinning wheels, hats, and cloth-ing. Shortly afterward several nail-cutting establishments were set up. In 1816 Lexington received comment for its six steam factories and other prosperous industries. Manufacturing in the interior of Kentucky, however, seems to have been unable to survive the competition made possible by the lower freight rates which attended the introduction of steamboats on the Ohio River. No doubt similar effects were produced in other western communities, then and later, as improved transporta-tion facilities gave increased advantages to some localities and impaired the possibilities of others.

"If we except the cordage, bale rope, bagging, and other articles of hempen fabric, manufactured in Kentucky, the chief part of the western manufactures originates in west Pennsyl-vania and Ohio," stated Flint's *History and Geography of the Mississippi Valley* published in 1832. "Glass is manufactured in various places, at present, it is supposed, nearly to an amount to supply the country. Manufactures in woolen and cotton, and pottery, in laboratories, as white and red lead, Prussian blue, and the colors generally, the acids and other chemical preparations, in steam power machinery, saddlery, wheel irons, wire drawing, buttons, knitting needles, silver plating, Morocco leather, articles in brass and copper, hats, boots and shoes, breweries, tin and other metals, cabinet work; in short, manu-factures subservient to the arts, and to domestic subsistence are carried on at various places in the western country with great spirit."

THE GROWTH OF WESTERN TOWNS

> Where late the savage, hid in ambush, lay,
> Or roamed the uncultured valleys for his prey,
> Her hardy gifts rough Industry extends,
> The groves bow down, the lofty forest bends;
> And see the spires of towns and cities rise,
> And domes and temples swell into the skies.

These closing lines from a "poem" recited by Return J Meigs at Marietta on July 4, 1789, breathe the exuberan optimism of the founders of countless towns which sprang up in the service of expanding trade and transportation and manu facturing. Some of these towns grew to be proud cities like Pittsburgh, Buffalo, Cincinnati, Louisville, Chicago, St. Louis, and New Orleans, boasting of populations ranging between seventy and one hundred and seventy thousand in the census of 1860. Others, like Detroit, Cleveland, Dayton, Toledo, Columbus, Indianapolis, Milwaukee, Memphis, and Nashville, made steady progress that pointed to further growth in later years. A host of other places gained the security of comfortable county seat towns or trading centers for prosperous farming communities. There were also the "paper towns"— each one sure to be a future metropolis—many of which became only soon-forgotten names or maintained a precarious and disheartening existence because their locations were without other justification than the dreams of speculators, honest or otherwise.

Points at which there was a break in transportation routes or strategic locations on waterways were the most promising sites for towns and future cities. Pittsburgh owed its early growth to its position at the forks of the Ohio River, where the principal land route across Pennsylvania met the main water highway to the West. Morris Birkbeck noted in 1817 that the town "contains about 7000 inhabitants, and is a place of great trade, as an entrepôt for the merchandise and manufactures supplied by the eastern states to the western." The business of portaging cargoes around the Falls of the Ohio gave occupation to many of the early inhabitants of Louisville. In 1826 a New York editor described the phenomenal progress of the new town of Buffalo at the western terminus of the Erie Canal. "Where but a few years since the croaking of frogs was the only music that broke the charms of solitude," he wrote, "the bugle from the decks of a procession of canal boats, mingles its notes with the merry peal of the hotel bells— the sturdy mariner of the lakes with his 'ho, heave o' is busy loading his vessel for a voyage to Detroit, or transhipping the products of the west, to be passed on the canal to an eastern market." Seven years later a Buffalo editor found it not unusual to see as many as thirty sailing vessels on the lake at one time. "The warehouses are full—many of the docks are filled six feet high with goods, and canal boats are constantly discharging fresh cargoes upon the top of the mass," he said. "All is hurry and activity; every thing carrying a sail or a steam engine is in constant requisition; and the jaded appearance of the dock clerks bears sufficient evidence of the task they daily accomplish."

Similar scenes were witnessed in Cleveland, Toledo, and other towns which came into existence at points where traffic on Lake Erie touched transportation routes by road or canal across Ohio, or in Detroit whose dreamy French-Canadian habitants found themselves out of place in the bustle and stir that transformed their village into a thriving American town after the opening of the Erie Canal. Cincinnati gained an early start and maintained a steady growth that by 1830 made it the principal western rival of Pittsburgh as a manufacturing and distributing center. By this time St. Louis had greatly outgrown the limits of the little village founded by Laclede and his French companions in 1764. Its inhabitants still had no reason to fear that their city would lose its position as the metropolis of the upper Mississippi Valley—a position based upon its control of the fur trade and the growing traffic of two mighty rivers. Then during the fifties, where once had stood an Indian village and later an ill-starred American fort and still later a struggling settlement, Chicago became the hub of a railway system, as well as a busy lake port, and grew in population by leaps and bounds, although not until after the Civil War did it overtake and outdistance St. Louis in the race for supremacy.

So the entire roll of the rapidly growing towns and cities might be called. There is a real fascination in the story of western town-building. Life and movement, buoyancy and boastfulness were everywhere in evidence. If in many cases fondest dreams were unfulfilled, in innumerable other instances the actual achievements exceeded the hopes and predictions of the founders. The building of hundreds of houses each year was common in many towns on sites which a year or two earlier were covered by forests. Often the annual growth was limited by the dearth of building materials and the lack of a sufficient number of workmen. It is true that in most cases there was little or no planning and much that was distinctly ugly in these upstart towns. Streets and alleys and vacant lots long remained filthy for want of adequate drainage and sewage systems. Hogs and cattle ran at large. For years, also, vestiges of their frontier village days remained. Alongside of "palatial" business blocks and well-built churches and attractive frame and brick dwellings were cabins and shanties of the first comers, and tree stumps were reminders of the original forest covering.

THE LAND OF OPPORTUNITY AND EQUALITY

This middle western frontier was the land of opportunity for thousands and hundreds of thousands of people during the six or seven decades which followed the establishment of the republic. Millions of acres of cheap and fertile land held out the promise of a competency to men and women of meager means who were willing to undertake the toil and hardship of pioneering. There were good wages to be earned in helping to build roads and canals and railroads, or in the manifold occupations connected with transportation. The springing towns called for armies of carpenters, bricklayers, plasterers, blacksmiths, and mechanics of all kinds. They also offered alluring inducements to merchants, lawyers, doctors, preachers, and school teachers. It is small wonder that the manufacturers and employers in the eastern States viewed with alarm the movement of population that played such havoc with their wishes for a cheap and constant labor supply.

It is obvious also that in the early stages of its development the frontier was a region where substantial economic equality prevailed—at least a real equality of opportunity. Neither wealth nor family availed much when it came to clearing land, building cabins, and making farms. Every man was cast largely upon his own resources, and he was known for what he could do, and not for what he had been—whether a success or a failure—in the place from which he had come. Initiative, resourcefulness, perseverance, and courage were the qualities demanded and respected in the new environment. Because this was true and because the opportunities for everyone seemed so unlimited the westerners were ardent champions of individual freedom, at the same time that they insisted on the maintenance of equality.

CHAPTER XI

FRONTIER FINANCE IN PROSPERITY AND DEPRESSION

RELATIVELY few settlers were able to migrate westward, purchase land, and maintain themselves until their new farms became productive, without borrowing money or obtaining credit, or both. Similarly the new western communities and States were obliged to seek eastern capital with which to build roads, canals, and railroads. In short, the frontier was a debtor region.

During periods of prosperity when, to use the words of an English observer, "the Progress of the Country" was the great western staple, this debtor status imposed no restraint on the spirits or activities of westerners. Unregulated banks providing easy credit and an inflated currency, were eagerly welcomed, while eastern capitalists and money-lenders were regarded with equal cordiality. But when panic and depression came these erstwhile beneficent agencies were viewed in a very different light by the people of the frontier. When loans were called in, and mortgages were foreclosed, and banks closed their doors, these institutions appeared suddenly to have assumed the role of monsters. The "money power" of the East likewise seemed a veritable ogre of greed and oppression to communities unable to pay the interest on stocks and bonds so blithely sold to finance internal improvements. The experiences gained in financing western development left the West with an ingrained antipathy to commercial banks in general and the two United States Banks in particular, and led to much bitterness in the attitude of the West and the East toward each other.

THE FINANCIAL NEEDS OF PIONEERS

There is no reliable data upon which to base an estimate of the percentage of the western migrants who were able to finance their own transfer to homes further west. Obviously a considerable number of them had lands and property to sell before they moved, and horses, wagons, and farming tools with which to make the journey and begin farming in the new environment. A smaller number, especially in the later stages of settlement, were men of relatively large means, able to migrate in fine style and even with companies of employees and tenant farmers. The migration of plantation owners with their retinues of negro slaves were notable features of the settlement of the southern cotton belt. On the other hand, such evidence as exists points to the fact that a large proportion of the early settlers were without means with which to equip themselves even for the westward journey, and that they borrowed from, or were helped by, more fortunate relatives or friends.

Upon arrival at their destination the settlers were confronted by their second basic financial need—money with which to buy land, or at least to make the initial payment if it were during the period when the Harrison Land Law was in operation. Doubtless in most cases the settlers brought this money with them. Letters, diaries, and reminiscences often tell us of the great care with which migrating families guarded the precious money-bag containing the wherewithal to purchase the land that had lured them westward. There is no way of proving in how many cases this money was borrowed, but there is reason to believe the number was not small. Down to 1820, while the credit system of land sales prevailed, the federal government became the creditor for the deferred payments. As has already been described, large numbers of settlers were unable or unwilling to make these payments and Congress was obliged to enact a series of relief measures; while much land eventually reverted to the government. By the time the Great Migration got under way after 1815 banks began to play their versatile and disastrous role in connection with land purchases, both speculative and bona fide. In any case, there is evidence that one cause of the financial difficulties of western settlers was their tendency to take up more land than they could pay for or make remunerative.

Even when payments on land had been met the financial problems of the settlers were not entirely solved. Log cabins cost little or nothing to build. Wild game and fruits and truck-patches provided much food. But shoes and clothing wore out and had to be replaced, and some essential groceries must be purchased. Western merchants were generally ready to extend credit until crops were harvested. The merchants, in turn, were carried by eastern mercantile firms and commission houses.

Banking and Currency in the West

The coming of banks of issue was hailed as the dawn of a new era in a region where debt was the general rule and where specie or any circulating medium was exceedingly scarce. The growth of the number of independent banks during the life of the first Bank of the United States was slow. Only twenty-nine were in existence in the entire country in 1800. There were eighty-eight in 1811 when the Bank's charter expired and several of these were west of the Alleghanies. Many of the evils of the unregulated issuance of bank notes, with woefully inadequate reserves, appeared even during this period. But until 1811 the Bank of the United States exercised a certain measure of control by its practice of calling for the redemption of the notes of banks which were thought to be unsound. Even so, it could do little to protect the holders of worthless bank paper.

When this partial control was removed in 1811 the number of private banks increased with great rapidity, until there were 307 such institutions in the country by 1820. The West had more than its share of this number, as legislature after legislature had yielded to the popular demand and granted charters, and as wildcat banks were established. This meant an enormous expansion of credit and currency, since the banks launched large issues of bank notes with virtually no regulation. Prices of land, farm products and commodities of all kinds rose rapidly. Neither speculators nor settlers gave sufficient attention to the question of whether the inflated currency had a sound basis or whether credit was extended beyond all bounds of safety. They easily dismissed any vagrant thought that eventually there must be a day of reckoning. Doubters were silenced by calling attention to the unexampled prosperity and the great progress that would make easy the payment of all loans and the redemption of all bank paper within a few years.

It is not difficult to discern the elements of disaster that were inherent in the situation. In the first place, banking was in the experimental stage, and often developed as an adjunct of other business enterprises. The bankers were nearly all amateurs. Few of them had any knowledge of the business based on experience. It had been discovered that notes could be issued in large amounts and placed in circulation, and that most of them might remain in circulation until worn out before being presented for redemption. This made it possible for the bank to lend many times the amount of actual capital which it possessed. But even among those who were thoroughly honest there was no certainty or agreement as to what constituted an adequate reserve for the redemption of their notes. The unscrupulous made no effort to find out.

As a matter of fact even the better banks were often started with only a very small part of their capital paid up in actual coin. In other cases specie was used only for exhibition purposes to inspire confidence and was later loaned to subscribers to stock, who gave as security the stock certificates thus purchased. In spite of such unpromising beginnings many such banks were able to achieve a position of security and permanence. But there were the "wildcat" and "saddle-bag" banks, which were launched by gamblers and other unprincipled individuals or groups, without any tangible assets whatever. A well-appearing man would come into a community with a supply of bright, new bank notes, and set up an office. This attractive paper would be loaned to eager borrowers on the most liberal terms in return for promissory notes. These, in turn, were sold to gullible but greedy note-shavers for cash at large discounts; and then the perpetrator of the fraud would take his departure between dusk and dawn. Thus the West was deluged by a flood of bank notes, many of which were absolutely worthless and a very large proportion of which could not possibly have been redeemed in currency.

During the years from 1814 to 1817 there was complete suspension of specie payments. Bank notes continued to circulate and were issued in ever increasing amounts—especially in view of the fact that they could not be presented for redemption. Nevertheless, they soon depreciated in value, and year after year the situation of the currency became more and more confusing. Some effort was made to gather information upon which to base a schedule of discounts to be applied in accepting the notes of various banks, but it was next to impossible to know the value of any particular issue at any given time. Moreover, counterfeiting was easy, widely prevalent, and difficult of detection. Professor McMaster illustrates the desperate condition by citing the situation in Zanesville, Ohio, where in 1817 "more than thirty kinds of paper were passing from hand to hand. There were bills of the Canton Bank, the Owl Creek Bank, the Virginia Saline, the Granville, the Perryopolis, the Mansfield and New Philadelphia banks, and the Saddlebag Bank, as that at Parkersburg was nicknamed from the fact that all its capital had been carried in a saddlebag from Pittsburg to Parkersburg. But most plentiful of all were the 'shinplasters' issued by bridge, turnpike, and manufacturing companies, city authorities and borough authorities, merchants, tavern-keepers, barbers, and shoeblacks, and ranging in value from three cents to two dollars." [1]

The defects and inconveniences in the currency situation were readily appreciated and people not in debt welcomed the resumption of specie payments. The dangers, to banks and borrowers alike, attending the enormous extension of credit were not apparent until curtailment and liquidation began. It seemed as though the millenium had arrived when men could go to a bank and borrow money with which to buy land, giving in return mortgages at appraisals based upon optimistically anticipated, rather than actual, valuations. Furthermore, these loans were of necessity for long periods, since short time loans are of little use to farmers, especially in a new country. Thus the western banks, unlike those in commercial centers, had a great preponderance of their assets "frozen" or tied up in securities which could not be quickly converted in case of a sudden demand for redemption of the large issues of bank notes.

[1] John B. McMaster, *History of the People of the United States* (1883-1913), Vol. IV, pp. 317-318. By permission of the D. Appleton-Century Company, publishers.

The Panic of 1819 in the West

Premonitions of approaching difficulties began to be felt with the chartering of the Second Bank of the United States in 1816 and were increased by the resumption of specie payments in 1817. A curtailment of loans soon became evident. To be sure the Second Bank with its numerous branches, five of which were in the West, was almost as reckless in its operations during its first two years as were the state and private banks. In 1819, however, Langdon Cheves assumed the presidency of the Bank and at once initiated measures to save the institution from ruin. The Bank now exercised all its coercive powers to compel the local banks to meet their obligations.

Even before this time the wrath of westerners had turned against the Second Bank, which they regarded as a gigantic engine of destruction designed for the purpose of annihilating the prosperity which they had been enjoying. In their constitutions of 1816 and 1818 the new States of Indiana and Illinois sought to prohibit the establishment of branches of the Bank within their borders. Ohio, Kentucky, and Tennessee joined Maryland, North Carolina, and Georgia in the attempt to tax the branches out of existence. Even after John Marshall's decision in the historic case of McCulloch vs. Maryland in 1819 the defiance continued, most notably in Ohio. Here the legislature reaffirmed the doctrines of the Virginia and Kentucky resolutions, and denied the protection of the laws to the branches within that State, even in cases of burglary and arson. The dispute was not settled until the decision was rendered in 1824 in the case of Osborn vs. Bank of the United States.

With the coming of the Panic of 1819 and the subsequent period of depression the rosy dreams induced by easy credit, inflation, and high prices were completely dispelled. Prices dropped to low levels. Lands, whether improved or wild, would not bring more than a fraction of their previous prices even where valuations had not been definitely exaggerated. Cotton prices tumbled rapidly because of decreasing demand from abroad. Agricultural produce would not bring prices sufficient to pay the charges for water transportation to New Orleans, much less for hauling across the mountains to eastern markets. Western newspapers were filled with long lists of lands to be sold for taxes amounting in some cases to only a few cents on a hundred acres. Bankruptcy was widespread. Worst of all, the West was deeply blanketed with debts and mortgages.

In the minds of westerners the Second Bank of the United States was the arch conspirator causing all this distress. But their resentment burned only slightly less fiercely against all banks. These institutions which so recently had seemed so kindly and generous now assumed a malevolent mien. Many of them closed their doors at the first approach of stringency. The others, in the effort to maintain solvency, brought all possible pressure to bear to collect their loans. Mortgages were foreclosed by the wholesale and banks incurred the popular odium which attaches to this process. In many instances public opinion made it difficult to sell the land on which foreclosure had been completed. Everywhere the people turned to their legislatures for protection, and stay laws, replevin acts, and other measures for the relief of debtors were enacted. Kentucky created the Bank of the Commonwealth, virtually without capital and with power to make a large issue of notes, which creditors were compelled to accept or submit to a prolonged postponement of collection of debts due them. The politics of the State were thrown into turmoil, the Supreme Court was legislated out of existence for declaring the relief laws unconstitutional, a new court was created, and two rival tribunals bade defiance to each other before sanity returned and the old court was restored to its prerogatives in 1826.

Recovery from the depression took place as the decade of the twenties advanced. Rising prices and relief measures enabled western farmers to pay off their mortgages and for a time the severity of the recent lesson was sufficient to inhibit any tendency to incur new indebtedness. The existing currency, including the circulating bank notes which had been curtailed by more than fifty per cent during the panic, was sufficient for all needs. The demand for credit likewise decreased, since hard times and the cash purchase provisions of the Land Law of 1820 diminished the volume of public land sales. Gradually open resentment toward banks died away, but throughout the West there were memories only waiting the proper occasion to be revived in full force. Especially was there a continued undercurrent of fear and distrust of the Second Bank of the United States.

The Western Background of the Panic of 1837

Unfortunately only fifteen years elapsed before the country was headed toward another and even more destructive crash. The western setting of the new crisis exhibited all the familiar factors that had preceded the Panic of 1819: wild speculation, reckless banking, inflation, and over-extension of credit.   To these were added other intensifying elements: the rage for internal improvements, Andrew Jackson's war on the Bank, and the Specie Circular.

Sales of public land, which had dropped sharply in 1820, began to mount slowly toward the end of that decade and by 1834 almost equalled the volume of the previous record year of 1819, when more than five million acres were sold.   In 1835 the sales advanced surprisingly, almost trebling the amount of any previous year, but that record was far out-distanced in 1836 when more than twenty million acres were sold.   The proceeds this year (nearly $25,000,000) were equal to the total of those for the thirteen years from 1820 to 1833.   Most of this land was bought on borrowed money, and a large part of the purchases were speculative in character.   This speculative mania has been described in a previous chapter.   "The farmer, the manufacturer, the city merchant, the county merchant, bought land and paid their debts, if paid at all, not with dollars but with overvalued acres," wrote Professor McMaster.   "Land bought from the government for a dollar and a quarter an acre was at once valued at ten or fifteen dollars an acre.   The more a man bought, and the more he borrowed to pay for it, the richer he was." [2]   Western steamboats, stage-coaches, taverns, and towns swarmed with land-buyers, and for every buyer there were several owners or speculators eager to sell at fancy

[2] John B. McMaster, *History of the People of the United States* (1883-1913), Vol. VI, p. 324. By permission of the D. Appleton-Century Company, publishers.

prices, promising certain wealth from future increases in value.

Speculation was by no means confined to agricultural land. This was heyday of the western town-boomers. New towns by the hundreds were plotted in the forests and on the prairies, and lots sold to avid purchasers at prices exceeding values in well-established eastern centers. When Harriet Martineau visited Chicago in 1835 she observed this mania of town-lot speculation in all its virulence. "I never saw a busier place than Chicago was at the time of our arrival," she wrote. "The streets were crowded with land speculators, hurrying from one sale to another. A negro, dressed up in scarlet, bearing a scarlet flag, and riding a white horse with housings of scarlet, announced the times of sale. At every street-corner where he stopped, the crowd flocked around him; and it seemed as if some prevalent mania infected the whole people." Thomas Ford also gave a vivid description of the scene. "Chicago had been for some time only one great town market. The plats of towns, for a hundred miles around, were carried there to be disposed of at auction. The eastern people had caught the mania. Every vessel coming west was loaded with them, their money and means, bound for Chicago, the great fairy land of fortunes. But as enough did not come to satisfy the insatiable greediness of the Chicago sharpers and speculators, they frequently consigned their wares to eastern markets. . . . In fact, lands and town lots were the staple of the country."

Once more the banks furnished the currency and credit with which to finance this orgy of buying and speculation. The number of private banks in the entire country in 1830 was reported to be 329; by 1834, after Jackson's veto of the bill rechartering the Second United States Bank, it had risen to 506, and by 1837 to about 800. Many of the newer banks, to use the words of a Louisville editor, had "perhaps an amount of capital in their vaults barely sufficient to pay the engraver of their notes." Bank capitalization often consisted of the promissory notes of the stockholders or of certificates of deposit in other banks. In other cases specie was loaned to new banks and exhibited for a short period and then passed on to perform a similar service for another institution. And yet all these banks put their notes into circulation with almost no limit other than the willingness of the public to accept them. From a per capita circulation of $6.69 in 1830 the issues of bank notes increased until in 1837 the per capita amount was $13.87. Both in number of banks and in the amount of circulating medium the West again had more than its share. Once more also the country was flooded with the worthless notes of defaulting banks, and the counterfeit-detector had to be kept at hand by every merchant.

Prices rose with the increase of the money supply, and as the region of diversified agriculture found growing market for its products in the expanding cotton-planting areas in the lower South. Wheat brought from two to three dollars a bushel in 1836, flour sold at fifteen dollars a barrel in Cincinnati and pork at twenty-five dollars a barrel in Chicago. Hogs running wild in the woods or in the streets of towns were worth seven dollars a hundred. Wages likewise mounted to new levels. Times were good, with prices high and money plenty.

As a consequence credit was also easy. Speculators and land-buyers found the banks ready and almost eager to lend them money with which to buy land, accepting the land itself as security, not at the purchase price but at prospective valuations. Again, as fifteen years earlier, the banks had their assets tied up in long-time loans and their resources anything but fluid. Neither banks nor borrowers saw any cause for worry, or if they did they were willing to take the risk. The country was booming, progress was on the march, and that person was foolish who did not seize the opportunity to get in line for the fortunes that were sure to come.

Then, as though not desiring to appear less enterprising and confident of the future than their citizens, the western States plunged into debt to finance roads and canals and railroads. After the opening of the Erie Canal and the beginning of projects by other eastern States designed to attract the trade of the West the commonwealths beyond the mountains caught the contagion. Not a western State escaped the rage for internal improvements at any cost. Every portion of every State demanded its share. If the southern States were less affected than those north of the Ohio River it was only because they lacked the means and the credit to undertake such ambitious progress.

Indiana, for instance, began building the Wabash Canal in 1832 and at the same time chartered several railroads. Four years later the legislature authorized the sale of bonds to the extent of ten million dollars, or an average of more than twenty dollars for every inhabitant of the State, to aid internal improvements. It was confidently expected that tolls and tariffs would soon produce an income sufficient not merely to pay the interest and principal of the debt, but even to relieve the people from taxation for the support of the government. Illinois was equally optimistic. In 1837 that State sold five million dollars worth of bonds to finance nine railroads. It was suggested that by selling these bonds abroad and taking advantage of the exchange rates, by depositing the proceeds in banks at interest until needed, and by other means, the improvements could be secured without cost to the State. No sooner had Michigan been admitted into the Union in 1836 when that State sought to rival its more populous neighbors in the mad scramble for canals and railroads. So the entire roll of the western States might be called, and each would be found pledging its credit for internal improvements to an extent far beyond the bounds of safety.

It is generally agreed that all this indulgence in reckless banking, speculation, and debt-creation was facilitated and encouraged by President Andrew Jackson's war on the Second Bank of the United States. Jackson paid little attention to the Bank in the first year of his presidency. But he was a westerner, thoroughly imbued with all his section's latent antagonism toward that institution. When his advisers convinced him that the Bank was being used in opposition to him by his political enemies he began his attack in each successive annual message. Although the charter would not expire until 1836, in 1832 the supporters of the Bank, with Henry Clay as their leader, decided to force the issue on the eve of the presidential election. A bill rechartering the Bank was introduced in Congress and passed. Jackson promptly vetoed it. Once more the Bank forces threw down the gage of battle and in the campaign of 1832 the Bank question was the main issue. Jackson emerged with a smashing victory which he interpreted, rightly or wrongly, as a vindication of his course with respect to the Bank.

The President now determined to destroy the Bank without waiting for the expiration of its charter.   In 1833, after having removed two Secretaries of the Treasury, he found in Roger B. Taney a man who was willing to carry out his wishes and withdraw the government deposits from the United States Bank and place them with private banks throughout the country.   To be sure, the money already deposited with the Bank was not immediately withdrawn, but no further deposits were made, and the Bank was compelled to place itself in readiness to honor drafts for funds already on hand as rapidly as they were made.

This action produced a temporary money famine.   The Bank of the United States throughout all its branches was compelled to call in its loans, refuse new ones, and curtail the circulation of its notes.   Somewhat the same necessity faced the state banks which were in debt to the United States Bank. Furthermore, in order to be placed on the list of "pet banks" to receive government deposits the local institutions were obliged to show that they were in a sound financial condition. The whole country experienced a period of depression, with unemployment, distress, and business stagnation.

In the West, especially, this depression was of short duration.   The years from 1834 to 1837 witnessed the worst features of the speculation, currency inflation, easy credit, and rage for internal improvements which have already been described.   The depression of 1833-4 caused a great outpouring of people into the West, eager to purchase land for farms and for speculative purposes.   As the steadying influence of the Bank of the United States ceased to be felt, the number of private banks increased rapidly with a corresponding expansion of the issues of bank notes.   Then, after deposits in the "pet banks" began, and when the sales of public lands increased by leaps and bounds, the available funds for loans multiplied indefinitely.   Individuals went to banks and borrowed money with which to buy land.   This money was paid into the land office, and then deposited in the nearest depository bank where it was immediately used in additional loans. Thus an endless chain or vicious circle was established.

By the summer of 1836 the federal government was greatly concerned about two problems connected with the enormous sales of public lands. One of these problems was that of the surplus piling up in the treasury, a temptation to extravagance and recklessness. The public debt had been paid in 1834 and each year there was an excess of income over expenditures of the government. As a remedy for this situation Congress passed the Distribution Law of 1836. In accordance with the terms of this law the Treasurer was to set aside five million dollars as a working capital and then, beginning on January 1, 1837, distribute the remainder among the States in four quarterly installments in proportion to the representation of the various States in Congress. To satisfy the strict constructionists this money was ostensibly to be merely deposited with the States, but there was no real expectation that it would be returned.

The other cause for worry was the growing doubt concerning the real value of the bank notes which were being received in payment for public lands. In 1835 President Jackson issued orders forbidding the reception of bank notes of small denominations. He sought also, without success, to secure a Congressional act requiring that payments to the government be made in coin. In this effort he was supported by Thomas Hart Benton, who thus gained his sobriquet of "Old Bullion." Failing to secure legislative approval, Jackson took matters into his own hands and, on July 11, 1836, issued his famous Specie Circular to all receivers of public money. "In consequence of complaints which have been made of frauds, speculations, and monopolies, in the purchase of the public lands, and the aid which is said to be given to effect these objects by excessive bank credits . . . and the general evil influence likely to result to the public interests, and especially the safety of the great amount of money in the Treasury, and the sound condition of the currency of the country, from the further exchange of the national domain in this manner," the receivers of the land offices were directed after August 15th to receive nothing but gold or silver in payment for land. Exceptions might be made until December 15th in favor of actual settlers and bona fide residents purchasing not more than 320 acres.

These two measures—the Distribution Law and the Specie Circular—had the effect of pricking the rosy-hued bubble that had been dazzling the eyes of the people of the West. The Specie Circular was the first to be felt, and many westerners were apparently dazed by it. There were various surmises as to its purpose. Some thought it was designed to fill the vaults of the "pet banks" preparatory to paying out the surplus revenue to the States. There were also rumors that the circular had been issued at the suggestion of New York speculators who had secured all the land they wanted and wished to throw obstacles in way of others doing likewise. "Whatever the object may be," declared a Lexington editor, "the western farmers may say, as the frogs in the fable said to the boys who were stoning them, 'what is fun to you is death to us.' " One marked effect of the refusal of the government to receive bank notes was a widespread destruction of confidence in the banks and their currency.

The Distribution Act brought about a sudden and almost complete curtailment of credit. Instead of making further loans, the depository banks were compelled to accumulate money with which to meet drafts from the Treasurer in order that that officer might make the quarterly distributions of surplus funds to the States.

The Panic of 1837 in the West

This then was the western background of the Panic of 1837 which ushered in a period of depression from which the country did not recover for five or six years. Banks suspended specie payments in 1837 and hundreds failed completely. Land sales for that year were less than one-third of those in 1836, and in 1838 they again fell off by more than one-half of the volume of 1837. Works of internal improvements were abandoned, leaving States heavily in debt for transportation facilities which they did not possess and the bond-holders with securities which were worthless or of little immediate value. Currency depreciated and prices and wages fell. Everywhere mortgages were being foreclosed and debts liquidated. Before the date for the fourth installment under the Distribution Act arrived, the treasury was facing a deficit rather than a surplus. The State of Mississippi entirely repudiated a debt of five million dollars.

Details of the distress throughout the West during this period need not be enumerated. Neither can space be given to the measures and circumstances which eventually brought recovery after long years of hard times. A few States apparently profited from lessons learned in the Panic of 1819 in regard to stay laws and extreme efforts at relief by legislation. This was notably true of Kentucky, where mutual aid and leniency to debtors on the part of the courts were the main reliance. A Lexington editor commented on the "property laws, stop laws, and the whole machinery of a relief system," which were being demanded in Mississippi. "It may be," he warned, "that the evils which you now suffer may be light in comparison with those to which you are hastening. Kentucky in a voice of thunder would admonish you to beware how you interfere with the obligations of contracts."

The experiences of the Panic of 1837 cannot be said to have led to any real appreciation of the evils of land-speculation or over-buying of land; nor did they long deter western States from again pledging their credit extensively for railroads and other public works. The defects of the banking system, however, made a more definite and lasting impression. Antagonism to unregulated banks of issue was vividly reflected in the constitution-making of the succeeding years, as, for instance, in Iowa and Wisconsin. A member of the Iowa constitutional convention expressed the sentiments of many of his fellows when he declared that "the whole concern of Banks, from big A down were a set of swindling machines, and now was the time for the people of Iowa to give an eternal quietus to the whole concern."

THE PANIC OF 1857 IN THE WEST

Severe and distressing as were the experiences during the period following the Panic of 1837, the lesson was not long effective after recovery took place. Settlers continued to pour into the West, including a large number of foreign immigrants after the European revolutions of 1848. By the time of the Panic of 1857 the Middle West had very largely passed out of the frontier stage. But the western background of that crisis was very much like that of the previous panics. In spite of deep-seated antagonism and efforts of regulation by general legislation, banks increased greatly in numbers and engaged in practices that showed little or no improvement over those in the past. Land speculation once more became prevalent. Railroad-building was in progress everywhere. Then there came a time when the demand for capital exceeded the supply and there was a money stringency. The close of the Crimean War brought curtailment of the European market for American grain. When the telegraph flashed the news of the failure of the Ohio Life Insurance and Trust Company in the mid-summer of 1857, the country again found itself in the throes of a panic, shared by the West together with all other sections except the South, which escaped the worst features because of the strong demand for cotton.

Thus the story of frontier finance has debt as its central theme. In part this chronic condition of debt was based upon the fundamental necessities of a developing region; in part it was due to recklessness of consequences. Periodically there came times of reckoning characterized by painful liquidation— either by the slow process of repayment or by repudiation, default, and failure.

CHAPTER XII

STATE-MAKING ON THE MIDDLE WESTERN FRONTIER

WESTERN DEMANDS FOR SELF-GOVERNMENT

"FINDING ourselves on the Frontiers, and being apprehensive that for want of a proper legislature, we might become a shelter for such as endeavored to defraud their creditors; considering also the necessity of recording Deeds, Wills, and doing other public business; we by consent of the people formed a court for the purposes above mentioned, taking (by desire of our constituents) the Virginia laws for our guide, so near as the situation of affairs would admit." Thus did the Watauga settlers describe and explain the organization of their "Association" when, in 1776, they petitioned the legislature of North Carolina to take them under its wing and create for them the county of Washington. They went on to express the hope that "we shall be considered as we deserve, and not as we have (no doubt) been many times represented, as a lawless mob." One year earlier, in his address to the delegates assembled to frame a government for Transylvania, Richard Henderson declared, "we have the right to make laws for the regulation of our conduct without giving offense to Great Britain or any of the American colonies."

Throughout the period of the Revolutionary War, as Professor Turner so clearly revealed, there was constant agitation for the creation of new States west of the mountains, not only on the part of land companies but on the part of the settlers as well. In a memorial to Congress in 1777 the frontiersmen of western Pennsylvania and Virginia asserted that they had "imbibed the highest and most extensive ideas of liberty" and as a consequence they would "with Difficulty Submit to being annexed to or Subjugated by (Terms Synonomous to them) any one of these Provinces, much less the being partitioned or parcelled out among them." Three years later, in another memorial to Congress, the settlers of this same section called attention to their remoteness from the cis-Alleghany region, from which fact "proceeds a different Interest & consequently a Coolness." Continuing they enunciated the doctrine "that the people have a right to emigrate from one state to another and form new states in different Countries, whenever they can thereby promote their own Ease & Safety."

More than a half century later, in 1836, the demands of settlers living west of the Mississippi River were expressed with equal vigor in a memorial asking for the creation of the Territory of Wisconsin. "That ten or twelve thousand free-men, Citizens of the United States, living in its territory, should be unprotected in their lives and property, by its courts of civil and criminal jurisdiction," declared the petitioners, "is an anomaly unparalleled in the annals of republican legislation." The request was granted and the Territory of Wisconsin was established. Within less than two years Congress was the recipient of an urgent petition that the jurisdiction be again divided and the separate Territory of Iowa be set up for the people living on the west bank of the Mississippi. The memorialists had no hesitation in asserting that "no Territory of the United States has been so much neglected by the parent Government, so illy protected in the political and individual rights of her citizens. . . . It will appear that we have existed as a portion of an organized Territory for sixteen months, with but one term of court." They considered themselves entitled to the granting of their request "by principles of moral right, by the sacred obligation that rests upon the present government to protect them in the free enjoyment of their rights, until such time as they shall be permitted to provide protection for themselves."

These typical selections from frontier political literature require no analysis to make their meaning clear. They speak eloquently of the westerner's ardent adherence to the doctrine of natural rights and the social compact theory, of his desire and aptitude for self-government, of his insistence upon autonomy, and of his distrust of absentee government. In other words, whenever a group of settlers found themselves beyond the pale of any organized government or within the jurisdiction of a government inattentive to their needs, they either proceeded with one accord to draw up rules and regulations of their own, or they sought by every possible means to secure the prompt extension of adequate governmental services to the region where they lived.

Frontiersmen recognized the need of political organization, but they were determined to have a deciding voice in their own government. One important chapter in the story of colonial politics is concerned with the long struggle of the frontier against the tidewater regions to secure legislative representation, lower taxes, agencies of local government, and protection against the Indians. When the delays and disappointments experienced in this contest became unbearable the frontiersmen exhibited their wrath in such demonstrations as Bacon's Rebellion in Virginia, the forays of the "Paxton men" in Pennsylvania, and the Regulation movement in the Carolinas. These episodes, however, were only the more spectacular events in the unceasing conflict which imbued the individualistic, liberty-loving westerners with a deep-seated distrust of governments remote from them and unsympathetic with their interests and needs. This same attitude was shared by later settlers as they crossed the mountains and advanced westward. Autonomous self-government at the earliest possible moment was their goal in every new community. It was, therefore, fortunate that at the time when the federal Constitution was being drafted the expiring Congress of the Confederation laid the foundations of a colonial system which made possible the orderly and certain attainment of this goal.

THE ORDINANCE OF 1787

The Ordinance of 1787, providing government for the territory northwest of the Ohio River, has had a significance in the history of the United States far exceeding the dreams of those members of the Congress of the Confederation whose affirmative votes resulted in its adoption on July 13th of that momentous year. From that day to this it has served as the basic charter of the unique American system of colonial or territorial government. Only the briefest sketch of the movements leading up to the adoption of this important document or of the origins of its various provisions can here be presented.

It must be regarded as fortunate that a report drafted by Thomas Jefferson and embodied in a so-called Ordinance of 1784 never became operative in its original form. This plan contained no provision for territorial preparation for statehood, but divided the Old Northwest into ten potential States, each of which might be admitted into the Union on an equal footing with the original States when it contained a population equal to that of the smallest State already a member of the Union. The vagaries which even a capable man like Jefferson might display were revealed in the method of dividing the territory by artificial straight lines, and by the names suggested for the new States. If his proposal had prevailed we should now be speaking of Chicago, Assenisippia; Cincinnati, Pelisipia; Duluth, Sylvania; and Detroit, Metropotamia; and there would be other States with names as classical in allusion and as difficult in pronunciation. This plan, for various reasons, was abortive, and the question of government for the western country remained in abeyance.

Then, in 1787, as was described in a previous chapter, a group of New England men, known as the Ohio Associates, presented an offer to purchase a large tract of land on the Muskingum River. The members of this organization were desirous of securing land beyond the Ohio, but as a condition to the purchase they insisted that a government be provided for the region where they proposed to settle. Thus the purchase and a plan of government were inextricably bound together. It is clear that neither could have been achieved without the other. Congress was badly in need of revenue for the support of the government, and the prospect of a large sale of public land was very attractive. Individually, also, many members of Congress became interested in the proposal after the agents of the Ohio Associates, to quote from the diary of the Rev. Manasseh Cutler, broached a plan "for a private speculation in which many of the principal characters in America are concerned." No doubt other and more praiseworthy motives also actuated the members of Congress. At any rate, on July

13th "An Ordinance for the Government of the Territory of the United States, north-west of the river Ohio" was adopted. Shortly afterward a law was passed authorizing the sale of 1,500,000 acres of land to the Ohio Associates.

The Ordinance of 1787 contained a bill of rights, a list of obligations and prohibitions, a plan for dividing the Territory into smaller units as population increased and advanced westward, and a system of government, although these features were not arranged in the order indicated. The bill of rights included the time-honored guarantees so dear to the hearts of English-speaking people, such as religious freedom, habeas corpus, trial by jury, right of bail, moderate fines and punishments, due process of law, and the obligation of contracts. In addition, a section dealing with the transfer and descent of property struck at the rules of primogeniture and entail which Thomas Jefferson had fought in Virginia. Property of intestates was to be divided equally between the children, and the widow was to have one-third of the property during her life. Finally, the Ordinance contained another statement that was reflective of the New Englanders' belief in, and prophetic of the westerners' insistence upon, public education. "Religion, morality and knowledge, being necessary to good government and the happiness of mankind," ran the classic words, "schools and the means of education shall forever be encouraged."

The obligations and prohibitions imposed by the Ordinance were equally interesting and important. With fine optimism it asserted that good faith should be observed in all dealings with the Indians, that their lands and property should never be taken without their consent, and that they should never be invaded or disturbed, "unless in just and lawful wars authorized by Congress." The States to be formed out of the Territory were to remain forever in the Union. The people of the Territory were to pay their share of the national debts and expenses. The legislatures of the future States were never to interfere with the disposal of the public lands by Congress. No tax was to be imposed on the property of the United States, nor were non-residents to be taxed more heavily than residents. The waterways leading to the Mississippi and the St. Lawrence were to remain free. Of far-reaching significance was the declaration that "There shall be neither slavery nor involuntary servitude in the said territory, otherwise than in punishment of crimes whereof the party shall have been duly convicted." Such a clause had been included in Jefferson's original report of 1784 and it was demanded by the Ohio Associates. Interestingly enough, this prohibition was included with the full acquiescence of the southern members of the Congress which adopted the Ordinance.

The section which dealt with the division of the Territory made provision for three or five States as circumstances might dictate. If only three States were to be created, then the boundaries between them were to be the lines which now separate Indiana from Ohio and Illinois from Indiana, except that these lines were to extend northward to the Canadian boundary. If five States should become desirable the two additional jurisdictions should be formed out of the northern portion of the Territory north of a line running east and west through the southern extremity of Lake Michigan. With some minor, though important, variations the present States of Ohio, Indiana, Illinois, Michigan, and Wisconsin correspond closely with the five divisions outlined in the Ordinance.

Important as were many of the provisions of the Ordinance of 1787 already described, the greatest significance of the document lies in the system of government aiming at, and culminating in, statehood which it laid down. With some modifications, this portion of the Ordinance was followed in all later acts establishing territorial governments in the United States. Moreover, the progressive system of government here provided was unique in the history of colonial government, in that it led by definite steps to statehood on an equal basis with the older States and with full participation in the government of the nation. Fortunately, whether by accident or design, it was calculated to meet the demands for autonomy on the part of frontiersmen. No matter how much they might chafe under Congressional delays or the vexations of a territorial status, they knew that ultimately they would attain their desires.

Three stages of government were prescribed, each successive stage giving the people greater participation than the one which preceded it. The first stage was simple, autocratic, and closely under federal control. A governor, a secretary, and three judges were to be appointed by Congress, (although the appointive power was soon transferred to the President, with the consent of the Senate, when the Ordinance was re-adopted by Congress after the Constitution went into operation). The governor and judges constituted the legislative body, with power to adopt such laws of the original States as appeared suited to territorial needs. When the adult, male population of the Territory numbered five thousand, the people were given the right to an elective legislature. This body was empowered to choose a Delegate to Congress, who might sit in the lower house of Congress and participate in the debates, but without the right to vote. This constituted the second stage of government. Then, when any of the divisions outlined in the Ordinance contained sixty thousand free inhabitants, the people were authorized to draw up a constitution and be admitted into the Union "on an equal footing with the original states in all respects whatsoever."

These, in brief, were the provisions of the Ordinance of 1787. In October of that year the Congress of the Confederation chose as Governor of the Northwest Territory the man who had been its presiding officer when the Ordinance was passed, Arthur St. Clair. In July of the following year he, together with the secretary and the judges, arrived in Marietta and the long history of territorial government in the West was begun. Before tracing the process by which the region north of the Ohio River was carved into self-governing commonwealths, however, it is necessary to turn our attention to events and movements to the southward of that stream, where the first States of the American Union west of the Alleghanies came into being.

The Admission of Kentucky and Tennessee

In earlier chapters we have followed the progress of events in Kentucky preceding, during, and immediately after the Revolution: the beginning of settlement, the short-lived Transylvania experiment, the hazardous times during the war, the great influx of settlers after the close of hostilities, and the disturbed state of the public mind during the period when the free navigation of the Mississippi River was abrogated by Spain. There is no doubt that some of the settlers were cordial to the idea of establishing an independent government in Kentucky, and even to the arranging of some form of accommodation with the Spanish in New Orleans. The general sentiment, however, seems at most times to have been inclined toward negotiations with Virginia and with Congress, looking toward statehood within the Union.

Late in the year 1784 a convention was held at Danville, at which the delegates passed resolutions favoring separation from Virginia. Two more conventions in the following year voiced the same request, and the General Assembly of Virginia yielded to the demand. But Virginia made her relinquishment conditional upon the admission of Kentucky by Congress before June 1, 1787. This condition introduced the prospect of delay and uncertainty, while the Kentucky settlers wanted immediate statehood. Within the next four years Virginia made three more offers to dissolve the ties binding Kentucky to that State, but each time circumstances prevented the Kentuckians from taking advantage of the offer. By this time, however, the Constitution of the United States had gone into operation, and States might now be admitted into the Union by simple act of Congress. In February, 1791, such an act was passed by Congress admitting Kentucky as a State on June 1, 1792.

Delegates assembled at Danville in April, 1792, for the tenth convention in the long series of gatherings connected with Kentucky's movement toward statehood. A constitution was drafted, which was patterned largely after that of Virginia, although it reflected the spirit of frontier democracy by providing for universal white manhood suffrage. By the first of June, 1792, Kentucky, with a population of perhaps one hundred thousand, had a state government installed and senators and representatives chosen and ready to give the West its first full voice in the affairs of the nation.

Meanwhile, in the valleys of the Tennessee and the Cumberland to the southward events were running a checkered course. The frontiersmen in this region were of the type of those who had migrated to the Watauga settlement after the

Battle of the Alamance, or they came from Virginia and had little love for the authorities of North Carolina within whose jurisdiction they were now living. Therefore it was apparently with some satisfaction over the prospect of ridding itself of a troublesome problem that the legislature of North Carolina, in April, 1784, ceded its western land to the federal government. Before the year ended the act of cession was repealed, in the hope of securing better terms from Congress at a later time. Before this time arrived, however, the settlers in the Tennessee region, realizing that they could hope for little or no help from North Carolina in the way of either civil government or military protection, had taken matters into their own hands.

The frontiersmen assembled at Jonesborough to consider their situation. The maintenance of a connection with the older counties of North Carolina was felt to be hostile to the interests of the western settlements. "They are the most numerous," it was declared, "and consequently will always be able to make us subservient to them; that our interest must be generally neglected, and sometimes sacrificed, to promote theirs, as was instanced in a late taxation act." Therefore, the convention drew up a constitution and named their organization the State of Franklin, hoping thereby to gain the sympathy and sponsorship of the aged Benjamin Franklin—a hope in which they were disappointed. At its first meeting in March, 1785, the legislature chose as governor John Sevier, who was by general consent recognized as the outstanding leader in the State of Franklin.

The new commonwealth maintained a turbulent and precarious existence for more than four years. Intrigues with the Spanish, troubles with the Indians, overtures to the Kentucky settlers, controversies with North Carolina, and ineffectual efforts to obtain recognition from Congress were among the episodes which marked its career. But it was internal dissension which brought an end to the State of Franklin. A political rival to Sevier arose in the person of John Tipton, who sought and obtained aid from North Carolina. For a time two sets of officials, the one representing North Carolina and the other the State of Franklin, endeavored to collect taxes and govern the harassed settlers. John Sevier was outlawed, but in 1789 he took oath of allegiance to North Carolina, was pardoned, and elected to the senate of the parent State. The State of Franklin was now only a name to be remembered, along with that of Transylvania, as that of an unsuccessful attempt to establish a self-created commonwealth in the West.

In 1789 North Carolina repeated its cession of its western lands and Congress accepted. Recognizing the claims of the settlers to some form of government, in 1790 Congress established the "Territory of the United States south of the river Ohio." The new territory, included the Tennessee region, the narrow strip of country just to the south which had been ceded by South Carolina, and in theory at least the land below the Yazoo line, still in the actual possession of Spain. The law specified that the inhabitants should enjoy "all the privileges, benefits and advantages" guaranteed in the Ordinance of 1787 and that the government should be similar, with the significant exception that the prohibition of slavery was omitted. The creation of the Southwest Territory satisfied the settlers temporarily and helped to allay the tendencies toward Spanish intrigue, especially since a number of the frontier leaders were appointed to important offices in the new government. Six years later, Tennessee drew up a constitution and was admitted into the Union on June 1, 1796, with John Sevier as governor, William Blount as one of the United States senators, and Andrew Jackson as representative.

OHIO: THE FIRST STATE IN THE OLD NORTHWEST

Neither of these first two western States can rightly be said to have been a product of the peculiar American process of state-making contemplated by the Ordinance of 1787 and followed by Congress. Kentucky had never been a Territory. Although Tennessee had passed through the territorial status, its people drew up a constitution without asking anyone's permission and Congress felt constrained to pass an act of admission without serious demur. Thereafter, however, it became the practice, followed in a majority of cases to admit no State into the Union until after Congress had passed an "enabling act" authorizing its people to draw up a constitution. This process was begun in the Old Northwest.

Although space will not permit, it would be instructive to narrate the history of the Northwest Territory during the period of its existence from 1787 to 1803. Many of the tendencies and episodes which characterized later territorial history were foreshadowed during this period. Arthur St. Clair was an able, honest, well-intentioned man, a veteran of the Revolutionary War. Yet his selection as governor of a western Territory was not a happy one. He was an autocrat and a Federalist in a region where democracy was in the air and where a constantly increasing number of the people were Jeffersonian Republicans. His defeat by the Indians in 1791 greatly weakened his prestige among the hardy frontiersmen whose heroes were successful Indian-fighters. The plan of government, also, was experimental and without precedent, so that numerous problems arose which taxed the ability of the officials to the limit and gave occasion for complaints upon the part of those who were not pleased with the solutions.

In 1798 the Northwest Territory was sufficiently populous to enter the second stage of government. A territorial legislature was elected. In the following year it assembled for its first session—and chose William Henry Harrison as Delegate to Congress. The settlers now had an agency through which to express their antipathies toward Governor St. Clair. The next few years were filled with bitter controversies over questions both trivial and serious, such as the provision of a seal for the Territory, the establishment of counties, the location of the seat of government, and the very liberal use of the veto power by the governor.

The advance to the second stage of government was only the prelude to a movement toward statehood, which was vigorously opposed by Governor St. Clair. Various motives contributed to the movement. Political partisanship was becoming a powerful force and the Jeffersonians were desirous of adding to their strength in Congress by the admission of another western State. Personal ambition to attain offices in the proposed government was clearly not lacking. Permeating the entire frontier society was the passionate desire for autonomy, the wish to escape from the leading strings of Congress and the control of officials in whose selection the people had no voice. It may be said, in passing, that these motives are discernible in most of the later movements which resulted in adding State after State to the Union.

As a preliminary to statehood for the more populous eastern section of the Territory, and in order to provide a government more closely identified with the needs of the scattered settlements in the western part, on May 7, 1800, Congress passed an act dividing the Northwest Territory. The region west of a line running roughly north from the Ohio opposite the mouth of the Kentucky became the Territory of Indiana. Then on April 30, 1802, Congress adopted an enabling act authorizing the people of Ohio to frame a constitution, at the same time restoring the western boundary to the line running through the mouth of the Great Miami River; while the northern boundary was to be an extension of the line running through the southern tip of Lake Michigan—both of which had been laid down in the Ordinance of 1787. The people proceeded at once to form a convention to draft a constitution. The resulting frame of government reflected the long opposition to Arthur St. Clair by depriving the governor of the veto and appointive powers. The justices of the supreme court were to be chosen for a term of years by a joint ballot of the two houses of the legislature. The suffrage was given to all male tax-payers over twenty-one years of age. On March 1, 1803, Ohio became a State. It need only be noted here that the Ohio constitution contained a provision regarding the northern boundary which was destined to give rise to a controversy with Michigan later.

The Admission of Indiana and Illinois

Indiana Territory, with William Henry Harrison as its governor, was allowed to enter upon the second stage of territorial government, whenever its inhabitants so desired, on the ground that they had already gained the requisite political experience as citizens of the Northwest Territory. In 1805 the region east of a line through the middle of Lake Michigan was cut off to form Michigan Territory. Four years later, in 1809, the area of Indiana was still further curtailed, after an exciting contest, by the creation of Illinois Territory west of a line running up the Wabash River to Vincennes and thence north to the Canadian border. The population of Indiana increased rapidly, especially after the close of the War of 1812, and a statehood movement developed as soon as the required sixty thousand had been reached. In the year 1816 Congress passed an enabling act, a constitution was adopted and on December 11th Indiana was admitted into the Union. Recognizing the justice of the complaint that a northern boundary through the southern tip of Lake Michigan, as prescribed by the Ordinance of 1787, would leave the new State with no frontage on the lake, Congress drew the line ten miles further north.

Illinois waited only nine years for statehood after becoming a Territory in 1809. Ninian Edwards of Kentucky served successfully as governor throughout the entire period. Factional controversies, Indian troubles preceding and during the War of 1812, and popular discontent because of federal regulations or inaction were among the problems which claimed his attention. In the spring of 1818 Congress passed an enabling act for Illinois, although the Territory was far short of having sixty thousand inhabitants. Despite the prohibition embodied in the Ordinance of 1787, the question of slavery was a lively topic of debate in the constitutional convention of that year; and the constitution contained a compromise on this subject, thus giving countenance to the fact that a number of slaves were actually being held in the Territory. Along the Ohio River slavery sentiment was strong, and it was not until 1824 that a persistent effort to secure a pro-slavery amendment to the Illinois constitution was decisively defeated.

Illinois became a State on December 3, 1818. The northern boundary marked an even greater departure than that of Indiana from the terms of the Ordinance of 1787. In the enabling act Congress permitted Illinois to extend northward about sixty miles along the western shore of Lake Michigan. The portion of the Illinois Territory north of this line was attached to the Territory of Michigan.

CHAPTER XIII

THE FURTHER SPREAD OF STATEHOOD

THE FIRST STATE IN THE LOUISIANA PURCHASE

SHORTLY after Ohio became a State and while Indiana and Illinois were advancing toward the same goal, the American process of state-making was put into operation west of the Mississippi River. Article three of the Louisiana Purchase Treaty contained the covenant that "The inhabitants of the ceded territory shall be incorporated in the Union of the United States, and admitted as soon as possible, according to the principles of the Federal constitution, to the enjoyment of all the rights, advantages and immunities of citizens of the United States."

Accordingly, the official transfer of the new purchase to the jurisdiction of the United States had scarcely been consummated at New Orleans on December 20, 1803, and at St. Louis on March 10, 1804, when on March 26th of the latter year Congress divided the acquired region by a line running west from the Mississippi on the thirty-third parallel. South of this line the Territory of Orleans was set up, under the governship of William C. C. Claiborne. The enormous area north of the line became known as the District of Louisiana and was attached for governmental purposes to the Territory of Indiana, although this arrangement was of short duration. The attempt to govern the people of St. Louis and other settlements in the present region of Missouri from Vincennes on the Wabash was unsatisfactory to everyone concerned. In 1805, therefore, what had been merely a district was constituted the Territory of Louisiana. Despite all his previous career in intrigue James Wilkinson seems to have stood high in the opinion of President Jefferson and he was appointed governor of the new Territory. After a stormy incumbency of less than two years in that office he was replaced by Meriwether Lewis, who had just returned from his great western exploration and was thus given recognition for his services.

Meanwhile, in the Territory of Orleans, Governor Claiborne was finding his hands more than full in governing a population composed of French, Spanish creoles, and a constantly increasing number of Americans. The Territory probably contained fifty thousand white inhabitants when it was created. Sentiment in favor of statehood soon developed, and early in 1811 Congress passed an enabling act. In the debates on this measure and in those preceding the final act of admission the next year, the Federalists in Congress ranged themselves in opposition, just as they had done in the effort to prevent the ratification of the Louisiana Purchase Treaty.

Not only party rancor, but sectional fear, and distrust of western democracy, were expressed in the tirades of New England Federalists against the admission of Louisiana. Representative Josiah Quincy was their most eloquent spokesman. Suppose, he suggested, it had been foreseen in the federal constitutional convention that "the whole population of a world beyond the Mississippi was to be brought into this and the other branch of the legislature, to form our laws, control our rights, and decide our destiny. Sir, can it be pretended that the patriots of that day would for one moment have listened to it?" He had heard of at least six new States to be created beyond the Mississippi, and it had been predicted that the mouth of the Ohio would ultimately be far east of the center of the nation. "You have no authority," he exploded, "to throw the rights and property of this people into a 'hotch-pot' with the wild men on the Missouri, or with the mixed, though more respectable, race of Anglo-Hispano-Gallo-Americans who bask on the sands, in the mouth of the Mississippi. . . . Do you suppose the people of the northern and Atlantic states will, or ought to, look on with patience and see representatives and senators from the Red river and Missouri, pouring themselves upon this and the other floor, managing the concerns of a seaboard fifteen hundred miles, at least, from their residence?"

All such fulminations were wasted. Louisiana was admitted into the Union on April 30, 1812. Its boundaries were identical with those of the Territory of Orleans, except that they extended eastward to the Pearl River. Thus Louisiana included the western portion of West Florida which had recently been seized by American frontiersmen and officially declared to belong to the United States, despite the protests of the Spanish. In order to avoid a duplication of names the Territory of Louisiana was renamed the Territory of Missouri, and the people were permitted to enjoy the second grade of government and elect a legislature. William Clark, the companion of Meriwether Lewis on the expedition to the mouth of the Columbia, was appointed governor, and served with conspicuous success throughout the entire period of the Territory's existence.

Mississippi and Alabama

The beginning of the movements leading up to statehood for Mississippi and Alabama in 1817 and 1819 must be sought in a period antedating that of the events which have just been narrated. When Tennessee was admitted in 1796 the Southwest Territory passed out of existence for all practical purposes. Georgia had not ceded her western lands lying just to the south of Tennessee. Spain still kept possession of the strip between the thirty-first parallel and the line passing through the mouth of the Yazoo River, in spite of the terms of Pinckney's Treaty of 1795. In 1798, however, the Spanish could find no further excuse for delay and they surrendered this region. Congress immediately constituted it the Territory of Mississippi. When, in 1802, Georgia belatedly ceded her western lands to the federal government the jurisdiction of the new Territory was extended northward to the Tennessee line. In 1812 frontage on the Gulf was afforded by the addition of the country between the Pearl and Perdido rivers.

Mississippi Territory was somewhat off the earliest routes of travel westward and as a consequence its growth in population was slow. As we have seen, this region was the center of violent Indian disturbances just before and during the War of 1812, and it was here that Andrew Jackson gained most of his fame as an Indian fighter. By the close of the war new roads had opened the way to Mississippi and its rich, black soil attracted an ever increasing number of settlers and plantation-seekers. In 1817 the Territory was divided by a line running south to the Gulf of Mexico from the Tennessee River at the mouth of Bear Creek. The same year witnessed the admission of the western division into the Union on December 10th as the State of Mississippi. It is interesting to note that here for the first time in western constitution-making was the instrument of government submitted to the voters of the State for ratification. Hitherto the constitutions had been put into force by promulgation. Thereafter the precedent set by Mississippi was followed in most of the new western States.

The eastern division of the Territory of Mississippi became the Territory of Alabama in 1817, but its probationary period was of brief duration. The westward movement was in full swing. Population increased rapidly, in 1819 Congress passed an enabling act, and on December 14th of that year Alabama became a State.

The Struggle over the Admission of Missouri

Scarcely had Alabama been admitted when the nation was stirred to its depths by a controversy connected with another statehood proposal. The population of Missouri Territory did not grow appreciably until the Great Migration after the War of 1812 got under way. Then the lower Missouri Valley began to receive a steady stream of settlers, a large proportion of whom were from the South. Although the inhabitants did not yet number sixty thousand, as early as 1817 Congress was asked to permit the people of Missouri to form a constitution; and in 1818 the legislature of the Territory repeated this request. A bill for an enabling act was accordingly introduced and came up for discussion in February, 1819. Shortly afterward on March 2, 1819, Missouri was divided and the Territory of Arkansas was created. The new Territory extended from the Louisiana boundary northward to the parallel 36 degrees 30 minutes, except that the parallel 36 degrees became the dividing line in the New Madrid region so that these settlements would be included in Missouri. Westwardly the Arkansas Territory extended to the one hundredth meridian, which in that latitude was the western boundary of the United States as determined by the recent treaty with Spain.

The bill for the Missouri enabling act failed to pass in that session of Congress. Representative James Tallmadge of New York introduced an amendment virtually making slavery impossible in the proposed State, and the House adopted the amendment. The Senate, however, refused to accede, and the two houses became deadlocked on the issue. During the ensuing two years the whole nation was thrown into turmoil by the first great sectional contest between the North and the South.

The main facts concerning the Missouri Compromise are so well known to every student of American history that they need not be repeated here. A brief statement will serve to show how the demands of the advancing frontier precipitated a sectional struggle on the slavery question. Southern leaders were by this time convinced that slavery was necessary to their economic and social welfare. Therefore, it was essential that they should maintain equality with the free States in Congress. The prospect of parity in the lower house was becoming poorer and poorer, since the free States were increasing in population much more rapidly than those favorable to slavery. In the Senate, however, equality would prevail as long as each section contained an equal number of States. Such a situation existed after the admission of Louisiana, and the balance had not been upset by the creation of the next four commonwealths. Indiana, a free State, admitted in 1816, was matched by Mississippi, a slave State admitted in 1817; and Illinois in 1818 by Alabama in 1819.

Now, however, the outlook was far from reassuring to southerners, as they surveyed the possibilities for additional States in the West. The treaty of February, 1819, with Spain, relinquishing the claims of the United States to Texas in return for the Floridas, seemed to close the door to the creation of new slave States in that direction. The prevailing opinion credited the Great Plains region with being inhospitable to white settlements—an opinion that was soon to be confirmed by the report of Stephen H. Long after an extensive exploration. As a consequence, Missouri, Arkansas, and Florida were the only possible States in sight which could be expected to favor slavery. On the other hand, Maine was already seeking admission, two more free States could be anticipated in the Old Northwest, and there was the region along the west bank of the Mississippi north of the proposed State of Missouri—a region clearly unsuited to slavery—out of which additional States might be carved.

It is not surprising, therefore, that southerners were thoroughly aroused to the vital necessity of securing the admission of Missouri with slavery in order to maintain the balance between the sections in the United States Senate. In this they were successful, but whether or not it was a real victory for the South is still a mooted point. Maine became a State in March, 1820; and after further delay Missouri was admitted on August 10, 1821, as a slave State, but with the express provision that in all the remaining portion of the Louisiana Purchase north of 36 degrees and 30 minutes "slavery and involuntary servitude, otherwise than in punishment of crime . . . shall be and is hereby forever prohibited."

Before leaving this subject it should be noted that, while slavery was the great moral question over which the people of the nation became aroused during the Missouri struggle, there were other issues involved. One was the question of the right of Congress to impose restrictions on an incoming State or dictate the contents of its constitution. Certain restrictions or obligations had been previously laid down by Congress in enabling acts, and this practice was frequently followed in later years. As a matter of fact the question was a rather futile one, since within limits there is nothing in the federal Constitution to prevent a State from amending its instrument of government after once having been admitted into the Union. The other issue was the right of Congress to prohibit slavery in the Territories. This point seemed to be settled by the provision forbidding slavery north of 36 degrees 30 minutes. How the frontier advance upset this decision thirty years later will appear in a subsequent chapter.

MICHIGAN AND ARKANSAS

Fifteen years now passed before another State was ready to enter the Union; and it was fortunate that at that time two Territories were seeking statehood, one as a free State and the other with slavery.

Michigan Territory, established in 1805, was enlarged and extended to the Mississippi River after the admission of Illinois in 1818. The first governor of the Territory was the ill-starred William Hull. After the War of 1812 he was succeeded by Lewis Cass, who served with great success until 1831. The population of the Territory in its early years was made up chiefly of descendants of the original French colonists, with an admixture of American fur traders. Detroit, on the eastern border, was the principal settlement, while the remaining inhabitants lived in small groups along the shores of the lakes—especially at the heads of Lake Michigan and Lake Superior, on Green Bay, and at Prairie du Chien on the Mississippi. The American settlement of the region was long delayed. The established routes of the westward movement were further south. Moreover, there was a general belief that the interior of Michigan was an uninhabitable swamp. But the completion of the Erie Canal in 1825 wrought a great change. As has already been seen, settlers now began to pour into Michigan in such numbers that the census of 1830 gave the Territory a population of about thirty-two thousand. In 1834 the jurisdiction of Michigan Territory was extended over the vast region west of the Mississippi, north of Missouri and reaching westward to the Missouri and White Earth Rivers.

Agitation for statehood for Michigan began in 1832. A vote taken that year showed an overwhelming majority in favor of the proposition. The interest of the people was temporarily distracted, however, by the Black Hawk War and by a severe epidemic of cholera which raged through the region. A census taken in 1834 revealed a population of more than eighty-seven thousand. Congress was thereupon asked to pass an enabling act. Without waiting for this action, the people of the portion of the Territory east of Lake Michigan elected delegates to a convention. This body met in May, 1835, and drafted a constitution which was ratified by the voters in October and under which state officials were elected. This was all done on the assumption that a Territory was entitled to form a state government when it had reached a population of sixty thousand, in accordance with the terms of the Ordinance of 1787. This document, together with the Congressional act establishing the Territory of Michigan, was relied upon by the constitution-makers when they fixed the southern boundary of the proposed State along the line running through the southern extremity of Lake Michigan. This action, however, precipitated a boundary dispute with Ohio, led to a complicated situation in Michigan itself, and delayed admission for fifteen months.

As we have seen, the Ohio enabling act set the line through the tip of Lake Michigan as the northern boundary of that State from the northwest corner to Lake Erie; but the constitution of Ohio contained a provision looking to a possible readjustment. There was no exact knowledge as to where this line would strike Lake Erie and there was fear that it might pass entirely to the south of it. To guard against such a contingency the Ohio constitution stipulated that in case this fear should prove to be well founded the northern boundary should, with the consent of Congress, run along a line from the southern extreme of Lake Michigan to the northern cape at the mouth of the Maumee River on Lake Erie—thus including the land where Toledo now stands. With this constitution Congress admitted Ohio without any further word about the boundary. The people of Ohio claimed that silence gave consent to the provision in their constitution, although they sought several times in subsequent years to secure confirmative action by Congress.

The statehood movement in Michigan caused the Ohio authorities to take action. Governor Robert Lucas secured from the legislature in 1835 an act extending the jurisdiction of Ohio into the disputed tract and providing for the election of local officials. The youthful Governor Stevens T. Mason and the legislature of Michigan were equally belligerent in making it a criminal offense for anyone to accept office in the area except under Michigan auspices. Soon the so-called, though fortunately bloodless, "Toledo War" was in progress.

The militia of each jurisdiction was called out, and Governor Lucas backed by about six hundred men confronted Governor Mason with about one thousand.

The situation was an embarrassing one for President Jackson. In response to his request, the Attorney General expressed the opinion that until Congress had given its consent, the Michigan contention regarding the boundary should be upheld. Yet the presidential election of 1836 was approaching and the large electoral vote of Ohio was not to be lightly placed in jeopardy. "Never in the course of my life," declared John Quincy Adams who warmly advocated the Michigan claim, "have I known a controversy of which all the right was so clear on one side, and all the power so overwhelmingly on the other; never a case where the temptation was so intense to take the strongest side, and the duty of taking the weakest was so thankless."

Commissioners were sent from Washington to make peace between the contending jurisdictions. In June, 1836, Congress passed an act authorizing the President to admit Michigan by proclamation whenever the people through a convention accepted the boundary desired by Ohio. To compensate Michigan for yielding the disputed tract the new State was given the peninsula between Lake Michigan and Lake Superior. A bill had already been enacted into law erecting the new Territory of Wisconsin out of the western part of what had previously been Michigan. In September a convention assembled at Ann Arbor and emphatically rejected the proposal made by Congress.

While the boundary dispute was raging the governmental situation in Michigan was anomalous. A full set of State officers, headed by Governor Stevens T. Mason, had been elected under the constitution adopted in 1835, and they were performing most of the duties of their positions. This government, however, was without legal status since it had not been recognized by Congress. President Jackson indicated that he still regarded Michigan as a Territory by appointing John S. Horner as acting governor. When Horner arrived in Detroit he was treated with such lack of respect that he soon betook himself to the region west of Lake Michigan. Nevertheless, the long controversy was now nearing a close. Despite their wrath because of the terms of admission which they regarded as flagrantly unfair to them, the leaders in Michigan realized that their case was hopeless. Congress held the whip hand. The addition of the northern peninsula had somewhat tempered the general resentment. Besides, the new State government was Democratic and political pressure was constantly being exerted. Accordingly, in December, 1836, a second convention, illegally constituted, met at Ann Arbor and accepted the boundary which Congress had prescribed and Ohio demanded. When President Jackson was notified, instead of issuing the proclamation authorized by Congress, he referred the matter back to that body. Here, after a protracted debate, Michigan was formally admitted as a State on January 26, 1837.

Before this date a new southern State had been added to the Union. It was for this reason that no sectional opposition had been raised to statehood for Michigan. Arkansas was without any considerable number of inhabitants when it became a Territory in 1819. Settlement progressed slowly, since the region was not easily accessible. Settlers moving down the Ohio and the Mississippi long found desirable locations before reaching Arkansas, and the same thing was true in some degree of those advancing up the Mississippi. In 1828 the western boundary of the Territory, previously at the one hundredth meridian, was fixed at the present line. The western portion became a part of what was expected to be the permanent Indian country set up in connection with the removal policy described in a previous chapter. The statehood movement in Arkansas was contemporaneous with that in Michigan, but its goal was achieved without difficulty. A constitution was drafted in the spring of 1836 and put into effect by promulgation. On June 15th of that year Congress admitted Arkansas as a State.

FLORIDA AND IOWA

Less than a decade after the admission of Arkansas and Michigan another pair of would-be States were knocking at the doors of Congress—Florida and Iowa. Once again the southern State succeeded in gaining admittance without disturbance or opposition. To be sure, the people of Florida desired statehood many years before their wish was granted. In 1838 they adopted a constitution and sought admission, but for seven years Congress turned a deaf ear to the request because there was no northern State ready to be admitted. Finally, a law of March 3, 1845, made Florida a State. The same law provided for the admission of Iowa, but imposed boundaries which the people refused to accept. Nearly two years passed before Iowa entered the Union.

The Iowa region was included in the various territorial jurisdictions of the Louisiana Purchase down to 1821. When Missouri was admitted the country to the northward was left without any territorial government—a fact that was of no significance for more than a decade, since there were almost no white inhabitants. In 1833, however, settlers began to flock to the fifty-mile strip along the west bank of the Mississippi known as the Black Hawk Purchase. Soon the need for courts and other agencies of local government became apparent. In 1834 the jurisdiction of the Territory of Michigan was extended over the region. Two years later it became a part of the newly created Territory of Wisconsin. Then on June 12, 1838, an act of Congress established the Territory of Iowa. The law was not passed until after there had been considerable debate, occasioned by the significance of the move to begin the process of carving Territories, with statehood in the offing, in the extensive area north of Missouri. Several eastern and southern members of Congress spoke rather vehemently in opposition to the measure. Some of them bitterly assailed the settlers of Iowa for having entered and held choice lands in direct violation of law. It will be remembered that it was in Iowa that the claim associations had their greatest vogue.

The first years of the new Territory were enlivened by petty but virulent bickerings between Governor Robert Lucas and William B. Conway, the territorial secretary, and quarrels between the governor and the legislative assembly. Even greater excitement was engendered by a boundary dispute with Missouri. This story cannot be related here; but it was an interesting coincidence that the man who had been chief executive of Ohio during the boundary controversy with Michigan was now the leader of the Territory of Iowa in its contest with Missouri. In both instances the contention which he supported was the winning one. For a time feeling ran high. Rival officials sought to collect taxes in the disputed tract, mails were stopped, property was seized, armed men gathered on either side of the border, and lead was being melted into bullets by the farmers. The question was not settled until 1848, after Iowa had become a State, when the Supreme Court of the United States handed down a decision supporting the Iowa claim.

Sentiment in favor of statehood began to be expressed early. The proposition was twice submitted to a vote of the people, once in 1840 and again in 1842, and each time the vote was in the negative. The certainty of increased taxation was the deciding factor. Most of the settlers had come from States where, during the years following the Panic of 1837, the burden of taxation seemed unbearable. As long as they remained a Territory the expenses of their general government were paid out of the federal treasury. In 1844 the question was again submitted, and by this time the popular attitude had changed so that a favorable vote was returned. Accordingly in August a convention assembled to draft a constitution. Under the boundaries set forth in this constitution the proposed State would have extended northward to the St. Peters (Minnesota) River, while a small region in what is now the northwestern corner would have been omitted.

This constitution was submitted to Congress. Under it, and before the people of Iowa had ratified it, admission to statehood was granted by Congress in the act of March 3, 1845, which extended the same privilege to Florida. But there was this difference: the boundaries proposed in the Iowa constitution were rejected. In their place Congress substituted boundaries which would have extended the State somewhat farther north than at present, but would have cut it off by a considerable distance from the Missouri River on the west. The reason seems to have been the determination of northern members of Congress to prevent, if possible, the admission of northern States with too generous boundaries, in order to leave room for a greater number of additional States, with a correspondingly greater representation of the North in Congress. This determination was strengthened, before the passage of the bill, by the joint resolution of March 1, 1845, providing for the annexation of Texas, out of which it was confidently anticipated that five slave States would ultimately be carved.

The act of March 3, 1845, did not result in the admission of Iowa. When the constitution with the boundaries substituted by Congress was twice submitted to the people of Iowa they rejected it both times. In May, 1846, a new constitutional convention assembled and drafted a new instrument of government, modelled in general upon the rejected constitution of 1844. The northern boundary, however, was placed along the parallel 43 degrees and 30 minutes. Since this compromise line had already been suggested by the committee on territories in the federal House of Representatives, all obstacles to admission were now removed. Accordingly Iowa became a State on December 28, 1846.

The Iowa constitution reflected the deep-seated antagonism to banks of issue which had been aroused in the West during the long period of depression following the Panic of 1837. The ninth article declared that "no corporate body shall hereafter be created, renewed, or extended, with the privilege of making, issuing, or putting in circulation any bill, check, ticket, certificate, promissory note, or other paper, or the paper of any bank, to circulate as money. The General Assembly of this State shall prohibit, by law, any person or persons, association, company or corporation, from exercising the privileges of banking, or creating paper to circulate as money."

THE ADMISSION OF WISCONSIN

One more State remained to be created in the Old Northwest. The Territory of Wisconsin as established in 1836 embraced all the country north of Illinois and Missouri and between Lake Michigan and the Missouri and White Earth rivers. Two years later the portion west of the Mississippi River was given a separate status as the Territory of Iowa. Even during the incumbency of the first territorial governor, Henry Dodge, agitation for statehood began in Wisconsin. As in Iowa the movement failed to gain wide support and for the same reason—the heavier taxation which statehood would entail. When the question was submitted to the people early in 1846, however, they voted overwhelmingly in favor of drawing up a constitution and applying for admission into the Union. In the meantime Congress had passed an enabling act, in order that Wisconsin might be paired with Texas which had just been admitted.

A Wisconsin convention drafted a constitution in 1846, but it was two years before statehood was achieved. Disappointment was caused by the boundaries prescribed by Congress, cutting the proposed State off from the Mississippi above the St. Croix River, but this was by no means the main cause of the delay. Conflicting political and economic viewpoints among the different areas of settlement within the Territory were the principal complicating factors. The southwestern portion was settled first and its people were ardent Jacksonian Democrats, many of whom had come from the southern States. The eastern border along Lake Michigan was settled largely by people from the North Atlantic States, with a constantly increasing number of recent immigrants from foreign lands. The southeastern corner contained a population very much like that of northern Illinois and Indiana, somewhat more conservative in their democracy than the people of the southwestern portion.

The radical Democrats had control of the convention of 1846 and they succeeded in embodying in the constitution a number of ideas and principles that were unacceptable to the people of the eastern and southeastern sections. One of these was the absolute prohibition of banks of issue and the circulation of any bank notes of denominations less than twenty dollars. Another was the requirement of residence for one year as a qualification for the franchise. There were other provisions that met with objections as being too radical. When the constitution came to a vote in the spring of 1847 it was rejected. Late in the same year another convention assembled and drafted a new constitution which removed some of the main objections to the first document. Especially was this true of the clause dealing with banking. The legislature was author-

zed to enact a general banking law if the question of chartering banks had first been referred to the people and approved
by them.   The law itself must likewise pass the gamut of a
referendum.   This constitution was ratified by a large vote,
and Wisconsin became a State in accordance with an act of
Congress dated May 29, 1848.

THE ADMISSION OF MINNESOTA

The Minnesota country was without territorial government
for a short period after the admission of Iowa and Wisconsin.
In March, 1849, however, the Territory of Minnesota was
established.   At this time the population was very small, num-
bering only 6,077 in 1850.   Moreover, settlements were confined to the section east of the Mississippi which had been
detached from Wisconsin when that State was admitted with
the St. Croix River as a portion of the western boundary.   The
more extensive region west of the Mississippi was still Sioux
Indian country.   The situation was greatly changed after
1851, when the Sioux ceded most of their lands.   The Indians
were treated with gross unfairness by the federal government,
by the traders, and by the settlers.   Nevertheless, the entire
area was now an open field for settlement, and such a stream
of people poured into the region that the census of 1860 credited Minnesota with 172,023 inhabitants.

Before this date, as might be expected with population
increasing so rapidly, a movement for statehood was launched
and pushed to fruition.   After considerable debate, during
which many southern members of Congress opposed the bill, an
enabling act was passed on February 26, 1857.   Bitter rivalry
between Republicans and Democrats featured the election of
delegates to the constitutional convention.   The result was
close and both sides claimed to have won the victory.   As a
result two bodies, each claiming to be the duly chosen representatives of the people, held sessions and each adopted a constitution.   Curiously enough the two documents were strikingly
similar, so much so that it was possible to agree on a compromise which was ratified by the people.   Minnesota entered the

Union on May 11, 1858. The chain of five States on the western side of the Mississippi River was now complete.

POLITICS IN THE WEST

Among the motives which, in all the Territories, inspired agitation for statehood were personal ambitions to obtain the many new offices which would thereby be created, the avidity of the national political parties to increase their voting power, and the sincere desire of aggressive pioneers to enjoy a voice in shaping national affairs. A study of the early history of any frontier commonwealth reveals the lively manner in which westerners availed themselves of the opportunities along these lines which statehood afforded.

Frontiersmen took to the game of politics with great zest. From the beginning the voting population was practically co-extensive with the number of white, adult males. The numerous offices in the State government were attractive prizes to be gained, even though the salaries were usually shockingly low. Besides, there were the more numerous smaller plums to be plucked in the rapidly increasing number of counties, townships, and towns. Political campaigning, especially after the inauguration of stump-speaking and mass-meetings, was an enjoyable diversion, satisfying a social need among frontier people much in the same way as did the religious camp-meeting. The hilarious campaign of 1840 was nowhere so colorful as in the West. With a frontier hero as a presidential candidate and with the log cabin, the coonskin cap, and the barrel of hard cider the glorified emblems of the Whig party, it was inevitable that westerners should march and shout and sing and attend monster mass-meetings.

The first newspapers in the western States were established primarily to serve as political organs or to obtain the government printing. Politics was the all-absorbing topic during campaign periods, both in the editorials and in the news columns. The editors as a rule were vigorous and aggressive in their espousal of candidates and parties. All too commonly they attacked opponents with a virulence and scurrility that make us gasp. In 1835 a Kentucky editor described a competitor of opposing political views as "one of the dirtiest villains, the most reckless liars, and ineffable paltrons, that ever walked." In a gubernatorial campaign in Iowa in 1859 a newspaper account of a speech by one of the candidates contained the statement that "he descended to the lowest depths of vulgarity and blackguardism. . . . No species of low circus-acting clownishness that he would not use for effect. Even his political friends admit that he is a blackguard, and yet some of them honor him for it." These quotations selected at random are by no means extreme: they could be duplicated indefinitely. They apparently did not meet with serious disapproval in frontier communities, although they frequently involved the editors in duels and other personal encounters.

As a section the West was naturally Jeffersonian Republican in national politics down to 1820, and it shifted its support with alacrity to Andrew Jackson when his star arose on the political horizon. For some of the same reasons that caused them to follow Jackson the westerners cast their votes for another frontier hero—William Henry Harrison—in the boisterous campaign of 1840. Ohio, Indiana, and Michigan, as might be expected, gave their electoral votes to Harrison, but so did Kentucky, Tennessee, Mississippi, and Louisiana. Only Alabama, Arkansas, Missouri, and Illinois returned Van Buren's electors. Thereafter, until 1856 the West was overwhelmingly Democratic. The most interesting exceptions were Kentucky and Tennessee which chose Whig electors down to and including 1852.

The middle of the decade of the fifties witnessed a break in the political alignment of the free States north of the Ohio River. The long-standing alliance between the grain-growing West and the cotton-planting South began to dissolve. Various reasons explain the change of sentiment. In the first place, the Mississippi River, so long depended upon by southerners to bind the West to the South as an avenue of transportation, had ceased to function in that capacity. Railroads were yearly identifying the West more closely with the East in economic interest. In the second place, the great outpouring of people during the fifties from the New England and Middle States and from northern Europe into the upper Mississippi Valley changed the social and political complexion of that region. Finally, the passage of the Kansas-Nebraska Bill with its repeal of the time-honored Missouri Compromise alienated many Democrats and led to the formation of the new Republican party. This party had its birth in the Old Northwest which the Ordinance of 1787 had pledged to freedom. Ohio, Michigan, Wisconsin, and Iowa gave their support to John C. Frémont and the new party in its first national campaign in 1856. Four years later all the seven free States of the West were enrolled under the Republican banner.

Economic motives no doubt in large measure explain the hearty welcome thus accorded the Republican party, which espoused free lands and opposed the further spread of slavery. But sincere idealism also played a part. There was real hatred of slavery as an institution in the region which had witnessed the manifold operations of the Underground Railroad. Even more widespread was the spirit of nationalism which pervaded the section which still bore the impress of growth and development fostered and encouraged by the federal government.

CHAPTER XIV

FRONTIER SOCIETY

"AMERICA does not belong to one age alone," wrote a distinguished English historian, A. F. Pollard, in a book published in 1925. "The East might wax old like a garment, but the frontier was always reverting to nature as it moved farther towards the West. That is why the nation is still so young. Some of its parts have reached the most finished phases of social development and are almost as *blasé* as Europe itself. But in the real America which lies beyond the Alleghanies they are—or were till the end of last century—beginning all over again and repeating in each community the experience of mankind and the progress of civilization." Continuing, he made the comment that "the frontier lay midway between the refinements of society and the savagery of the wilderness; and the pioneer was a cross between the friends he left behind and the foes he went to meet."[1]

The Frontier in Romance and Reality

The romantic interpretation of the frontier is to be found in the writings of three main groups: those who had never seen it, or only hastily, but who looked forward to it as the land of hope for the race or the individual; those who have given expression to the ideals and dreams and aspirations of the pioneers; and those who have looked back wistfully to the vanished life of the frontier as one of color and adventure and freedom.

Such writers as Blake, Byron, John Filson, and C. W. Dana fall into the first of these groups. Another typical illustration is to be found in Francis Baily's apotheosis of the frontiersmen contained in the journal of his western tour in 1796

[1] A. F. Pollard, *Factors in American History* (1925) pp. 136-137. By permission of The Macmillan Company, publishers.

and 1797. "Happy men!" he wrote, "who, ignorant of all the deceits and artifices attendant on a state of civilization, unpracticed in the vices and dissipations of degraded humanity, unconscious of artificial and unnecessary wants, secluded from all those pomps and ridiculous ostentations which serve to enslave one-half a nation for the gratification of the other; unshackled with the terrors which fanaticism and superstition inspire; enjoying equally the free blessings which nature intended for man, how much, alas! how much I envy you!"

Turning to the second group of writers dealing with the frontier in a romantic manner, it is to be noted that the pioneers themselves wrote very little about their own life.   Timothy Flint was one of a very small number of early western authors who have left us contemporary accounts that approach adequacy.   He was a keen and indefatigable observer of men and events, and many of his descriptions entitle him to be classed with the realists. Yet he also sensed and expressed the romantic side of the westward movement and the forward-looking spirit of the frontier.   "What mind," he asked "ever contemplated the project of moving from the old settlements over the Alleghany mountains, and selecting a home in the West, without forming pictures of new woods and streams, new animals and vegetables, new configurations of scenery, new aspects of men and new forms of society."   Flint himself was frequently so enraptured with the prospect that he expressed himself in poetic form.   For instance, in 1820, when he viewed the potential development along the Missouri River, he wrote:

> And then anticipation, rapt away,
> Forestalls thy future glory, when thy tide
> Shall roll by towns, and villages, and farms,
> Continuous, amidst the peaceful hum
> Of happy multitudes, fed from thy soil;
> When the glad eye shall cheer at frequent view
> Of gilded spires of halls, still vocal with the task
> Of ripening youth; or churches, sounding high
> Hosannas to the living God.

J. K. Paulding, although not a resident of the West, also gave expression to the hopes and aspirations of the pioneers in a poem containing the following lines:

Hence comes it, that our meanest farmer's boy
Aspires to taste the proud and manly joy
That springs from holding, in his own dear right,
The land he ploughs, the home he seeks at night.

Other contemporary writers in this group might be quoted to illustrate the statement made by Frederick J. Turner that "the men and women who made the Middle West were idealists." The pioneer, in Turner's words, saw "beyond the harsh life of the log hut and the sod house to the home of his children, where should dwell comfort and the higher things of life, though they might not be for him."

The most romantic of all writers dealing with frontier life are to be found among those of recent years and the present time. The dull and prosaic and sordid sides are all forgotten or neglected by these writers, and the glamorous features are retained to make us believe in a time and a place where men were free and adventure was met at every turn. "The frontier!" exclaimed Emerson Hough in his little book entitled *The Passing of the Frontier.* "There is no word in the English language more stirring, more intimate, or more beloved. . . . It means all that America ever meant. It means the old hope of a real personal liberty, and yet a real human advance in character and achievement. To a genuine American it is the dearest word in all the world." [2] It is not necessary to give further illustrations of this backward-looking view, which mourns for the finished romance of the days that will never return.

On the other hand, writers of the realistic school of recent years have sought to depict the pioneer as a figure of much less than heroic proportions and to throw doubt upon the beneficial effects of the frontier experience. This is especially true of those who have attempted a description and an evaluation of American culture. Says Louis Mumford, one of the most sympathetic of this group of critics, in his delightful little book entitled *The Golden Day:* "What happened was just the reverse of the old barbarian invasions, which turned the Goths and the Vandals into Romans. The movement into backwoods America turned the European into a barbarian."

[2] Emerson Hough, *The Passing of the Frontier* (Vol. 26, *The Chronicles of America*), p. 152. By permission of the Yale University Press, publishers.

As a matter of fact, if realism necessarily implies emphasis on the sordid and brutal and degenerative aspects of life, there were realists among numerous contemporaries of the pioneer period who saw the frontier through glasses that were not rose-tinted. Among these, of course, were English and eastern writers who could see nothing but the crudities and brutalities of the conspicuous frontiersmen, easterners who were alarmed at the exodus to the West and were quick to depict the seamy side, and preachers who were shocked at the irreligious habits of westerners. For instance, Thomas Ashe's *Travels in America*, 1806, was so critical that even *Niles' Register* gave much space to ridicule and refutation. Ten years later H. B. Fearon gave his English readers a picture scarcely less unfavorable.

William Faux, writing in 1823 of *Memorable Days in America*, added still darker colors. "The traveler," he wrote, "who must necessarily often mix with the very dregs of society, in this country, should be prepared with plain clothes, or the dress of a mechanic; a gentlemanly appearance only exciting unfriendly or curious feelings, which defeat his object, and make his superiority painful." Kentucky was bad enough, but when he crossed into Indiana he felt "quite out of society; everything and everybody, with some exceptions, looks wild, and half savage." A writer in *The Quarterly Review* in 1809 described the westerners as "a worse race than the Indians upon whose border they trespass"; and the same magazine several years later predicted that "long ages must pass away before the population, now thinly spread over the immense vale of the Mississippi, will become sufficiently dense to render any part of it a desirable habitation for civilized beings." Harriet Martineau, Mrs. Trollope, and Charles Dickens were other writers whose strictures, in the main well founded, aroused the ire of westerners.

Somewhere between the brightly colored visions of the romanticists and the deeply shaded pictures of the super-realists lies the true portraiture of frontier society. Generalizations, here as elsewhere, are likely to be misleading. It is certain that a pioneer community in which most of the people hailed from New England exhibited different characteristics from one the inhabitants of which came from the back country of Virginia or the Carolinas. Both of these types of settlement differed from those where foreign-born settlers were numerous. Moreover, the state of society in any given region depended to a considerable extent on the length of time which had elapsed since the first settlements were made.

The pages which follow will be devoted to an estimate of the personal characteristics and qualities developed or accentuated by frontier life, and of the most salient features of society in the middle western frontier. Frequent recourse will be had to the writings of contemporary observers who, because of long association or keen discrimination, were competent to express judgment.

THE BACKWOODSMEN

The first-comers in every frontier region, at least until the prairies of Illinois were reached, were of the class to whom the name "backwoodsmen" has been generally applied—a class typified by some of James Fenimore Cooper's characters. Hector St. John de Crèvecoeur described these people in the late colonial period in his classical *Letters from an American Farmer*. "By living in or near the woods," he wrote, "their actions are regulated by the wildness of the neighborhood. . . . The chase renders them ferocious, gloomy and unsociable. . . . That new mode of life brings along with it a new set of manners, which I cannot easily describe. These new manners being grafted on the old stock, produce a strange sort of lawless profligacy, the impressions of which are indelible. The manners of the Indian natives are respectable, compared with this European medley." Crèvecoeur hastened to add that there were some individual exceptions and numerous group exceptions, as in the case of the Moravians, the Quakers, and the New Englanders. But he concluded his description by saying: "Thus are our first steps trod, thus are our first trees felled, in general, by the most vicious of our people; and thus is the path opened for the arrival of a second and better class."

Later writers who came in contact with backwoodsmen in

the country north of the Ohio River described them in much the same terms as Crèvecoeur, but frequently they were less severe in their judgments. Timothy Flint testified that before he went into the West he had heard "a thousand stories of gougings, and robberies, and shooting down with the rifle," but that he had traveled unarmed thousands of miles in the wilderness without being insulted, much less being in danger from the frontiersmen. "He carries a knife, or dirk in his bosom," wrote Flint of the typical backwoodsman, "and when in the woods has a rifle on his back, and a pack of dogs at his heels. An Atlantic stranger, transferred directly from one of our cities to his door, would recoil from an encounter with him. But remember that his rifle and his dogs are among his chief means of support and profit." The kindly Morris Birkbeck admitted that the frontier was always a place of retreat for "rude and even abandoned characters, who find the regulations of society intolerable. . . . These people retire, with the wolves, from the regular colonists, keeping always to the outside of civilized settlements." At another time, however, he felt called upon to assert that "they are not savage in disposition, but honest and kind; ready to forward our wishes, and even to labour for us, though our coming will compel them to remove to the 'outside' again."

Since they depended largely upon the hunt for their subsistence, the backwoodsmen lived lonely, isolated lives, far apart from each other, and they resented the coming of the regular settlers. Henry O'Reilly cited the instance of a man named Hincher in western New York who lived twelve miles from his nearest neighbor. He looked with jealousy upon the arrival of newcomers who would disturb the tranquillity of the "neighborhood." It was not infrequent to find men of this type moving two or three times in a single year, building a rude cabin in each place and then abandoning it or selling it to some settler.

The continuous life in the woods gave these people an appearance that was often noted by travelers. Morris Birkbeck declared he could tell the extent of the clearings in which people lived by observing their color. "Buried in the depths of a boundless forest," he said, "the breeze of health never reaches these poor wanderers; the bright prospect of distant hills fading away into the semblance of clouds, never cheered their sight: they are tall and pale, like vegetables that grow in a vault, pining for light. . . . The blood, I fancy, is not supplied with its proper dose of oxygen from their gloomy atmosphere, crowded with vegetables growing almost in the dark, or decomposing; and, in either case, abstracting from the air this vital principle."

It was of this type of individual that the fiery John Randolph spoke in Congress, when he said: "I had as lief be a tythe-proctor in Ireland, and met on a dark night in a narrow road by a dozen white boys, or peep-of-day boys, or hearts of oak, or hearts of steel, as an exciseman in the Allegheny mountains, met, in a lonely road, or by-place, by a backwoodsman." It was these people, together with the river men, with their ferocious curses and boasting, and their rough and tumble fighting in which eyes were often gouged and ears and noses torn, who gave many travelers their first impression of the westerners. Easterners were all too ready to attribute similar characteristics to all the people of the West. Our chief concern, however, is not with them, but with the much larger class of real settlers who felled the trees and transformed the country into a land of homes. It was not until their coming that there was anything that can be called society on the frontier.

Frontier Traits and Qualities

Contemporary observers, as well as modern writers, agree that frontier society was characterized by social democracy. This is entirely natural. In an environment where there was substantial economic equality there was no basis for social distinctions. Neither wealth nor family standing nor previous position in life meant much in the early years of settlement. All stood on an equality in facing the tasks of cutting down trees, building cabins, putting in crops, and stringing fences. Grinding labor, with little leisure, was the common lot. When a man needed help in performing some of the larger tasks his neighbors were glad to rally to his assistance. Otherwise the individual was expected to stand or fall according to his own abilities and labor. There was no occasion to give lip service to equality as a theory or ideal: equality was an inescapable fact. Thus it was that anyone was regarded with suspicion who sought to live or demean himself in ways that differed conspicuously from those of the settlers in general. This does not mean that superiority was not recognized, when that superiority displayed itself in greater ability to do the things demanded by frontier life. The notables among pioneers were those who excelled in such activities as Indian fighting, rail-splitting, corn-husking, stage-coach driving, or the maneuvering of flatboats.

"There is in the West a real equality, not merely an equality to talk about, an equality on paper," wrote the keen and impartial Michael Chevalier in 1835, "everybody that has on a decent coat is a gentleman; every gentleman is as good as any other, and does not conceive that he should incommode himself to oblige his equal . . . he expects no attention from others, and does not suspect that his neighbor can desire any from him. In this rudeness, however, there is not a grain of malice; there is on the contrary an appearance of good humour that disarms you. The man of the West is rude, but not sullen or quarrelsome." Chevalier was also deeply impressed with the fact that the law of the westward movement was the law of armies. "The mass is everything, the individual nothing."

Where self-reliance was imposed by the environment as a condition of success, the individual who met the test was likely to be imbued with a high degree of self-confidence. Inventive resourcefulness was another quality developed by life on the frontier. When people moved into the West and began life anew under the most primitive conditions they were obliged to make the best use of the slender means at hand. They knew what they wanted to do, but in the early years they lacked the equipment with which such things had been done in the older settled communities. Few tools and no nails were available for use in the building of a cabin. New methods of providing shelter had to be learned. Chairs and beds and other articles of furniture were necessarily left behind, and substitutes had to be devised. So it went, through the whole range of activities essential to existence and economic success.

When these two traits or qualities of self-confidence and resourcefulness were applied in the realm of material things they were generally beneficial. But when confidence in self, based upon economic success, was extended into other fields it was not always justified by the results. Transferred into the political sphere this attitude made it easy and natural to believe that every man of sound mind and adult years was capable of holding and administering any office of government. This same trait of the pioneer inclined him to believe that what he did not know or could not do were not worth knowing or doing; and so he was apt to ridicule and resist the activities of those who sought to introduce some of the elements and aspects of culture into the region. The success of inventive resourcefulness in solving problems in the material realm, as they arose, may also have contributed to the tendency to deal with all questions in a similar manner and on an emergency basis.

Frontiersmen were optimistic people. Hope and expectation of improving their condition were among the motives impelling them westward. They endured the labor and hardships of the early years because they knew that their labors would be rewarded and the hardships would be forgotten in the better times that were sure to come. Growth, progress, movement were everywhere in evidence in the rapidly developing frontier regions, and the spirit of optimism was the natural result. Many observers of pioneer life were impressed with this optimism and some of them became its eloquent apostles. "The West is a young empire of mind, and power, and wealth, and free institutions, rushing up to a giant manhood with a rapidity and power never before witnessed below the sun," wrote Lyman Beecher in 1835. "And if she carries with her the elements of her preservation, the experiment will be glorious."

In an address before the Historical and Philosophical Society of Ohio in 1850 William D. Gallagher expressed his conviction that "to suppose that we are here to see but a segment of the old circle traveled over again, is to give mankind a place in the scale of being lower than that which I have heretofore assigned them. . . . It is my firm belief, that out of the crude materials now collected and collecting in this mighty North-West . . . are to come arts and institutions and education, better fitted for the uses and enjoyments of man, and more promotive of those high developments that are within the capacities of his nature, than anything which the world has yet seen."

Frequently this optimism led westerners across the border line into boastfulness concerning the superiorities of their particular region or into comparisons unfavorable to the East or Europe. For instance, Timothy Flint related an anecdote which, he said, was well known in the West, of a preacher from Kentucky, who was preaching in a neighboring State on the topic of the happiness of heaven. "In short, my brethren," said the preacher when he reached his climax, "to say all in one word, heaven is a Kentuck of a place." Gilbert Imlay, writing to a friend in England in 1792, pointed out numerous respects in which Kentucky society excelled that of the old world. A European might doubt this statement, but said Imlay, "a few years residence with us teaches him that important truth, and self-conviction is always the most lasting." Another illustration of this self-complacent, boastful spirit was given by James Hall. "One would have thought," he wrote, referring to the people of Ohio and Indiana, "they were speaking in parables, who heard them describing the old thirteen states as a mere appendage of the future republic—a speck on the map of the United States—a sort of out-lot with a cotton field at one end, and a manufactory of wooden clocks at the other; yet they were in sober earnest." Of course, in reading the impressions of travelers it must always be kept in mind that westerners enjoyed "tall stories" and that they found great fun in "stuffing" strangers who seemed too inquisitive.

Pioneer farmers were scarcely less migratory than the backwoodsmen whom they succeeded. For this reason among others, frontier society did not become static. Restlessness was in the air. There seemed so much to be done, so much to be gained, and such a short time in which to accomplish it before the entire country would be settled. Reports of better lands further west were for many people too alluring to be resisted. Travelers from the eastern States or from Europe, where families were accustomed to live in one locality through successive generations, were much surprised at, and rather critical of, the nonchalant manner in which people in the West changed their abodes without any apparent necessity or reason. "Though they have generally good houses," wrote Timothy Flint, "they might almost as well, like the Tartars, dwell in tents. Everything shifts under your eye. The present occupants sell, pack up, depart. Strangers replace them. Before they have gained the confidence of their neighbors, they hear of a better place, pack up and follow their precursors." Flint lamented the absence of "those permanent and noble improvements which grow out of a love for that appropriated spot where we were born, and where we expect to die."

Other traits of westerners may be briefly mentioned. One of these was aggressiveness. "Personal resistance to personal aggression, or designed affront," remarked Morris Birkbeck, "holds a high place in the class of duties." This characteristic may have been innate with many frontiersmen, but it was also developed and accentuated by life in a region where such an attitude was often necessary to self-preservation or success. Again, the pioneers were tolerant, within limits. Differences of creed or social viewpoints, or even personal idiosyncracies were seen to be of little consequence so long as people devoted themselves to the common tasks of life on the frontier. Tolerance was apt to cease, however, when individuals or groups sought to conduct themselves in ways that were markedly different from those of typical frontier people. Finally, there was the trait of hospitality exemplified by the familiar phrase, "the latch-string is always out." Strangers traveling through the country were seldom denied such rude accommodations as pioneer cabins afforded. One important factor in producing this far-famed western hospitality was the loneliness which inclined the settlers to welcome visitors, whether acquaintances or strangers.

HEALTH AND DISEASE ON THE FRONTIER

An aspect of frontier society which deserves some consideration is that which is concerned with health and vital statistics. It was assumed by numerous writers contemplating the benefits of life in the wilderness that general good health would be one of its blessings. This assumption does not seem to have been borne out by the actual facts. Timothy Flint summarized the situation quite accurately when he wrote that "there appears to be in the great plan of Providence a scale, in which the advantages and disadvantages of human condition are balanced.—Where the lands are extremely fertile, it seems to be appended to them, as a drawback to that advantage, that they are generally sickly."

This statement is corroborated by numerous other contemporary writers. The first settlements were mainly in the forest where the sun's rays could not destroy the generally prevailing miasma, or on the low lands along streams or in the vicinity of stagnant water. The first clearings did little to improve the situation. Birkbeck noted that the settlers "ignorant of the dangers they were incurring, found good land along the course of the rivers; and there they naturally fixed their cabins, near enough to the stream to dip out of it with a bowl." Most of the towns were similarly located, their founders "prefering convenience or profit to salubrity. . . . Short-sighted and narrow economy! by which the lives of thousands are shortened, and the comfort of all sacrificed to mistaken notions of private interests." Charles F. Hoffman, writing in 1833, found conditions equally unhealthful in the newly settled prairie regions where, in the hope of securing crops the first year, newcomers arriving in June were turning over the sod with its carpet of tall grass, weeds, and wild flowers, "and allowing the accumulation of vegetable decomposition to be acted upon by a vertical sun, and steam up for months under their very nostrils."

It was generally agreed that life in environments and under conditions such as these caused the wide prevalence of ague, with its alternating chills and fever, and other types of malarial diseases. Much more fatal were the epidemics of typhoid fever which swept western communities, especially in seasons of low water. Newspapers often devoted much space to the ravages of these diseases. The year 1823, for instance, was one in which there was much sickness in the Ohio Valley. Many communities in Ohio were said to have few families that were not affected. In Kentucky numerous families had lost "two or three of their members, and in others six or eight are sick." Still more dreaded was the terrible scourge of cholera which proceeded so rapidly to a fatal termination for large numbers of its victims. "There are not enough well persons left to take care of the convalescent and later the dead," runs a newspaper report from Lexington in June, 1833, "It is useless for any one to attempt to guess how many have fallen. Three hundred would probably be a reasonable computation." A Little Rock newspaper contained several columns filled with accounts of the ravages of the cholera epidemic in the Mississippi Valley. Similar visitations in other years caused equal consternation.

There is also evidence that, because of exposure and poorly constructed dwellings, frontier settlers were particularly susceptible to respiratory diseases such as bronchitis, diphtheria, pneumonia, and tuberculosis. Among small children cholera infantum or cholera morbus in the summer and croup in the winter were widespread and greatly dreaded.

The horrors of epidemic periods on the frontier were enhanced by the great dearth or unavailability of physicians. Medical science was still in its early stages, and at their very best even the most honest and skilful practitioners could do little to check the progress of most of the diseases. On the other hand, "quack doctors" flourished in such a situation— especially the herb doctors who peddled sure-cure panaceas for all sorts of ailments. Concoctions almost as weird as that brewed by the witches in *Macbeth* had a wide currency. Many of the so-called remedies may have been harmless; others were no doubt efficacious for certain illnesses; but seldom was there any definite knowledge to serve as a guide in their use.

No dependable vital statistics give any accurate knowledge of either birth-rate or death-rate on the frontier. Travelers frequently commented on the large number of children that swarmed out of settlers' cabins, and there is no doubt that large families were the general rule. On the other hand, there is ample evidence that the rate of infant mortality was extremely high. Some writers estimate that at least one-half of the babies died before reaching the age of four. It is equally certain that early graves claimed a shockingly great proportion of the mothers who brought these large families into the world and endured the physical and psychological hardships of frontier life.

Social Life on the Frontier

It is pleasant now to turn to an aspect of pioneer life that is far from being doleful or somber. The backwoodsmen deliberately chose isolation and resented the coming of neighbors because it limited their opportunities to pursue the type of existence they enjoyed. The pioneer farmers, on the other hand, were not ungregarious. Frontier conditions imposed isolation and loneliness upon them, but they welcomed the arrival of new settlers, both because of increased economic advantages and because of greater prospect for companionship. Although for the greater part, the lives of the pioneers were spent in perpetual toil, they seized with great avidity upon every occasion to enjoy the society of their fellow settlers.

From miles around the settlers came to help a newcomer build his log cabin. The women folk prepared a bountiful repast, visiting all the while to make up for the long periods of solitude. Similar opportunities came at log-rolling time. After a settler had felled the trees to make a clearing, the neighbors gathered to assist him in rolling the heavy logs into piles. Friendly rivalry occurred among the men to prove their strength or among groups to see which could make the largest heap of logs in a given time. Competition also added zest to harvesting grain, when there were often races between cradlers to see which could reach the end of the row first; or at corn-husking bees to determine the championship in this line. To be sure, there was usually an abundance of whiskey on all such occasions and the fun at meal time and in the evenings was likely to be rude and boisterous, sometimes ending in wrestling and rough-and-tumble fighting in which there were no rules or restraints. In addition to preparing hearty meals for the men folks, the women were apt to parallel the activities in the fields with a "quilting bee" or a "sewing bee," thus making play of work and displaying their skill with the needle.

Later, when small towns appeared, shooting matches, horse-racing, and other sports offered welcome diversion. Court days in the county seat towns were sure to attract a large gathering of settlers from the surrounding country. Some of those in attendance were interested in the cases being tried, but more of them came merely for the sake of visiting or engaging in the various contests of skill or strength that were always afoot.

Weddings, of course, were occasions of great festivity on the frontier. To travel a long distance on horseback or in a jolting wagon, and then merely listen to a brief ceremony and go home again, was far from the pioneer's thought or intention. Feasting, sometimes at the homes of the parents of both the bride and groom, was confidently expected. At night the strains of the fiddle were heard as, hour after hour, the young people danced the square dance or the Virginia reel. Later, when the newly married couple had established themselves in a home of their own, a "house warming" occasioned another social gathering.

Thus the social life of frontier people in the early years was largely a by-product of their need for assistance in performing many of the tasks necessary to their existence. Social life for its own sake came later when the country had become more thickly settled, and the most arduous labors of pioneering had been completed. The following chapter will deal with the cultural beginnings which were an accompaniment of the growth of western towns.

CHAPTER XV

CULTURAL BEGINNINGS

MUCH has been written, especially in recent years, concerning the anti-cultural aspects of life on the frontier. It is obvious that regions undergoing the processes of settlement did not furnish an environment congenial to the growth of cultural ideas or institutions. Michael Chevalier recognized this fact in 1835 when he pointed out that the pioneer "has been obliged to occupy himself much more with the cultivation of the soil than of himself." In *A Plea for the West* written the same year, Lyman Beecher remarked that: "No people ever did, in the first generation, fell the forest, and construct the roads, and rear the dwellings and public edifices, and provide the competent supply of schools and literary institutions."

It is unquestionably true that frontier society was inclined to view the possessor of intellectual attainments or cultural interests with ridicule and contempt. Persons exhibiting superior educational acquirements often found themselves at such disadvantage that they hastened to conform to the general pattern in speech and manners. As Timothy Flint expressed it, "an unwarrantable disdain keeps back the better informed and more powerful minds from displaying themselves." On the other hand, it is safe to say that few frontier communities were without some individuals who appreciated cultural activities and facilities, and were ready to co-operate in securing their introduction at the earliest opportunity. After all is said, there is less reason for surprise that the frontier experience delayed cultural development than there is that the cultural advance was so early in making its appearance.

RELIGION ON THE FRONTIER

Except for the few instances in which whole congregations migrated to the West, taking their ministers with them, church-going was not possible during the early stages of settlement, since there were no churches. The pioneers, however, were not irreligious, as was sometimes charged by critical writers. They responded eagerly to every opportunity to hear religious teaching from ministers and itinerant preachers. Among the earliest acts passed by the House of Delegates of the short-lived Transylvania colony was one "to prevent profane swearing, and Sabbath breaking"; and the first legislative bodies of the new western States hastened to enact laws to protect and encourage religious observances. On the other hand, the forms and practices of religion underwent many changes in the process of adaptation to frontier conditions in the region west of the Alleghanies.

There were Roman Catholics among the first settlers west of the mountains, especially in Kentucky, but for many years the chief centers of Catholic influence were in the old French towns, such as Detroit, Vincennes, and St. Louis. Members of the Protestant Episcopal Church were apparently few in number in the West until long after the frontier era had come to a close. Congregationalists early gained a foothold in the New England settlements at Marietta and in the Western Reserve in Ohio. Later, as a consequence of the large migrations from New England following the opening of the Erie Canal, this denomination came to exert a strong influence throughout the upper Mississippi Valley, not only in the religious field but particularly in the promotion of education. The Congregationalists early joined with the Presbyterians in a plan for cooperation in the establishment of new churches.

The three denominations which had the largest number of adherents on the middle western frontier were the Presbyterians, the Methodists, and the Baptists. Presbyterians were apparently in the lead numerically in Kentucky and Tennessee during the later years of the eighteenth century, since Scotch-Irish predominated among the settlers who poured into that region after the American Revolution. By 1800 several presbyteries had been established west of the mountains under the jurisdiction of eastern synods; and before long western synods appeared—the first being the Synod of Kentucky organized by David Rice. The Presbyterian Church, however, clung to its insistence upon an educated clergy, and its ministers retained their fondness for doctrinal sermons—gloomily Calvinistic. For these reasons it can scarcely be said that Presbyterianism was popular on the frontier, where the demand was for a religion that was more adaptable to the everyday life of the pioneers.

This demand was admirably met by the Methodists. Under the leadership of the zealous, strongly evangelistic Bishop Francis Asbury, this denomination had a rapid growth in the West. Its preachers proclaimed a democratic gospel—one which placed great emphasis upon equality in the sight of God and upon individual responsibility, rather than upon any doctrine of predestination. The Methodist form of local organization was also well suited to frontier conditions, since it included not only ordained ministers but lay exhorters and class leaders. But the most significant contribution of Methodism to the religious life of the pioneers was the itinerant preacher or circuit-rider. Scores of the preachers of this type traveled through the western country on horseback, preaching nearly every day in the week in pioneer cabins, in outdoor places, or wherever people could assemble to hear their teaching. Some of these circuits were hundreds of miles in length. In spite of every hardship, with only a pittance for their pay, these missionaries rode their circuits year after year. Not less important than their preaching was their influence over the isolated families in whose cabins they were welcome guests and bearers of tidings from the outside world.

The Baptists, likewise, early proved their adaptability to frontier needs. By 1800 they were well organized in Kentucky and Tennessee and within another decade they had several Associations, embracing numerous churches north of the Ohio River. They depended more on local, established preachers than upon itinerants, and were less inclined to emotionalism in their preaching than were the Methodists. On the other hand, their democratic form of church organization and their evangelical aggressiveness appealed to the pioneers and led to a rapid growth in membership.

Some writers are inclined to doubt whether religion in certain of its aspects can be counted as a cultural force on the frontier. This attitude of skepticism is based upon the crudeness of some of the preachers, and especially upon the extreme emotionalism manifested in what is known as the Great Revival, which raged through the West during the opening years of the nineteenth century. Presbyterians, Methodists, and Baptists all joined in this widespread evangelistic activity, but the last two were the denominations which entered into the movement most wholeheartedly and continued its practices the longest as a part of their regular policy. Revivals were under way in the West as early as 1797. The device of the camp-meeting was soon adopted, because it fitted the needs of pioneer peoples. It served some of the same social purposes as the wedding, the house-raising, or the log-rolling, only on a larger scale. No single pioneer family or group of families was able to supply food and shelter for the ever-increasing crowds that attended the preaching services as the movement gained momentum. As a consequence meetings were held in groves, and people came long distances in their wagons, with bedding and provisions, prepared and eager to spend several days. The intense excitement evoked by the revival spirit, together with the opportunity for human companionship, provided a welcome relief from the loneliness of pioneer life.

It is generally agreed that the Great Revival reached its highest point in the huge meeting at Cain Ridge in Kentucky in August, 1801, lasting without interruption from Friday until the night of the following Wednesday. Thousands of people— some estimates place the number as high as 25,000—gathered from all parts of Kentucky, from Tennessee, and even from north of the Ohio. Preaching on the part of seven or eight preachers was almost continuous from morning until late at night. It was at night that the scene at this and similar meetings was most impressive: the huge, milling crowd, the hundreds of torches flaring against the dark background of the surrounding forest, the hoarse voices of the preachers, and the cries and wailing of those under conviction of sin. The emotional frenzy was also expressed by remarkable physical manifestations. Men, women, and children fell to the ground by the hundreds and lost the power to move, so that they had to be carried to places where they would not be trampled upon.

Others were seized with an uncontrollable jerking which became unbelievably violent. Still others "would start up suddenly in a fit of barking, rush out, roam around, and in a short time come barking and foaming back. Down on all fours they sometimes went growling, snapping their teeth, and barking just like dogs."

The Great Revival continued throughout the West at least down to 1805, when the movement seems to have abated somewhat. The camp-meeting and periodic revivals, however, became permanent institutions among such denominations as the Methodists, the Baptists, and the Cumberland Presbyterians. Catherine C. Cleveland, the most competent authority on this great religious upheaval, expresses her belief that the beneficial results outweighed the detrimental. She attributes the growth of the philanthropic spirit in the West, the beginning of the temperance movement, the awakening of many people to the evils of slavery, and other similar changes of attitude largely to the effects of this stirring revival. Among the church organizations themselves the results were seen in a phenomenal increase in membership; in the scism among the Presbyterians eventuating in 1810 in the separate establishment of the Cumberland Presbyterian Church; and in the appearance of the Campbellite or Christian Church. In general, to quote Miss Cleveland, "the forces set in motion must be reckoned with as important factors in the development of western society in the years that followed."

EDUCATIONAL BEGINNINGS

"Religion, morality and knowledge, being necessary to good government and the happiness of mankind, schools and the means of education shall for ever be encouraged." In these words did the drafters of the Ordinance of 1787 seek to inspire the people of the new commonwealths to be formed beyond the mountains. Congress gave added force to this admonition by granting the sixteenth section of each township of the public lands to the States as they were admitted for the maintenance of schools. Most of the new constitutions contained clauses dealing with education. For example the Indiana constitution of 1816 contained the stipulation that "It shall be the duty of the general assembly, as soon as circumstances will permit, to provide by law for a general system of education, ascending in regular gradations from township schools to a State university, wherein tuition shall be gratis and equally open to all."

Despite all these encouragements and expressions of pious hopes, progress in the establishment of state systems of public education was slow and beset with many reverses. In fact, with a few exceptions, the frontier period had passed before the ideal of free public schools was realized in any of the midwestern States. Those regions which received large numbers of settlers from New England, New York, and Pennsylvania were first to lay adequate foundations for a system of public education; while the sections where emigrants from the southern States predominated were the most backward in developing educational support. The people of the frontier were intent upon the problems and labors of settling a new country. They were poor and opposed to any project that would increase taxes without prospect of immediate economic benefit. Elementary education was not wholly unappreciated, but the plan of tax-supported schools, open to all, was an idea of slow growth which gained wide acceptance only after the first stages of frontier development had been achieved. Ohio and Michigan were the earliest to make notable progress in the establishment of public school systems.

It would be a mistake, however, to assume that the Middle West was without educational facilities during the pioneer period. As soon as any region received a nucleus of settlers schools of all kinds began to appear—elementary schools, academies, seminaries, and so-called colleges and universities. Although most of these institutions were exceedingly crude and rudimentary in character, they reveal an educational fermentation that modifies the picture presented by the slow development of statewide school systems at public expense. Many of these early schools were public in the sense that they were supported by local levies or rate-bills, and frequently children of indigent parents were admitted free of charge. Others were "subscription schools" maintained, at least in part, by those whose children were in attendance. The growing cities, such as Cincinnati, Lexington, Louisville, Detroit, and Chicago, made the greatest advancement, and by 1840 could boast of public school systems which cared for a majority of their children of school age in attractive, commodious buildings. In the smaller towns and throughout the rural areas in the log school houses, with their split-log seats and benches and oiled-paper windows, migratory and usually illy-prepared teachers taught the children of the pioneers the rudiments of reading, writing, and arithmetic. Terms were short, school books were woefully scarce and inadequate, and the pay of the teachers a mere pittance. Yet poor as most of these schools were, many a faithful teacher succeeded in inspiring his pupils with a thirst for knowledge, and by his presence in the frontier homes as he "boarded around" he exercised a cultural influence that extended beyond the school room.

Private grammar schools and academies were numerous. The latter were peculiarly adapted to frontier needs, and performed a valuable service. Some of them had a brief existence; others succeeded in maintaining themselves for considerable periods. The educational experiments of the period were not unknown in the West. For instance, in the newspapers and the journals of travel for the period between 1820 and 1840, one may read of Lancastrian schools of "instruction mutuelle"; of Pestalozzian establishments; of agricultural schools. In St. Louis a group of "professors" offered to teach most of the languages and all the sciences. They promised to impart proficiency in the Hebrew language in twelve lessons, and in Greek and Latin with proportionate ease.

A notable feature of the educational history of the middle western frontier is the large number of colleges and universities which were founded and given legislative charters before the Civil War. Mortality was very high among these institutions projected with high ambition and local enthusiasm. Out of forty-three colleges launched in Ohio during this period only seventeen are now in existence. In Tennessee only seven out of forty-six are still in operation; in Missouri only eight out of eighty-five. A few of these defunct colleges never actually opened their doors to students. The others struggled along for varying periods and then succumbed. Catastrophes such as

fires were sufficient to bring total discouragement to some institutions. Internal dissensions and bitter rivalries wrecked
others. But the most common cause of failure was lack of
success in securing the necessary funds for maintenance.

While every effort was made to secure local support, most
of these frontier colleges were largely dependent upon the
generosity of eastern donors for funds in their early years.
Strong appeals for aid were made, especially in the years of
panic and depression. "What will become of the West," asked
Lyman Beecher in 1835, "if her prosperity rushes up to such
a majesty of power, while those great institutions linger which
are necessary to form the mind, and the conscience, and the
heart of that vast world? . . . We must educate! We must
educate! or we must perish by our own prosperity. . . . And
let no man at the East quiet himself, and dream of liberty,
whatever may become of the West." He warned especially
against sending misfits and failures to the West to be its teachers. "The men, who, *somehow*, do not succeed at the East, are
the very men who will succeed still less at the West." So
numerous were appeals of this kind and so importunate the
pleas for financial aid that several groups were formed in the
eastern States, similar to the influential "Society for the Promotion of Collegiate and Theological Education at the West."

State universities were established by law early in the history of each western commonwealth, but pioneer days had
passed before most of them actually opened their doors. With
these exceptions the colleges of the frontier period were founded
by the various religious denominations. Those churches which
insisted upon an educated clergy, such as the Catholics, the
Presbyterians, and the Congregationalists, were earliest to
establish colleges in the West. Late in the pioneer period the
Methodists and the Baptists joined in the movement, and the
former, especially, soon made up for their late start by establishing a large number of institutions. The Congregationalists
and the Presbyterians had early adopted a policy of co-opera-
tion and non-competition in their western missionary and
educational activities, and as a result numerous colleges were
founded under their joint auspices. Before the Civil War
about fifteen different religious denominations were instrumen-

tal in establishing colleges in the region west of the Alleghanies.

Most of the colleges of this period, while professing to be institutions of higher learning, would fall considerably short of the standards of a good modern high school. On the other hand, they did not differ greatly in quality from a majority of their contemporary eastern colleges. Many of the instructors were graduates of Harvard, Yale, Princeton, and other eastern institutions of high rank, and they labored valiantly in the face of the most discouraging handicaps. The "Yale Band" who founded Illinois College in 1829, and the equally famous "Iowa Band" who in 1847 established the institution now known as Grinnell College in Iowa, furnished notable examples of the devotion of these early educators on the frontier. Despite their meager resources, their inadequate equipment, and their restricted curricula, these pioneer colleges exercised a cultural influence which it would be difficult fully to evaluate. Many of them,—to mention only Center, Denison, De Pauw (originally Indiana Asbury), Franklin, Kenyon, Knox, Oberlin, Marietta, and Western Reserve, out of a long list—survived the long struggle for existence, steadily improved their standards, and are now among the best of the nations' institutions of higher learning.

Two colleges founded very early in the pioneer period in the West deserve special mention because of the high quality of instruction they offered and because of their widespread cultural influence. One of these was the first American institution of higher learning west of the Alleghany Mountains—Transylvania Seminary, founded in 1783. The name was changed to Transylvania University in 1798. Even during its early years the fame of this school gave to Lexington, Kentucky, the title of the "Athens of the West." In 1818 Horace Holley came to the presidency and in the succeeding decade he advanced the institution to real collegiate standing, with a student body ·of more than four hundred, representing fifteen States, and with instruction in liberal arts subjects, medicine, and law. The faculty contained such men as Constantine Rafinesque, the eminent scientist; Mann Butler, the Kentucky historian; Robert H. Bishop and James Blythe, both of whom were later western college presidents; and Daniel Drake and

Charles Caldwell, leaders in the medical profession. The other notable institution of the early pioneer period was Miami University at Oxford, Ohio. It was founded in 1809 and attained collegiate rank in 1824, when Robert H. Bishop became its president. One of the members of the Miami faculty whose name became widely known was William Holmes M'Guffey, author of a series of readers which were used in the elementary schools throughout the West down to comparatively recent years.

Professional education received some attention in the Middle West before 1840. It has already been noted that Transylvania University early offered instruction in law and medicine. There were several other law schools and five or six other medical schools, among which were the Medical College of Ohio at Cincinnati and the Louisville Medical College. The training of ministers was given special attention in a half-score theological schools or seminaries, a majority of which were established by the Presbyterian denomination. Although there was a growing professional interest among teachers, no colleges or schools devoted primarily to teacher-training were in existence in the region before 1840.

OTHER CULTURAL AGENCIES AND ACTIVITIES

Supplementing the schools and colleges, and in many cases exceeding them in real influence, were other cultural agencies and activities which made an early appearance in frontier society. Subscription libraries and book stores reveal a growing taste for good literature; and book-publishing concerns were established. Newspapers and gazettes devoted considerable space to literary productions. Westerners themselves began to write fiction, essays and poetry of varying degrees of merit. Dramatic productions, home-talent and professional, made a wide appeal, as did also the lyceum. Debating societies and singing schools multiplied. In short, in the growing towns an indigenous culture gradually developed and helped to create a taste for the better things of life, although music and art, as was perhaps natural, lagged far behind and had little attention during the pioneer era.

Books were extremely scarce on the frontier. A literate family was regarded as fortunate if it possessed a Bible, an almanac, and some such book as Hervey's *Evening Meditations*. An occasional family brought a more extensive library from its eastern home. That there were in many communities, however, groups of settlers who wanted books is shown by the fact that subscription libraries began to appear here and there at an early date—even before 1800. Vincennes had such a library of more than two hundred volumes by 1808, including history, geography, biography, and poetry. The library at Lexington was begun about 1795: by 1837 it contained more than six thousand volumes. Cincinnati had several subscription libraries of fair size by 1840. St. Louis, Dayton, and numerous other towns supported similar enterprises. Stores devoted exclusively to books were slow in appearing, but general stores and news-papers offices had books for sale. These included, in addition to a preponderance of religious works, many of the classics, contemporary English novels, scientific treatises, and the poetry of Milton, Byron, Pope, Burns, Addison, and others. Scott and Byron were the favorites among frontier readers. By 1840 western publishing houses were issuing a surprisingly large number of locally-printed books. Cincinnati was the greatest center of this industry. It is estimated that by 1840 the print-ing houses of that city were turning out as many as a half-million bound volumes annually. Of these a majority were school books and the remainder consisted of a variety of orig-inal works and of reprints of English novels and other books. No copyright law at that time prevented "piratical" printing.

Before the close of the pioneer era a large output of writings from the pens of midwestern authors had found its way into print. Much of this writing was devoid of any literary merit. Unfortunately, although perhaps naturally, such frontier fic-tionists as possessed real talent failed to produce stories or novels based on the normal life of the people whom they knew so well. Thus they are of little help to us in interpreting the frontier experience. Two of the most prolific western writers of fiction in the period between 1820 and 1840 were James Hall and Timothy Flint—both of whom wrote books of travel which reveal their keen observation and which are valuable as source material. Yet in his fiction Hall, while drawing his themes from his own environment, selected the picturesque and even the melodramatic, as in the *The Harpe's Head; a Legend of Kentucky*. Flint, who knew the midwest thoroughly, chose rather to write novels about the Far West which he had never seen, as in *Francis Berrian, or the Mexican Patriot* and *The Shoshonee Valley*. John M'Clung and Frederick William Thomas, two other popular western novelists, laid the scenes of their stories in the eastern states. Only Caroline M. Kirkland, in a book called *A New Home,* approached a realistic depiction of frontier life as the author observed it.

Poetry held a place not far below that of fiction, both in the interests of frontier readers and in the efforts of early western writers. One important outlet for the urge to versify was found in song-making, most often in writing new words for familiar airs. A large number of religious songs were the work of western writers, especially during the periods of revivalist fervor. Original political songs were also popular. Another group of poets adopted the satirical mood and no doubt expressed views of frontier life which were at least as nearly realistic as the imaginative poems of the more romantically inclined. Representatives of the latter group found abundant material for themes in the stirring episodes of Indian wars and other conflicts in the West.

A large part of these writings appeared in the columns of the rapidly increasing number of newspapers, gazettes, magazines, and other periodicals which constituted the most influential literary product of the frontier period. The first newspaper west of the Alleghanies was *The Kentucky Gazette,* established at Lexington in 1787 by John Bradford. Newspapers appeared in rapid succession in the towns which marked the progress of western settlement. By 1840 a total of three hundred and fifty-four western newspapers were reported in the census of that year. Many of these sheets were established to serve as political organs. In many cases the owners derived their most dependable income at first from contracts for government printing—laws, proclamations, and official notices. Advertising was meager in the early years. Subscription lists grew slowly and pay was far from certain. Nevertheless, editors wielded a powerful influence in frontier communities. In the heat of political campaigns and in the midst of other controversies they often expressed themselves so vigorously as to draw them into violent personal encounters resulting occasionally in the death of one of the parties.

A large majority of these journals were issued weekly, but during the decade of the eighteen twenties newspapers began to appear daily in some of the larger towns, such as Cincinnati and Louisville. Comparatively little local news of a personal nature was contained in these papers. Local political news and accounts of commercial and economic progress received some attention. It was not unusual for half the space to be devoted to news, often a month or more old, regarding events and movements in eastern States and foreign countries. A "Poet's Corner" or column with some other similar heading was found in nearly every paper, and frequently considerable space was given to prose literary productions of a nondescript character. After a time special periodicals, issued weekly, bi-weekly or monthly, made their appearance to serve as purveyors of entertainment or instruction along literary, religious, educational, and scientific lines.

Rivaling the editor in popularity in pioneer society was the orator and public speaker. For people whose vocabularies were extremely limited the orator who possessed a stentorian voice and a gift for florid, extravagant language seems to have had a strong fascination. This fascination no doubt helps to explain the eagerness with which frontier people flocked to listen to the interminable sermons of camp-meeting preachers, the spread-eagle Fourth of July orations, the stump-speaking of political campaigns, and the pleas of attorneys in jury trials.

Interest in the drama was manifested at a very early period in the western settlements in the presentation of amateur theatricals. Thus, in 1799 the students of Transylvania University presented two comedies, *The Busy Body* and *Love a la Mode,* and within a few years Lexington boasted a theater. In 1801 a theater was opened in Cincinnati with the performance of *The Poor Soldier* by a group of amateurs, who later presented *She Stoops to Conquer.* "Thespian societies" were formed in Louisville, St. Louis, Detroit, and numerous smaller towns in the early years of their existence, and there is evidence of a real interest both in this form of self-expression and in the drama itself. Later, beginning about 1810 professional troupes of players made their appearance in the West and soon established circuits embracing the larger towns, where their productions apparently met with a hearty welcome. Edwin Forrest, then at the beginning of his histrionic career, was seen in several western cities during the winter of 1822-3, and returned a few years later when he had attained considerable fame. Before 1840 western audiences had witnessed performances by such famous actors and actresses as Junius Brutus Booth, Mlle. Celeste, Clara Fisher, Charles Kean, James H. Hackett, Dan Marble, and Ellen Tree.

The other fine arts can scarcely be said to have gained even a foothold in the Middle West during the frontier period. Group singing, without accompaniment, was conducted in churches, and in some of the larger places singing societies were popular. Singing masters were conducting schools in Cincinnati and Marietta and other villages as early as 1802. The Harmonical Society and the Euphonical Society were names of organizations in existence in Cincinnati by the end of the next decade. This vocal music was largely a social activity and in no sense approached the status of an art. Instrumental music was even less developed. Pianos were extremely rare. The fiddle and the flute were the most common musical instruments. Their players were usually entirely self-taught and their music was heard by the public most frequently at dances and other social gatherings.

Appreciation of painting and sculpture was very rudimentary, and opportunities for instruction in either of these subjects were virtually non-existent. It is true that a painting academy was opened in Cincinnati in 1812, but its character is reflected in the advertisement of the instructor offering to paint signs and do other similar "practical" work. Some indifferent sculpturing was done in the West, especially by Hiram Powers, whose "Slave Girl" gained wide notoriety because of its nudity. Far more popular than these artistic efforts were the figures in such exhibitions as the Museum of Wax Works opened in Cincinnati in 1815.   In a word, persons who devoted, or desired to devote, their time to the painting of pictures or the sculpturing of figures were quite generally regarded as effeminate and use-less in frontier society.